Post-Truth Public Relations

This book explores the purpose, practice and effects of public relations (PR) at a time that has been variously described as an era of populism, post-truth and fake news. It considers how PR processes have contributed to the current social condition of post-truth and what constitutes PR work in this environment.

Post-Truth Public Relations: Communication in an Era of Digital Disinformation proposes that while we can now look back upon the last 80–100 years as a period of classical PR, that style is being supplemented by the emergence of a post-classical form of PR that has emerged in response to the post-truth era. This new style of PR consists of a mixed repertoire of communicative work that matches the new geometry of digital media and delivers a mix of online engagement and persuasion in order to meet the needs of increasingly partisan audiences. Using contemporary case studies and original interviews with PR practitioners in several countries, including China and the Philippines, the book investigates how PR workers have reconciled their role as communicative intermediaries with the post-truth era of digital disinformation.

This thought-provoking book will be of great interest to researchers and advanced students interested in the changing nature of PR and its practice.

Gareth Thompson is a Senior Lecturer at London College of Communication, University of the Arts London. He has worked in public relations in the corporate, finance and technology sectors for over 20 years, as well as teaching the subject in London and at the French business school, ESCEM, in Poitiers.

Routledge New Directions in PR & Communication Research

Edited by Kevin Moloney

Current academic thinking about public relations (PR) and related communication is a lively, expanding marketplace of ideas and many scholars believe that it's time for its radical approach to be deepened. **Routledge New Directions in PR & Communication Research** is the forum of choice for this new thinking. Its key strength is its remit, publishing critical and challenging responses to continuities and fractures in contemporary PR thinking and practice, tracking its spread into new geographies and political economies. It questions its contested role in market-orientated, capitalist, liberal democracies around the world, and examines its invasion of all media spaces, old, new, and as yet unenvisaged.

The **New Directions** series has already published and commissioned diverse original work on topics such as:

- PR's influence on Israeli and Palestinian nation-building
- PR's origins in the history of ideas
- A Jungian approach to PR ethics and professionalism
- Global perspectives on PR professional practice
- PR as an everyday language for everyone
- PR as emotional labour
- PR as communication in conflicted societies, and
- PR's relationships to cooperation, justice and paradox.

We actively invite new contributions and offer academics a welcoming place for the publication of their analyses of a universal, persuasive mindset that lives comfortably in old and new media around the world.

Public Relations in the Gulf Cooperation Council Countries
An Arab Perspective
Edited by Talal M. Almutairi and Dean Kruckeberg

Public Relations as Emotional Labour
Liz Yeomans

Climate Change Denial and Public Relations
Strategic Communication and Interest Groups in Climate Inaction
Edited by Núria Almiron and Jordi Xifra

Post-Truth Public Relations
Communication in an Era of Digital Disinformation
Gareth Thompson

For more information about the series, please visit: www.routledge.com/Routledge-New-Directions-in-Public-Relations–Communication-Research/book-series/RNDPRCR

Post-Truth Public Relations

Communication in an Era of Digital Disinformation

Gareth Thompson

Routledge
Taylor & Francis Group

LONDON AND NEW YORK

First published 2020 by Routledge

2 Park Square, Milton Park, Abingdon, Oxon OX14 4RN

605 Third Avenue, New York, NY 10017

Routledge is an imprint of the Taylor & Francis Group, an informa business

First issued in paperback 2021

British Library Cataloguing-in-Publication Data
A catalogue record for this book is available from the British Library

Library of Congress Cataloging-in-Publication Data
A catalog record has been requested for this book

ISBN: 978-1-138-36860-6 (hbk)
ISBN: 978-1-03-217570-6 (pbk)
DOI: 10.4324/9780429429125

Typeset in Bembo
by Aptara, India

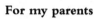
For my parents

Contents

Illustrations

Figure

Tables

Acknowledgements

Firstly, thanks to many colleagues and students at London College of Communication (LCC), University of the Arts London, and elsewhere, for discussions on some of the themes that appear here. In particular, I would like to thank my LCC colleague Michal Chmiel for many fruitful conversations and for allowing me to include his work on social psychology, collective narcissism and post-truth in Chapter 6.

I first explored the idea of post-classical public relations in an article in *Public Relations Review* in 2017 on Islamic State's recruitment communications. The paper was presented at the 23rd BledCom International Public Relations Research Symposium in July 2016, so I thank the BledCom programme committee of Ana Tkalac Verčič, Dejan Verčič and Krishnamurthy Sriramesh, along with Maja Jančič and others at University of Ljubljana in Slovenia for their welcome each year and the intellectual stimulation and feedback from colleagues that follows. At the 68th Annual International Communication Association (ICA) Conference in 2018 in Prague, Czech Republic, I presented a summary of the transition from classical to post-classical public relations at a preconference session. I am grateful to Lee Edwards of London School of Economics and Chiara Valentini of Aarhus University, Denmark for organising the day on *Theories in Public Relations: Reflections and Future Directions* on 24 May at Charles University, Prague and to all attenders for their commentary and contributions.

I am grateful to the staff of Cumberland Lodge for their kind invitation to a timely conference on *The Politics of (Post) Truth* in October 2018 when I started writing. I thank the organising committee of the colloquium, along with all participants at the event, and, in particular, Steve Fuller of the University of Warwick for a useful follow-up conversation and for sharing a copy of his book, *Post Truth: Knowledge as A Power Game* which is referenced here.

I am indebted to the following LCC MA Public Relations postgraduates for bringing an international outlook to the project through interviews conducted in their home countries and gratefully acknowledge their research contributions:

Miguel Cortez for his interviews with public relations people and journalists, plus analysis of government public relations materials and other research work conducted in The Philippines in 2017 into the populist performance of President Rodrigo Duterte, which appear in Chapter 7.

Xiran Xu for his research and interviews with a *Wuamao* (government-paid social media content poster) and others in China in 2018, that feature in the case study on the contemporary public relations and propaganda of the Chinese Government in Chapter 8.

Yaqi Zhang for her research into the promotion of ideology, nationalism and military capability in the 2018 Chinese film, *Operation Red Sea* for Chapter 8.

Some charts, tables and other material have appeared in journal articles and I am grateful to the reviewers of the following papers for their suggestions for improvement and to publishers for permission to include them:

Thompson, G. (2016) An analysis of the interaction of public relations practitioners with Wikipedia and other user generated content. *Journal of Communications Management,* 20 (1), 4–20.

Thompson, G. (2017) Extremes of engagement: the post-classical public relations of the Islamic State. *Public Relations Review,* 43 (5), 915–924.

Series editor Kevin Moloney of Bournemouth University was gently persistent in encouraging me to develop the ideas that appear here in book form and, along with Jacqueline Curtoys at Routledge, stewarded me through the early stages with great efficiency. Thanks to you both and also to Routledge's Matthew Ranscombe, Tarun Soni and Shashank Gupta who oversaw the text through to the printed pages that follow.

Richard Bailey, with whom I shared an office during my first PR job in 1987 and followed into teaching the subject at universities some years later, commented on a draft at short notice as the book neared completion. Thank you for a sage set of observations on this project and others over 30 years as a colleague and friend. Adrian Sledmere also kindly took time to read over a draft and I am grateful for his sharp eye for typos and other blemishes in the text.

All errors and omissions that remain are mine.

Gareth Thompson
Mount Ephraim Farm, Kent, September 2019

1 Introduction

This book explores the purpose, practice and effects of public relations (PR) at a time that has been variously described as a period of populism, post-truth and fake news. The aim is to consider how PR processes may have contributed to the current social condition of post-truth and what constitutes PR work in this environment. Using contemporary case studies and original interviews with practitioners in several countries, the book investigates how PR people have reconciled their role as communicative intermediaries with an era of digital disinformation. The practitioner interviews are intended to find out more about what Anne Cronin (2018, p. 2) has described as "the enhanced significance of PR and other promotional forms" in the contemporary life and, in particular, how this function has contributed to "disenchantment with contemporary representative democracy." With that challenge in mind, the interviews and accompanying text probe how PR has been used as part of broader efforts to create new truths during a period of digital disinformation. Some historical perspectives are offered on the place and role of PR in relation to the turbulence in communications and society that is attributed to post-truth phenomena. The accelerated development of modern PR is most commonly traced to the interwar period in the United States and other developed economies, but there are arguably earlier instances of the practice, such as the Sophists of Ancient Greece, that may helpfully inform the current consideration of PR topics, and which will be discussed here in relation to post-truth.

While PR has long been searching for its essence, my proposition is that the classical era and style of PR that lasted over 80 years between around 1930 and 2010 is coming to a close. The cultural component of PR and the way it is practiced is influenced by the environments in which it operates including national culture, the organisational culture of individual PR firms, the commercial culture of the industries in which clients operate and so on. Similarly, the communications management aspects of PR cannot be isolated from broader consideration of communication topics that relate to PR such as media, communications technology, the nature of the audience and the modes of communication used in PR work. The decision to consider the way PR is acting in an era of digital disinformation is prompted by the prominence of the communicative component in modern society, accompanied by a corresponding prevalence of online modes of economic exchange. So instead of physical goods, more and more goods and services – Netflix films, for example – are abstract outputs of a communicative form of capitalism. This dematerialisation has underpinned the development of large global businesses based on information such as Facebook, Google, Twitter and many others (Dean, 2009). Generally speaking, the PR industry adapted swiftly to digital communications and integrated these platforms into day-to-day work. So despite PR having some distinctive features, such as the points of difference with advertising, for example, my perspective is that PR work and the digital modes of communication used within it need not be bracketed off as a separate discipline, but considered within a broad realm of communicative expression when considering its place in the contemporary context of post-truth.

Peak public relations

There has arguably never been more PR activity in society as evidenced by the number of people currently working in the field and the amounts spent on PR services. Yet this peak in volume does not seem to have produced better debates on contentious issues as a result of the rhetorical contributions of PR people to the public sphere. Similarly, while the expansion of higher education in advanced economies has led to more educated citizens, there are few signs that this has led to more thoughtful political discourse. So considering how PR relates to the post-truth era means considering the scope of work PR people do alongside how PR has contributed to the current post-truth condition. This question is explored here through examples of post-truth PR and analysis of how PR operates in social conditions of digital disinformation and division. Specifically, the book's interviews provide some evidence of how workers in the field have integrated the media technologies of online media and computational communications into PR. While PR remains a process and commercial practice that combines the creation and curation of communications value, a post-classical variant or post-truth PR has arisen as a consequence of the need to compete in the new economics of attention. So my proposition here is not that this new style of post-truth PR accounts for all of modern practice, but rather that post-truth PR is a variant of the classical PR of the past 80 years or so that responds to and sometimes takes advantage of the post-truth condition in society.

At its corporatist peak from around 1990 to 2010, PR was feted as a discipline that could serve the public good by enabling a two-way rhetorical discussion that ensured all voices were heard in a fully functioning society (Heath, 2006, p. 96). In 2007, Aldoory and Sha (p. 339) summarised the dominant theoretical paradigm in PR scholarship at the time with their reflection that after 30 years of testing and refinement, Grunig's situational theory of publics and related work was now a "highly-regarded and well tested theory that has been integrated into the excellence theory" and as such represented the first "deep theory" in the field. Grunigian excellence theory, which appeared from 1984 onwards, offered a welcome and reassuring theoretical shelter for PR, a field that had emerged with relatively fragile underpinning in the 1920s alongside scientific management in the United States. Grunigian capture of the global PR academy with the US-derived excellence doctrine was not matched by a decisive territorial capture – nor even a secure and settled permanent academic home – for the discipline within either communication or management studies. Yet if measured in terms of revenues, people employed, university courses on the subject and journal articles citing the Grunigian ideal, the application of excellent PR on behalf of primarily corporatist interests was a success. However, there was uneasiness with aspects of the "best practice" orientation to thinking about PR and PR education in some quarters, which stirred a wave of critical scholarship. Heath and Toth's *Rhetorical and Critical Perspectives of Public Relations* appeared in 1992 in the United States and L'Etang and Piezcka published *Critical Perspectives in Public Relations* in the United Kingdom in 1996, which offered a rich set of analyses of PR work from innovative, varied and often challenging critical perspectives. After a decade of important contributions from critical scholars around the world, Moloney (2006) provided perhaps the most thorough and specific critique of the Grunigian orthodoxy with his conceptualisation of PR as a Niagara-like flow of "weak propaganda" in *Re-thinking Public Relations*. Over the next decade, as what Moloney (2006, p. 168) called the Grunigian "implied judgement" that PR would soon become a balanced two-way dialogue failed to materialise in practice, book-length critiques appeared that further questioned that excellence theory including Johanna Fawkes' (2015) exploration of what she called the "shadow" of excellence theory in *Public Relations Ethics and Professionalism: The Shadow of Excellence*. Yet as a share of all writing on PR topics over these years, critique was relatively rare, and theoretical variants, extensions and applications of the theory of best practice or excellent two-way PR were the main thrust of research for around 30 years.

A period of around 80 years – dating from the 1923 and 1928 publication of Edward Bernays' first books on public opinion and propaganda, respectively, up to around 2010 – can be described as the era of classical PR. Classical PR is characterised by a mixture of practice and theoretical orthodoxies, which saw PR as largely organisational and corporatist. In this view, even propaganda contributed to the general public good, in Bernays' (1928) view by increasing general knowledge and "keeping open an arena in which the battle of truth may be fairly fought." Eighty years later, in describing the positive roles that PR can play in society, Coombs and Holladay (2007) made a remarkably similar point with their characterisation of PR as contributing to a marketplace of ideas. So my claim is that a sustained wave of innovation in PR and public communication ran from the mid-1920s in the United States and around the same time for many developed economies in Europe and elsewhere up until around 2010. The timing is not precise and the start point for PR activity in different parts of the world may be either side of these periods. Similarly, the real development of PR in terms of both techniques and volume of activity occurred in a more concentrated period of around 60 years following World War II, a duration that fits Kondratiev's conception of long surges of growth lasting around 40–60 years continuously yielding to another era with different characteristics.

Post-classical public relations: a new style for the post-truth era

There are several components to the post-classical style and in the December 2017 edition of *Public Relations Review* (Thompson, 2017, p. 921), I suggested five features derived from analysis of the extreme PR of the Islamic State. The point I elaborated and propose to develop further here is that these themes have wider application. Thus, after first two chapters outlining what I mean by Classical and Post-Classical Public Relations, this book is organised around following themes of PR in the era of digital disinformation and post-truth:

1. A mixed repertoire of approaches
2. The rhetoric of certainty and division
3. Disregard for facts
4. A performative dimension to public communication
5. Computational data-driven PR and online engagement.

Since my central claim is that a post-classical style of PR has emerged in the past ten years and that this period has contributed to a communications landscape of digital disinformation and post-truth, I attend here to defining what I mean by style and also the period of classical PR that preceded these developments. I do not claim, for example, that the post-classical style of PR replaces the classical. Just as in the case of modernism and arts and crafts architecture in the 1920s and 1930s, the nomination of a post-classical style does not account for all PR any more than modernism and arts and crafts accounted for all architecture in that period. Rather it is a genre of practice that is present in certain cases at a certain time and which requires analysis. Putting architecture to one side, is it not surprising that in a field as concerned with image, persuasion and representation as PR, that we do not pay more attention to matters of style? Quentin Crisp, wrote with typical elegance that:

> Fashion is not style. Nay, we can say more: Fashion is instead of style. Fashion is a way of not having to decide who you are. Style is deciding who you are.
> – Crisp (1978)

In this reading, the stylistic or aesthetic dimensions of communication include representation and in particular deciding which "realms of reality" are included for display and which are excluded, a process central to the selective nature of PR, which is close to what Ranciere called the "distribution of the sensible" in political discourse (2004, p. 7). The making and distribution of "sensible" ideas in society and sense-making has been a high-profile function of PR during the past 80 years or so of the era of classical PR. This interpretation is consistent with the logic of PR contributing to the "social construction of meaning" in society to use Gordon's term (1997) from a paper that introduced thinking from sociology that seeks to explain the process of interpersonal and group interactions through the use of communicative symbols. Braun (2014) revisited these ideas and argued that the definitional interpretation of PR as a constructor of meaning in society through symbolic interactionism offered a sound theoretical base for the field overall.

This view of style aligns with the work of Harold Lasswell (1949, p. 38) who asserted, in an essay entitled *Style in the Language of Politics*, that "style is not to be dismissed as ornamentation." Ankersmit (2002, p. 135) went further countering suggestions of opposition between style and content to assert that "style sometimes generates content." This conceptualisation is important for the way it moves style beyond a thing of flimsy or fashion into the domain of communicative repertoire, particularly in relation to content. So the proposal here is that style can usefully be placed much more centrally in PR as a way of classifying the repertoire of display, language and performance used to engage with audiences. In this way, style helps us in understanding the work of some of today's post-classical PR actors and also offers the beginnings of a holistic and PR-oriented explication of contemporary communication topics such as authenticity, post-truth and performativity. It is also relevant to considering PR in terms of the aesthetics of communication and social constructivism, which leads to seeing PR as a basis for argumentation in society that creates realities for citizens and consumers.

Uneven vocality in the marketplace of ideas

In a crowded yet often apathetic modern political sphere, there is tough competition for attention. This condition has produced a performative mode of political communication that prioritises entertainment and performance over substantive policy explications. The past ten years have seen a class of media-savvy political entrepreneurs emerge, whose rise owes more to performative PR than solid policy proposals. While their arrival has often been disruptive, the emergence of these communicative entrepreneurs in politics is a logical evolution from the realisation that a confected promotional presence on social media can become a substantive asset and platform for campaigning. The electoral success of political operators such as Donald Trump and Italy's Five Star Movement are striking examples suggesting that post-truth PR has enabled a promotional process that has simultaneously charged public life with a combination of artificiality and grandiosity. In the contest for attention in the modern public sphere, some populist politicians and other public figures deliberately breach the norms of civic discourse, adopting an excessively aggressive and strident tone in their public communication. This example from politics is one component of how the post-classical style of PR has developed in response to conditions in society in the post-truth era, with others summarised in the following table.

Table 1.1 The post-truth condition in society and its PR components

Societal condition	PR component
Divided society	Rhetoric of division
Multi-channel communications	Mixed communications repertoire
Fact fatigue	Emotional narratives, disinformation
Digital dominance	Social media influencers and computational communications
Low attention/media overload	Rude and aggressive communication style

While the arrival of a post-truth style of PR is a response to the emergence of new conditions in society and the media, it is also a natural progression from the way US PR man Edward Bernays' used stunts in the 1920s and 1930s. The pseudo-events created by PR people in order to gain audience attention (Boorstin, 1962) also permeated the media from the 1960s onwards. Alongside earnestly promoting the benefits of corporate social responsibility (CSR) to corporates and public alike throughout the 1980s and 1990s, PR people were party to the industrial-scale manufacture of entirely synthetic news events that were created with the sole purpose of generating media interest and news coverage. These pseudo-events became prevalent in PR work and media consumption, perhaps especially so in the fields of celebrity and politics. Regardless of the sector, the mode of operation is constant. Media confections are designed and distributed by PR people, which match the needs of mass media but are light on facts, focusing instead on general intentions and feelings. In the distribution phase, when these narratives and visual materials are passed on to journalists, the media is largely compliant – or at least turns a blind eye – while gratefully accepting the ready-made content that has been presented to them.

Robert Heath (2009) offered a resolution to such critical questioning on the contribution of PR to media and society in his presentation of PR as a process of rhetorical enablement that ensured all voices are heard in public debate. He went on to claim that the outcome of this process of information exchange and rhetorical representation of opinion in the public area (the "wrangle in the marketplace" of competing priorities) was a fully functioning society in which all views were heard and account taken of them. Challenges to this optimistic conceptualisation of PR came from various quarters, including critical PR scholars and those concerned with the use of PR in civic activism. Kris Demetrious (2015), for example, was concerned about the effects of uneven distribution of vocality, most typically between the rhetorical volume and sophistication available to civic activists when confronting well-funded corporate or government interests, when she pointed out in an echo of Habermas that some voices are louder than others.

Similar complaints about a rhetorical resource imbalance in PR equations – alongside concerns about its relationship with the truth – were made by Plato and other critics of the early relationship intermediary work of the Sophists. Plato's criticism of the Sophists centred on their lack of regard for truth, dismissal of expertise and the insubstantial aspects of their rhetorical game playing in society for financial gain. For Plato, who offered a comprehensive analysis of the role of political leaders in *The Republic*, effective governance required a combination of truth and expertise, rather than nimble rhetoric. Truth was embodied in unchanging, absolute facts and derived its certainty from pure reason, such as exists in the unchallengeable logic of mathematical proof. Intriguingly – despite his concern about the sometimes dishonest public argumentation used by Ancient Greece's rhetorical virtuosos, the Sophists – Plato gives two instances in *The Republic* where he considers it acceptable for the ruling classes to deceive ordinary citizens in the wider interest of society at large. One of these instances was presented as "the noble lie" as it ensures content citizens and peaceful society by telling people that they are born into fixed strata in society, which in turn determines their place, their options for work, marriage and so on. Around 2,000 years later, in his book, *Propaganda*, Edward Bernays would make a similar point that it was the work of the PR counsellor to persuade the people what is best for them, when working on behalf of powerful interests such as governments.

At the current time of dislocation in economics, politics, society and technology, PR is again adapting and finding a place for its communicative labour. The post-classical form of PR practice that has emerged to meet these conditions in the post-truth era is the focus of the chapters that follow. In particular, the questions I seek to address are how do we make sense of this modern style of post-truth or post-classical PR, what is the scope of this form of communicative labour and how is it practised?

References

Aldoory, L. and Sha, B. (2007) The situational theory of publics: practical applications, methodological challenges and theoretical horizons. In: Toth, E. (Ed.) *The Future of Excellence in Public Relations and Communications Management.* New Jersey: Lawrence Erlbaum Associates, pp. 339–362.

Ankersmit, F. (2002) *Political Representation.* Stanford, California: Stanford University Press.

Bernays, E. (1928) *Propaganda.* New York: Horace Liveright.

Boorstin, D. (1962) *The Image: A Guide to Pseudo-events in America.* New York: Vintage.

Braun, S. (2014) Can we all agree? Building the case for symbolic interactionism as the theoretical origins of public relations. *Journal of Professional Communication,* 4(1), 49–70.

Coombs, T. and Holladay, S, (2007) *It's Not Just PR: Public Relations and Society.* Oxford: Blackwell.

Crisp, C. (1978) Naked is the best disguise. *New York Magazine,* 20 November, 106.

Cronin, A. (2018) *Public Relations Capitalism.* Basingstoke: Palgrave.

Dean, J. (2009) *Democracy and Other Neoliberal Fantasies: Communicative Capitalism and Left Politics.* Durham, North Carolina: Duke University Press.

Demetrious, K. (2015) *Public Relations, Activism, and Social Change. Speaking Up.* London: Routledge.

Fawkes, J. (2015) *Public Relations Ethics and Professionalism: The Shadow of Excellence.* London: Routledge.

Gordon, J.C. (1997) Interpreting definitions of public relations: self-assessment and a symbolic interactionism-based alternative. *Public Relations Review,* 23(1), 57–66.

Heath, R. (2006) Onward into more fog: thoughts on public relations research directions. *Journal of Public Relations Research,* 18(2), 93–114.

Heath, R. (2009) The wrangle in the marketplace: a rhetorical perspective of public relations. In: Toth, E., Heath, R. and Waymer, D. (Eds.) *Rhetorical and Critical Approaches to Public Relations II.* New York: Routledge, pp. 17–36.

Lasswell, H. (1949) Style in the language of politics. In: Lasswell, H. and Leites, N. (Eds.) *The Language of Politics: Studies in Quantitative Semantics.* New York: George W Stewart, pp. 20–39.

L'Etang, J. and Piezcka, M. (1996) *Critical Perspectives in Public Relations.* London: International Thompson Business Press.

Moloney, K. (2006) *Re-thinking Public Relations.* London: Routledge.

Ranciere, J. (2004) *The Politics of Aesthetics: The Distribution of the Sensible.* Translated by G. Rockhill, London: Bloomsbury Academic.

Thompson, G. (2017) Extremes of engagement: the post-classical public relations of the Islamic State. *Public Relations Review,* 43(5), 915–924.

2 Classical public relations

An introduction and some definitions

In 2012, Krishnamurthy Sriramesh and Dejan Verčič defined public relations (PR) as an occupation, a cultural practice, a social science and a social technology, that at its essence was concerned with processes of communication and relationship management in order to effect change:

> Public relations operates as a specific form of management of communication and relationships. It is strategic in its intent and focused on the production of envisioned changes among groups of people, organizations or the society at large.
>
> —Sriramesh and Verčič, (2012, p. 1)

The combination of communication and relationships proposed in this definition manifests itself in society as PR workers undertaking a specialised form of advocacy in the public sphere who act economically as paid promotional intermediaries on behalf of an internal or external/third-party client. The expansion of the field in the past 100 years – as judged by number of people employed or value of the market – confirms that PR people have proved agile and adaptable in pursuing this niche within the field of modern work Paolo Virno called "communicative labour" (2004, p. 57). According to the *2018 PR and Communications Census*, (PRCA, 2018), the sector in the United Kingdom expanded by 7% between 2016 and 2018 and is valued at £13.8bn. The scale and pervasiveness of the resulting activity means that PR techniques have become a "supportive mainstay" of a wider promotional culture, supplying a form of "information subsidy" to society (Davis, 2005, p. 149). As Jonathan Rutherford (2018) elaborated, communicative labour is immaterial, has no end product and is an example of an area of social life – he lists relationships, imagination and intuition as others – in which "what counts as a measure of productivity is performance" as judged by market-directed criteria such as the function, utility or profit it delivers to a third party, such as the client of a PR firm. Including PR within Virno's envelope of communicative labour here confirms its role as concerned with the management of communications and relationships on behalf of an individual or organisation in their interest, whether the client is a commercial corporation, campaign group, individual politician or celebrity. This line of argument emphasising the communicative dimension of PR and the role of the PR worker as agent of an end client is not intended to counter the Grunigian orthodoxy that PR is a management function itself, but rather to suggest that the *primary* concern of PR people – and of the clients who commission and pay for their services – is most often with the particular task of management of communication with publics.

In this formulation, PR is a management support function that provides advice and services in matters of communication and relationships with publics. Unlike the creative arts and professions such as medicine and law, PR is not undertaken for its own sake in the manner of the art for art's sake (*l'art pour l'art*) slogan from the eighteenth century France attributed to the philosopher Victor Cousin. Rather, alongside the other fields of communicative labour that make up the modern promotional industries (Wernick, 1991) PR is never done for its own sake but on behalf of organisations or individuals who seek promotional or persuasive advantage, for which they pay PR advisers. In this way, PR work goes beyond Bourdieu's (1984, p. 359) "cultural intermediary" categorisation, which included a more loosely defined range of "petit bourgeoisie" service providers in the fields of presentation and representation. Instead, the particular communications work of PR people can be included within the more specific scope of "promotional intermediaries" (Davis, 2005, p. 150) who play a key role in the production, consumption and promotion of commodities and culture.

The historical roots of classical public relations

National histories of PR have demonstrated the varied ways in which PR became visible in this promotional intermediary role over time, providing specialist communications management services to different areas of industry and the public sector that have required this function and been able to fund specialist service providers. There has been variance over time, between countries and sectors of industry that have identified a need for communications management in the form of PR. For example, the rapid growth and success of heavy industries such as engineering and steel manufacturing in Germany led to companies in that sector such as AEG, Krupp and Siemens undertaking planned communication from the late nineteenth and early twentieth century, alongside the beginnings of state and municipal PR efforts (Bentele and Wehmeier, 2003, p. 202). This mixed adoption of PR in German industry and politics was reflected in the subtitle of a chapter on the relationship between PR and societal culture in Germany – "between the iron cage and deliberative democracy" by Bentele and Seiffert (2012, p. 131) – which saw PR expand in support of the corporations that enabled the post-war economic miracle of Rhineland capitalism (*Wirtschaftswunder*) and the wider national and international promotion of Germany Inc. (*Deutschland AG*).

In contrast, prominent historical accounts of PR in the United Kingdom have prioritised civic PR and the way PR was used in support of an expanding state. Grant (1994) described how PR established itself in peacetime government against a flow of sentiment from some quarters in British politics that all such propaganda activities should be wound down after the end of World War I. The documentary film-maker, John Grierson, and the head of the Empire Marketing Board, Sir Stephen Tallents, are singled out in Grant's account (1994, p. 19) as "instrumental in introducing and legitimating the concept of government publicity during these years." With legitimacy established, new PR roles were created and activity undertaken in fields of national welfare such as health education, as well as on behalf of state-owned enterprises such as the General Post Office, for which Tallents worked from 1933 before moving to the BBC as its first head of PR. L'Etang's (2004) history of the post-war growth of PR in the United Kingdom emphasises the role of PR in local government and in explaining the benefits of the National Health Service and other welfare innovations of the post-war Labour government, as well as educating citizens on their new rights and responsibilities. Although L'Etang's account rightly picks out the emphasis post-war practitioners in the United Kingdom placed upon accurate and educational PR, there was also a distinctly promotional dimension to the Labour government's PR in the way it pushed new policies and celebrated the expansion of public services. Indeed, the growth of the official political PR apparatus that had been built during the Labour government to promote the new welfare state was confronted immediately by Prime Minister Winston Churchill after his return to power in October 1951. According to Sir Thomas Fife Clark, who served as the Prime Minister's PR adviser from 1952 to 1955 as well as later working as director general of the Central Office of Information (COI), Churchill abhorred the idea of using the newly expanded state PR infrastructure to disseminate policy ideas to the public. Whenever Churchill wished to communicate to voters, his preferred method was to deliver a speech in the Parliament or elsewhere or make a direct broadcast to the nation, which the news media would report in full. In contrast to the Labour Government of Clement Attlee, Churchill was opposed to giving journalists information about government actions through PR channels or even assisting newspapers on technical matters such as letting them have an advance copy of a platform speech. He was hostile to the way the Labour Government had promoted itself and its policies using PR, and has disdain for journalists and their requests for information: "Let them find out for themselves. The Public Relations Officers and the Central Office of Information set up by the Socialist government must be abolished." (Fife Clark, 1973).

The emergence of classical public relations in United States and Europe

The term PR has been described as "an artefact of American culture" (Sriramesh and Verčič, 2012, p. 1) and PR development in the United States is prominent from a historical perspective, perhaps most notably because of the legacy of Edward Bernays, in both the development of the practice and his books on *Crystallizing Public Opinion* (1923), *Propaganda* (1928) and *Public Relations* (1945). PR found a promotional role in the expansive US economy of the 1930s, as well as in other nations as a form of mass communication and relationship management at the beginning of the era of classical PR. Classical PR is characterised by a mixture of practice and theoretical orthodoxies, in which PR is a largely organisational and corporatist activity. In this view, even propaganda contributed to the general public good, in Bernays' (1928) view by increasing general knowledge and "keeping open an arena in which the battle of truth may be fairly fought." Eighty years later, in describing the positive roles that PR can play in society, a similar point was made by Robert Heath in his characterisation of PR as a "rhetorical enactment" or process (2001, p. 31) that enabled organisations to communicate well and also to contribute to a fully functioning society, by enabling all voices to be heard.

During the period from around 1920 to 2010, in which the practice of a classical style of PR developed, a body of PR theory began to build in the academy. The dates are not intended as precise markers but offered as an indicator of the start point in this explication, with the classical period following on from the theorised early "emergence of the professional field" from the mid-nineteenth century to 1918 in Bentele's (1997) periodical model of PR history, and the publication of Bernays' books on public opinion (1923) and propaganda (1928) in the United States. In the final years of World War I, Bernays had worked with Walter Lippman on US President Woodrow Wilson's campaign to persuade American voters to enter the war. As Steve Fuller (2018, p. 41) has pointed out, this "rhetorical coup" by Bernays and Lippman was a "remarkable PR feat, considering the United States was never officially attacked and that the war itself was happening more than three thousand miles away on a continent, Europe, that this nation of immigrants had been more than happy to leave." While Lippman pursued journalism as a career and later theorised on media and cultural topics, Bernays launched himself in New York in the professional-sounding business of "PR counsel" in 1919, an occupation Lippman later critiqued as "the manufacturing of consent." Bernays imported aspects of the psychology of the individual into his work, such as the concept of the subconscious mind, which had been pioneered by his uncle, Sigmund Freud. One of Bernays' innovations for PR practice was his application of this body of knowledge to the management of communications for the mass market, blending the idea of subconscious messaging with theories of crowd psychology and the herd instinct of citizens. Bernays' codification of a science of persuasion for the mass market in various books followed a line of similar developments in the emerging science of management and marketing. In 1911, FW Taylor published *The Principles of Scientific Management*, which laid out a system for analysing and improving productivity in which workflow and systems were prioritised over the individual worker. These ideas were implemented in the development of assembly line manufacturing by industrialists such as Henry Ford. The application of a systematic approach to advertising was the focus of Claude Hopkins' 1923 book, *Scientific Advertising*, in which he outlined an approach based on testing and measuring advertising effectiveness. As in Bernays' books on PR, Hopkins advocated the use of ideas from psychology and behavioural science in marketing, which were implemented through the process of split testing and of coupon-based customer tracking and loyalty schemes. The aim was to minimise losses from unsuccessful adverts while multiplying the gains from profitable ones. These books fitted into the broader movement to scientific management by helping to scientifically sell (through salesmanship in print/advertising) the mass produced goods produced by systemised manufacturing. The idea that human behaviour could be codified and that rules and systems matter more than people was a US cultural construct that was further shaped by the fast growth and laissez-faire industrialisation USA of the 1920s and 1930s. During this period, the field expanded to include personal relations and success literature, including the psychology of positive thinking and the famous book on *How to win friends and influence people* by Dale Carnegie in 1936.

Growth of a new industry of communicative labour

The origin of the word propaganda dates from the Roman Catholic Church's naming of a 1622 group during the Counter-reformation which was tasked with distributing to non-Catholic countries a set of religious ideas and messages that had been specified by their doctrinal client of senior clergymen. In this role, the Congregation for Propagation of the Faith (*Congregatio de Propaganda Fide*) can be viewed today as one of the first formally constituted in-house PR departments. Since then, like the Catholicism that was linked to the original definition of propaganda, PR has been what it has had to be over time and proved agile and adaptable in pursuing its niche of communicative labour or promotional intermediary work. Bernays himself was nimble in taking advantage of the laissez-faire economics of the 1920s America and quickly built a PR practice serving commercial and political clients. In doing so, he worked as a promotional intermediary alongside the first wave of management consulting firms and other specialist business service providers emerging at the time. In 1927, a year after the management consulting firm McKinsey was founded, the Hill and Knowlton PR agency opened its first office – and by 2018, employed staff in 80 different offices in 40 countries. Another firm that grew significantly before being absorbed into Hill and Knowlton in 2001, was founded by another influential US government PR operator from World War I, Carl Byoir, whose eponymous PR agency was set up in New York in 1930. In considering other firms founded in the United States that were still in the top ten global agencies table in 2018, there was a pause until post World War II when Fleishman Hillard started trading in 1946, followed by Edelman in 1952 and Burson Marsteller in 1953. In this reading, PR was part of the battalion of marketing communications firms that served the growing fast-moving consumer goods companies in the post-war era. Alongside the stable consensus politics of the time, the mass marketing of strong brands to consumers in steadily expanding Western economies provided a stable business for international brand companies such as Coca Cola, Procter and Gamble and Unilever, which few industries could beat for sustained returns during the 45 years up to 2010.

As the corporations and brands that the PR firms served opened up branches overseas in the post-war expansion of Western economies, the heads of several large US PR agencies took the opportunity to support their multinational US-headquartered clients in Europe and beyond. From the 1960s onwards, this led to the cultural export of classical PR throughout Europe and into the major commercial centres of Asia. Bob Leaf was appointed head of Burson Marsteller's international operations in 1975 and went on to establish offices for the firm throughout Europe and into Asia, where his ventures included setting up the first official Chinese Government approved PR firm (Leaf, 2012). The relationships aspect of PR was at the core of practice at this time and Leaf recalled that post-war PR "really was about relations with various publics" including federal and local government, potential customers and employees (Leaf, 2019). Despite it being a time when "nearly all politicians and businesses in the United Kingdom and United States were reported on positively," media relations – or more specifically the generation of "favourable publicity" – was also a priority and what Leaf described as "the main activity of the PR professional, whether in house or consultancy."

Public relations and post-war transnational institutions

The post-war period of growth for Western economies and for the PR sector has been described as the era in which "international PR starts" (Watson, 2018, p. 115). The impetus came not only from the expansion of North American commercial interests, but a commitment in Europe and beyond to new institutions focussed on the promotion of international understanding. For example, the United Nations Charter was signed on 26 June 1945 by 50 countries and the term "public information" was adopted by the United Nations (UN) as the goal of the newly established PR and communications arm, the United Nations Department of Public Information (UNDPI) when it was set up in 1946. In addition to the efforts of the UNDPI to communicate the organisation's goal of global governance and peacekeeping, the United Nations Educational, Scientific and Cultural Organisation (UNESCO) was also swift to initiate several projects on these themes in the early 1950s. UNESCO projects undertaken under the "for a better world" theme included exhibitions, posters explaining the role of education and sponsorship of the International Society for Education through Art, which argued for a new type of public engagement in peacetime that went beyond the transitional propaganda of the immediate post-war period. UNESCO's promotion of the UN's global governance work was a persuasive PR task that involved "a considerable amount of mental engineering in the shadow of the aggression of World War II," according to Duedahl (2016, p. 3). Other institutions to emerge from this shadow included the International Monetary Fund (founded in 1944), World Bank (founded in 1945), NATO (founded in 1949) and the Council of Europe (also founded in 1949). The post-war project of re-construction and transnational co-operation followed an era of PR in Europe described by Bentele (1997) in his stratified model as media relations and political propaganda under the Nazi regime in the case of his native Germany. If the Nazi Party association is put aside, this descriptor can be fairly applied across the continent for government communications throughout the 1930s and 1940s as nations shared a common goal of state-level communications in order to achieve nationalistic war goals. This genre of national propaganda was typically dual purpose, with messages to maintain morale at home targeted at the local population and propaganda for an external audience that stressed the military strengths of the country in order to discourage enemies and project power abroad.

Conformance for relational advantage

Outside the specifics of wartime propaganda, peacetime PR in the period immediately before and after World War II was focussed on achieving a relational advantage for clients with publics. This advantage was derived from communications that persuaded them to be favourable to the product, service or policy idea being propagated. Such improved relations with the public, with markets and other parties were the defining outcome of PR activity at the time. The communication approach was typically sensitive to the context in the way it was delivered, with an emphasis on conformance with the norms of mainstream society – and often the uncontroversial middle ground of politics – in order to maximise appeal. In this way, PR acted as an agent that introduced information, opinion and interests to the public sphere and public debate, as summarised in the following table.

Table 2.1 Classical and post-classical public relations

	Relationship to society and context	Public relations outcome	PR process
Classical PR	Conformance	Relational advantage	Sensitivity to others, rationality and civility
Post-classical PR	Non-conformance	Solitary and distinct positioning	Focus on self and incivility

Conformance, sensitivity to context, the use of rational argument and a civil tone were the ingredients that PR people put together to practice classical PR in order to generate relational advantages on behalf of clients. Conformance with dominant political norms sometimes extended to close relationships between PR people and governments, as PR operators attached themselves to political clients. In the United Kingdom, for example, the advertising executive turned PR man, the late Tim Bell, followed his previous employer Maurice Saatchi of the Saatchi and Saatchi advertising agency in to the House of Lords in 1998 as Lord Bell, as a reward for his work for the Conservative Party. Bell formed a close working relationship with the Conservative Party under Margaret Thatcher, and the access, contacts and influence in political life that this gave him led to rapid expansion of his PR consultancy, Bell Pottinger. Lord Bell was reported by one ex-journalist at the time to open calls to journalists with "Hello, my love" regardless of gender, in a combination of "chummy familiarity and false deference" (Burt, 2012, p. 33). The patterns of interaction between PR people and journalists during this era were based on a relationship of power imbalance, according to Cave and Rowell (2014, p. 84), that was "rarely one of equals," in which journalists had become like "babies in a high chair, waiting to be spoon-fed their stories" (Davies, 2007, p. 97).

Views varied among leaders of PR firms as to whether practitioners should make themselves available to help the communications management of any side of an argument on behalf of any type of client, and on how ethical considerations should influence the decision. In an approach that can be traced back to the Sophists, Tim

Bell of Bell Pottinger took the view that any company or individual had the right to be represented and make their case well, regardless of whether others may consider their activities or character unattractive, anti-social or even unethical. His eponymous firm made a speciality of offering PR services to "highly sensitive geo-political PR accounts and other controversial clients" including the Pinochet Foundation; Syria's first lady, Asma al-Assad; the governments of Bahrain and Egypt; Oscar Pistorius, after he was charged with murder and Alexander Lukashenko, the Belarusian dictator (Sweney, 2017). The firm collapsed in 2017 after its role in a racially themed PR campaign on behalf of the Gupta family in South Africa was made public, leading to widespread criticism in the media, clients withdrawing their accounts and expulsion from the Public Relations and Communications Association (PRCA) for unethical practice. In contrast, after over 60 years in the PR industry, which included serving as a founder of the Chartered Institute of Public Relations (CIPR) and PRCA in the United Kingdom, Tim Traverse Healy (2014) wrote in his *Credo* on PR that "the argument that we are like lawyers, available to either defend or prosecute is untenable." Instead, he argued, the purpose of PR was to contribute more positively to society by enabling "a balance between the intentions of the institutions we represent and the legitimate concerns of their community and constituency."

Operating in a less-partisan manner than Tim Bell, Alan Parker, founder of the London-based financial and corporate PR firm Brunswick, cultivated personal relationships with politicians on the left and right, with Labour Prime Minister Gordon Brown and future Conservative Prime Minister David Cameron both attending his wedding in 2007. Like Tim Bell with his Conservative political interests, since founding Finsbury in 1994, Roland Rudd has also been active in the political sphere, both through support for the Labour Party and taking leadership roles in campaign groups such as Business for New Europe which he chairs. Conformance for relational advantage extends to involvement with the arts and charities, mingling senior PR executives with high-level media and business people. Roland Rudd, for example, is a trustee of the Tate art galleries in London, where the board is chaired by Lionel Barber, editor of the *Financial Times* and fellow trustees include several senior business people. The mode of PR offered by these firms and others is about establishing and maintaining strategic relationships that in turn enable influence, through promotional activity based upon a common understanding of a pro-business agenda that reflects the goals of corporate media owners, such as the Murdoch family's News International. In this reading, the practice of classical PR is not just acting in support of corporate interests but also operating within and enabling a corporatist model of interaction within the public sphere which has endured in the United States and in European democracies for over 30 years. It is a corporatist model (Thompson, 2016) within which PR delivers value to internal and external clients as a result of its interactions with predominantly privately owned media institutions which in turn produce content that reaches audiences. The scope of influencing activity by PR operators within this corporatist model can extend to public policy engagement, through sponsorship and other

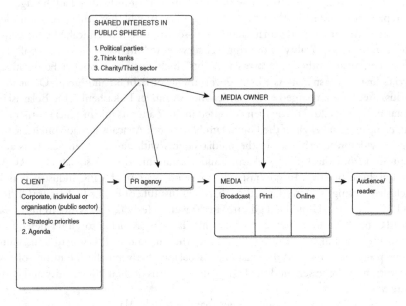

Figure 2.1 A corporatist model of media relations

involvement with actors on the policy field such as think tanks. With the exception of the BBC and similar state-funded media, the commercial interests of privately owned media defined the channels for engagement and the nature of interaction, which are now – after many years of refinement – well established. As can be seen by the charitable and political interests of successful senior PR executives, conformance and sensitivity manifests itself in the form of shared interests (with clients and media) in areas of the public sphere, such as support for certain political parties (in the form of finance or positive coverage), public policy interests (through sponsorship of think tanks or giving policy ideas space in papers) and charities. Alongside the conditions of economic and political consensus that prevailed in many developed nations, this corporatist model of PR interaction was both a sign of and a contributor to the state of relative civility and stability that resulted from a cosy cooperation amongst elite political and corporate interests. Rather than being seen as a handicap, these linkages remained favourable synergies for PR practice and business development. For example, when the corporate PR firm Seven Hills launched in the United Kingdom in 2010, it emphasised its differentials as a "new kind of campaigning communications agency, that would combine branding expertise, high-profile creative platforms and social media techniques, while maintaining a particular focus on working with entrepreneurs and growth businesses" (Vanity Fair, 2014). Four years later, the two founders were pictured in warm embrace with BBC Business Editor Kamal Ahmed and *Director* Magazine editor Lysanne Currie, showing how the new approach to social media and campaigning communications appeared equally reliant on old-style cosy relationships with key journalists and politicians. Another assessment of the business, which put founders Michal Hayman and Nick Giles in *GQ*'s 100 most influential people in Britain, gushed:

> Hayman is connected in Whitehall, while Giles, with more of a techy background, has a network that spans Silicon Roundabout to Silicon Valley via Hong Kong. Lord Bilimoria, chairman of Cobra Beer is a friend and client, as are Peter Jones and Sir Richard Branson. Their dinners, often held at The Corinthia hotel in London, attract a stellar array of guests, including government ministers and entrepreneurs.
>
> –GQ (2014)

The public sphere and classical public relations: the centre ground

If Sophists were the original middlemen offering communicative services, modern PR workers are worthy successors who have developed the processes of the promotional intermediary into an occupation that aspires to professionalism, with the associated professional institutes and growth in the provision of undergraduate and postgraduate degrees in the subject area. As well as featuring in academic literature on PR (Edwards, 2012, 2018, for example) the intermediary role has also appeared in cultural references to the work of PR people, such as John Betjeman's (1978, p. 114) poem, *Executive*, in which the executive of the poem's title is "partly a liaison man, and partly P.R.O." This poetic portrayal offers a neat insight into how the role of PR is that of an agent acting on behalf of a principal, in a role of liaison with and management of an intermediate realm of public communications and relationships.

Tim Traverse Healy used the term "public sphere" in his *Credo* and advocacy of the kind provided by the modern specialisation of classical PR is an obvious functional development in response to an information economy in which corporate and political interests seek influence in the modern public sphere of "mediated publicness" (Thompson, 1995). In contrast to advertising that was a form of sales pitch intended to advance specific commercial interests, PR was intended to promote the broader interests of corporations in the public and political spheres through the exercise of influence and opinion management, generating a "manipulated public sphere" of acclamation. (Habermas, 1991, p. 201). This development was part of a "transformation of the public sphere's political function [...] from the journalism of private men of letters to the public consumer services of the mass media" in which the public sphere served as a "platform for advertising" (Habermas, 1991, p. 181). In this mediated environment, the presentation of information to citizens and its consumption is both de-materialised and de-spatialised. Modern media systems such as television, the world wide web and social media platforms – and innovations such as the telegraph, newspapers and radio before that – ruptured longstanding norms of time and space, which meant that for most people in a society, unless they saw an event or were told of it by a fellow citizen, they had no experience of it and no way of knowing about it. Media places itself between events and people, often at a considerable physical distance but simultaneously generating a sense of closeness and even intimacy in the case of television and social media.

However, unlike genuine real-life discussions, the communicative set-pieces in the mediated public sphere such as TV newscasts are neither intimate nor does the unidirectional communication format offer opportunity for dialogue. TV news reporters, for example, are not able to engage directly with their viewing audience, sense their reaction and adapt their output accordingly, since despite often broadcasting to millions, the audience is not directly visible to the broadcast professionals who are mediating public discourse. So while media expands the range of events and information that can be absorbed, the wider lens on the world offered by media systems – which can include a role for PR people and processes in determining the style of presentation and even the scope of what is made visible – almost always comes with an angle. The media channel along with several other actors including the individual reporter, the politician giving an interview to the corporation giving a TV station access for a factory visit, all have a set of interests they represent and may seek to advocate, while consumers may or may not be conscious of these angles and certainly have no control over them. These aspects along with the incursion of "commercial communications and self-interested communications" in the public sphere led Moloney (2006, p. 177) to prefer the phrase "public domain," by which he meant the areas of public life, including "the institutions of the public, commercial and voluntary sectors" that give rise to PR work.

The media and classical public relations

From the start, mass media has been an institution that PR people have sought to influence as part of their communications management role. It was a dominant target of PR work in the classical PR era before technological change enabled mass-market internet and the widespread adoption of social media, which led in turn to a decline for many forms of printed mass media, including newspapers, and media relations work remains an important component of modern PR work for many firms and in-house teams today. PR has relied on media in order to distribute messages, exploiting its role in the middle between senders and receivers. The importance of the PR and media combination in society arises in view of the centrality of media in modern life and the way media can be used to project power. Classical PR relied on media as a channel for distribution of messages and also for their amplification. Even highly visual PR campaigns depended on the existing media in order to reach audiences. For example, in World War II, the photographer Lee Miller created a series of images as part of the UK's Ministry of Information's (MOI) campaign to communicate with women in order to maintain good morale and emphasise their role in winning the war as well as specific goals such as promoting shorter hairstyles for women working in factories in order to prevent accidents and encouraging women to continue to dress with style. Following the success of two series of photo stories early on in the war under the titles Wartime Fashion and Lifestyle and Women and the Home Front, when female conscription was introduced in 1941, these were followed up by the Women in Uniform series. All of this content was distributed through the medium of women's magazines, including *Vogue*, which the MOI saw as an important channel through which to reach a female audience. Audrey Withers, the *Vogue* editor who worked with the MOI on the campaign summed up the interaction between the MOI and British Vogue, describing a two-way interaction that was based on the distribution reach of *Vogue* and other publications:

> Women's magazines had a special place in government thinking during the war because with men in the forces, women carried the whole responsibility of family life and the way to catch women's attention was through the pages of magazines which in total were read by almost every woman in the country.
>
> They sought advice from us too – telling us what they wanted to achieve and how best to achieve it. We were even appealed to on fashion grounds. The vogue was for shoulder length hair. Girls working in factories refused to wear the ugly caps provided, with the result that their hair caught in machines and there were horrible scalping accidents. Could we persuade girls that short hair was chic?
>
> –Roberts (2015, p. 19)

All forms of media, whether print, broadcast or online, play an important role in society by establishing facts and shared truth. In doing so, media draws the boundaries of broadly agreed "centre ground," both by scoping and informing debates on topics of contention in society, and arriving at a consensus view. All sides of the debate may have been influenced by PR work acting on behalf of interested parties, before balance emerges. Habermas was critical of this smoothing over bumps to create a middle ground, claiming that the process represented a "refeudalisation of the public sphere" (1991, p. 194). This interaction of the media with state and corporate PR interests was seen in similarly critical light by Chomsky and Herman (1994) as the manufacture of consent in society in order to support a public interest that they claimed was built upon sometimes dubious informational foundations.

Classical public relations and the post-war consensus

One example of this refeudalisation was the fusing of politics and capitalism in the post-war Keynesian consensus, in which economic policies of state involvement in industry and the pursuit of high levels of employment became accepted as the norm by policy makers on the left and right in many developed countries. The overall result was an extended period of relatively balanced, moderate centrist policies throughout the post-war Keynesian era, during which capitalism and democracy functioned "incredibly well" together according to the German political theorist, Wolfgang Streeck, although he has since said that he sees that era as an aberration (O'Brien, 2019). The centrality of the PR functions of communication and persuasion in establishing this consensus was pointed out in Gabriel Almond and Sidney Verba's (1963, p. 8) description of Britain in their 1963 book, *The Civic Culture*, in which they reported a "pluralistic culture based on communication and persuasion, a culture of consensus and diversity." In their analysis, consensus had resulted from vigorous communication and persuasion activity in the public sphere, that had a cultural as well as political dimension, resulting in a relatively low volatility in British politics in the post-war period compared with the flux in the years leading up to the Brexit vote and its immediate aftermath. In analysis of the UK's contemporary political difficulties, *The Economist* (2019) contrasted the contemporary sense of a "collapse of legitimacy" of the political class with what Almond and Verba had described as a "high degree of faith in political institutions" at the time of their early 1960s study.

From the 1970s onwards, the counter-doctrine of neo-liberal economics which combined market liberalisation with deregulation of sectors including finance was promoted in similar ways, using PR, as Susan George acknowledged in a speech to the *Conference on Economic Sovereignty in a Globalising World* in 1999 in Bangkok:

> Starting from a tiny embryo at the University of Chicago with the philosopher-economist Friedrich von Hayek and his students like Milton Friedman at its nucleus, the neo-liberals and their funders have created a huge international network of foundations, institutes, research centers, publications, scholars, writers and public relations hacks to develop, package and push their ideas and doctrine relentlessly.
>
> –George (1999, p. 5)

The role of PR in promoting neo-liberalism and the way in which it "reinforces the neoliberal order" (Cronin, 2018) became a "default" setting, according to Kristin Demetrious and Anne Surma (2019, p. 106) in their introduction to a special edition of *Public Relations Inquiry* on the theme of "The intersection between public relations and neoliberalism." A cover of *The Economist* magazine in June 2017, with the title "Britain's missing middle" was one indicator of the end of this era and the beginning of a collapse of the neo-liberal consensus that had endured for around 40 years ("The summer of discontent," 2017). According to *the Financial Times* chief economics commentator, Martin Wolf (2018), the sustained damage of the 2008 financial crisis ten years on marked the end of "a dominant consensus for liberalisation and shifted political energy towards populist extremes."

The peak of a "monstrous industry"?

Alongside economic and political turbulence, a varied set of signals began to suggest that the classical PR era was reaching a peak. In financial markets, the rising market profile and salary of Sir Martin Sorrell, chairman of the marketing services group WPP, offered a useful indicator of the importance – or self-importance – of the PR, advertising and marketing communications business. The peak was signalled when in 2014, Sorrell earned £43m and was named as the highest-paid chief executive in the Financial Times Stock Exchange list (FTSE) of the top 100 quoted companies in the United Kingdom (FTSE 100), beating bankers, insurers and oil company CEOs by some margin. For what was essentially a people-based service business, the pay package of WPP's CEO was unusually high and brought criticism from shareholders, as well as sections of the media. The extraction of profits from the

PR and marketing communications sector was not unusual. The more substantial change was that a sizeable proportion of the sector was now controlled by financial managers in quoted holding companies – such as Omnicom and WPP – who were focussed solely on making the most of their invested asset and achieving the best returns for shareholders. In the larger cases, PR firms were no longer controlled by practitioners but by financial managers with little experience of working in the PR and marketing fields. One notable variation on the financialisation of PR through the acquisition of firms through holding companies was the September 2006 acquisition of the London financial PR firm Financial Dynamics, by the consulting and corporate investigations group, FTI Consulting. Financial Dynamics had previously been owned by its managers and the private equity investor Advent International, and with a price tag of $260m achieved, the *Financial Times* reported on this new peak for financial value in the PR sector:

> The deal represents the highest price ever paid for a financial public relations company, underlining the increasing value that corporate clients place on issues such as reputation management. It is also the first time a financial PR firm has been acquired by a consulting company, rather than a media or marketing group.
>
> –Wighton (2006)

In political PR, as well as contributing to the public sphere as consultants to politicians, towards the end of the classical era from around 1990, some operators moved from advising on presentation to getting elected and becoming political actors themselves and making policy. Peter Mandelson, the Labour Party's Director of Communications from 1985 to 1991 went on to serve as Trade and Industry Minister in Tony Blair's government and later as a European Commissioner with the trade portfolio. PR's capture of politics was arguably complete after the 2010 election, which saw the formation of a coalition government by Conservative Prime Minister, David Cameron, whose only job outside politics had been PR manager for a broadcaster, supported by a Deputy Prime Minister, Nick Clegg, whose only jobs outside politics had been roles in PR and lobbying firms. In October 2018, after leaving politics, Clegg moved back into the PR field when he was appointed Vice-President, Global Affairs and Communications at Facebook. As well as its presence in national political life, PR was also pervasive in arts and culture, with political spin featuring widely in popular TV series such as *The Thick of It* in the United Kingdom and *The West Wing* and *Veep* in the United States. The combination of ubiquity and ambition of the peak PR period found expression in the academic sphere with Robert Brown's (2014) book, *The Public Relations of Everything*, in which he argued that until around 2010, "dominant theorists had tailored a suit much too small for the realities of PR."

In 2003, in an interview for the documentary film, *The Corporation*, Noam Chomsky criticised PR as a "monstrous industry" (Achbar and Abbott, 2003) inferring that it operated solely on behalf of corporate and governmental interests against citizens and society. In his book *Propaganda and the Public Mind*, which was first published in 2001, Chomsky (2015, p. 165) had already traced the PR industry's goals and purpose back to the work of Edward Bernays and Walter Lippman in the aftermath of their work around World War I in the United States. According to Chomsky (p. 165), the justification for regimenting the public mind was because "we are the good guys and smart guys and they are stupid and dumb, and therefore we have to control them for their own good" which was possible because the PR industry had "marvellous techniques" at their disposal for this purpose. In the commercial sphere, the goal was to create what Chomsky called "fancied wants" in order to drive demand and to focus the public's attention upon consumption using PR and related promotions as tools of "domination and control."

For the latter years of the period of classical PR, critics such as Chomsky characterised PR as a secretive, persuasive and sometimes deceptive tool used by powerful interests that either hired PR firms or in-house specialists to spin for them. For most of the public, for most of the time, the communicative labour of PR people seeking to promote and influence them was indeed invisible or at least hard to detect in everyday consumption of media. Yet from around 2010 onwards, as citizens became more literate in classical PR techniques and cynical to the motives of those who deployed them, they became resistant to the once reliable modes of civic engagement deployed by politicians and corporations. While at one level it may seem a positive thing that citizens are more conscious of attempts to use PR to control the "public mind," to use Chomsky's phrase, the reality is that such understanding is only partially developed. The result, therefore, is not a positive sense of participation through being able to express their point of view in the public sphere, but instead a rather negative view that PR is part of a wider process of disinformation and control to which they are unwillingly subjected.

References

Achbar, M. and Abbott, J. (2003) *The Corporation*. Directed by M. Achbar. Canada: Big Picture Media Corporation.

Almond, G. and Verba, S. (1963) *The Civic Culture: Political Attitudes and Democracy in Five Nations*. Princeton: Princeton University Press.

Bentele, G. (1997) PR-Historiographie und functional-integrative Schichtung: Ein neuer Ansatz zur PR-Geschichtsschreibung [PR historiography and functional-integral stratification: a new approach to PR historiography]. In: Szyszka, P. (Ed.), *Auf der Suche nach Identiat: PR-Geschichte als Theoriebaustein [The Quest for Identity: PR As Theoretical Constituent]*. Berlin: Vistas, pp. 137–169.

Bentele, G. and Seiffert, J. (2012) Public relations and culture in Germany: between the "iron cage" and deliberative democracy. In: Sriramesh, K. and Verčič, D. (Eds.) *Culture and Public Relations: Links and Implications*. London: Routledge, pp. 124–141.

Bentele, G. and Wehmeier, S. (2003) From literary bureaus to a modern profession: the development and current structure of public relations in Germany. In: Sriramesh, K. and Verčič, D. (Eds.) *The Global Public Relations Handbook: Theory, Research and Practice*. Mahwah, New Jersey: Lawrence Erlbaum, pp. 199–221.

Bernays, E. (1928) *Propaganda*. New York: Horace Liveright.

Bernays, E. (1928) *Crystallizing Public Opinion*. New York: Boni and Liveright.

Bernays, E. (1945) *Public Relations*. Boston, Massachusetts: Bellman.

Betjeman, J. (1978) *The Best of Betjeman*. London: Penguin.

Bourdieu, P. (1984) *Distinction*. London: Routledge.

Brown, R. (2014) *The Public Relations of Everything: The Ancient, Modern and Postmodern Dramatic History of an Idea*. London: Routledge.

Burt, T. (2012) *Dark Art: The Changing Face of Public Relations*. London: Elliott and Thompson.

Carnegie, D. (1936) *How to Win Friends and Influence People*. New York: Simon and Schuster.

Cave, T. and Rowell, A. (2014) *A Quiet Word: Lobbying, Crony Capitalism and Broken Politics in Britain*. London: Bodley Head.

Chomsky, N. (2015) *Propaganda and the Public Mind*. London: Pluto Press.

Chomsky, N. and Herman, E. (1988) *Manufacturing Consent*. New York: Random House.

Cronin, A. (2018) *Public Relations Capitalism*. Basingstoke: Palgrave.

Davies, N. (2008) *Flat Earth News*. London: Vintage Books.

Davis, A. (2005) Placing promotional culture. In: Curran, J., and Morley, D. (Eds.) *Media and Cultural Theory*. London: Routledge, pp. 149–163.

Demetrious, K. and Surma, A. (2019) In ordinary places: the intersections between public relations and neoliberalism: Special Issue, Editorial. *Public Relations Inquiry*, 8 (2), 105–108.

Duedahl, P. (2016) Introduction: out of the house: on the global history of UNESCO 1945-2015. In: Duedahl, P. (Ed.) *A History of UNESCO: Global Actions and Impacts*. Basingstoke: Palgrave Macmillan, pp. 3–29.

The Economist. (2017) The summer of discontent. 3 June, pp. 20–24.

The Economist. (2019) The followership problem. 4 May, p. 31.

Edwards, L. (2012) Exploring the role of public relations as a cultural intermediary occupation. *Cultural Sociology*, 6 (4), 438–454.

Edwards, L. (2018) *Understanding Public Relations: Theory, Culture and Society*. London: Sage.

Fife Clark, T. (1973) *Churchill and the Press*, The Papers of Sir Thomas Fife Clark. (FICA 3/2), University of Cambridge: Churchill Archives Centre.

Fuller, S. (2018) *Post Truth: Knowledge As a Power Game*. London: Anthem Press.

George, S. (1999) *A Short History of Neoliberalism*. Proceedings of the Conference on Economic Sovereignty in a Globalising World, Bangkok, 24–26 March 1999. Available at: https://numerov.com/dspace/es/232490.pdf

GQ. (2014) GQ and EI's 100 Most Connected Men 2014, *GQ*, 8 December. Available at: https://www.gq-magazine.co.uk/gallery/100-most-connected-men-2014

Grant, M. (1994) *Propaganda and the Role of the State in Inter-War Britain*. Oxford: Oxford University Press.

Habermas, J. (1991) *The Structural Transformation of the Public Sphere*. Cambridge, Massachusetts: MIT Press.

Heath, R. (2001) A rhetorical enactment rationale for public relations. In: Heath, R. (Ed.) *Handbook of Public Relations*. Thousand Oaks, California: Sage, pp. 31–50.

Heath, R. (2006) Onward into the fog: thoughts on public relations' research directions. *Journal of Public Relations Research*, 18 (2), 93–114.

Hopkins, C. (1923) *Scientific Advertising*. New York: Moore

L'Etang, J. (2004) *Public Relations in Britain*. London: Lawrence Erlbaum Associates.

Leaf, R. (2012) *The Art of Perception*. London: Atlantic Books.

Leaf, R. (2019) 7 questions for managing brand perceptions. *Influence*, Q2, 52–53.

Moloney, K. (2006) *Rethinking Public Relations*. London: Routledge.

O'Brien, H. (2019) Wolfgang Streeck on why Brexit offers the best path for Britain. *New Statesman*, 22–28 March, p. 18.

PRCA (2018) PR and Communications Census 2018, London, Public Relations and Communications Association. Available at: https://www.prca.org.uk/sites/default/files/PR%20and%20Communications%20Census%202018.pdf

Roberts, H. (2015) *Lee Miller: A Woman's War*. London: Thames and Hudson.

Rutherford, J. (2018) How the decline of the working class made Labour a party of the bourgeois left. *The New Statesman*, 21–27 September, pp. 34–39.

Sriramesh, K. and Verčič, D. (2012) *Culture and Public Relations: Links and Implications*. London: Routledge.

Sweney, M. (2017) Bell Pottinger: key players and controversial clients. *The Guardian*, 5 September. Available at: https://www.theguardian.com/business/2017/sep/04/bell-pottinger-thatcher-pr-clients

Taylor, F.W. (1911) *The Principles of Scientific Management*. New York: Harper & Brothers.

Thompson, G. (2016) Public relations interactions with Wikipedia. *Journal of Communication Management*, 20 (1), 4–20.

Thompson, J. (1995) *The Media and the Modernity: A Social Theory of the Media*. Cambridge: Polity Press.

Healy, T.T. (2014) *Credo*, Stephen Waddington Blog, 3 March. Available at: https://wadds.co.uk/blog/2014/03/03/public-relations-credo-tim-traverse-healy

Vanity Fair. (2014) Seven Up. *Vanity Fair*, July, p. 51.

Virno, P. (2004) *A Grammar of the Multitude: For an Analysis of Contemporary Forms of Life*. Los Angeles, California: Semiotext.

Watson. T. (2018) What history tells us about public relations. In: Waddington, S. (Ed.) *Platinum*. London: Chartered Institute of Public Relations, pp. 113–117.

Wernick, A. (1991) *Promotional Culture: Advertising, Ideology and Symbolic Expression*. London: Sage.

Wighton, D. (2006) FTI pays $260m for financial dynamics, *Financial Times*, 11 September. Available at: https://www.ft.com/content/d961ef16-41b9-11db-b4ab-0000779e2340

Wolf. M. (2018) Crash landing. *Financial Times (Life and Arts Section)*, 21–22 July, p. 9.

3 Post-classical public relations

A new style of public relations work for the post-truth era

The premise for this book's proposition of post-classical public relations (PR) is that many theories, models and historically derived approaches to PR from the past 100 years or so no longer reflect some aspects of PR work in the twenty-first century. A Google search for the clause "PR is dead" currently yields 209 million results, which while disappointing at one level provides some support for this premise. There are many variants on the theme: "Media relations is dead," for example, as well as counterarguments: "PR isn't dead: it is just different." The phrase is the title of a book by Robert Phillips (2015), who worked in PR for a couple of decades rising to run the Europe, Middle East and Africa (EMEA) operations of Edelman. His book offers some tactical insights – most emphatically that the old ways of controlling messages are no longer relevant to the twenty-first century media landscape and not effective in a world of autonomous and widespread social media – alongside some more strategic observations on the need for corporations to be more participative in their communications than controlling. Perhaps most interestingly, he calls for communications directors to see their role as citizenship officers or activists responsible for channelling the civic energy of staff and customers, with the aim of creating what he calls public value.

These and other calls for change by practitioners suggest the need for a new way of thinking about the contemporary PR that reflects today's professional practices, alongside the changes in media, culture and society that are shaping PR work. As already stated in Chapter 1, the dominant theory and descriptor for PR for over 30 years has been Grunig and Hunt's (1984) four-fold typology. This reflected a view of the way PR developed in the United States for the late nineteenth and early twentieth century and was practiced in the 1970s and 1980s, in the media and social context of that time. So while Grunig and Hunt's work has provided an enduring descriptor of PR work of a certain period, it is of less value in describing and analysing the varied purposes and modes of the contemporary practice, partly because it could not reasonably anticipate the effects of communication technology on the ways people share information online today. The chapter that follows lays out a view on the emerging post-classical style of PR that is developing to cope with the current post-truth era, along with some consideration of the conditions in society and the media in particular, that have driven the development of new modes of practice.

Convergence

While innovations in communication technologies have been important in driving change in the way PR and media workers operate, the biggest strides of innovation have been a result of convergence of what were previously separate media, channels, pieces of hardware or technologies. In the media sector, Jenkins (2006) described this convergence as "the flow of content across multiple media platforms, the coopera- tion between multiple media industries, and the migratory behavior of media audi- ences." While at the end of the twentieth century there were examples of common ownership of different media types – such as Rupert Murdoch's proprietorship of Sky television and Fox alongside newspaper assets such as *The Times* and *The Sun* in the United Kingdom as well as *The Wall Street Journal* in the United States – these media categories were readily distinguishable from each other and operated in different ways. The advent of mass-market internet, including the availability of high bandwidth on mobile networks enabled desktop PCs and smart mobile phones with the capability to access multiple forms of media, including news, TV and cinema, which were previously purchased separately, distributed on different media and then consumed on separate devices.

The impetus for this change came from beyond the engineering momentum for merging technologies and included cultural and commercial motives. In the media and marketing services sector, between 1985 and 2018, Martin Sorrell built up WPP into a services business employing over 130,000 people in 400 companies in advertising, media buying, analytics, research and PR. The global network that resulted represented an anticipation of the globalisation of marketing communic- ations in the 1990s alongside an erosion of the boundaries between the different types of agencies, and the need for them to work together in order to solve clients' communications challenges. In a digitally converged media landscape, clients expect their agencies to work together, or even merge into one service provider such as WPP, in order to produce campaigns and messages that work globally across all types of media. The scope of PR activity in this environment extends to understanding Search Engine Optimisation (SEO) in order to integrate SEO techniques into PR work. This includes managing the creation of content such as news releases in SEO- conscious ways and ensuring keywords are used in ways that deliver clear searchable messages and enhance search rankings. PR content and the results it generates in the form of earned media (media coverage in mainstream media) are now a key currency in the economy of digital attention, since press coverage is one of the top ranking factors in the Google search algorithm.

The role of social media

Digital media platforms such as Facebook, Instagram and Twitter depend on at least some of their media consumers also acting as producers of content, or actively participating in online conversations and communities in order to generate network effects that make the media service valuable and engaging to audiences.

One consequence of this role of consumers, employees and even Presidents of the United States as participants in the social media messaging chain is the loss of control that PR people used to be able to exercise over the messages that were developed and distributed on behalf of their organisation. The impact of social media on media infrastructures and economics has been addressed by numerous writers, as well as in PR books that have stressed the positive prospects of social media for PR (Philips and Young, 2009, for example). For the professional institutes, the need for content, narrative and engagement made social media an ideal new media "territory" or field of practice that was ripe for capture by PR rather than advertising agencies, for example. Valentini's (2014, p. 171) reflection on the effect of social media on PR made the point that initial assessments by many practitioners were that new media formats would enable more symmetrical two-way communication and engagement between publics and organisations than were possible using the traditional media channels, producing a "dominant public relations discourse" that "using social media is good." While the underlying functional characteristics of social media suggested this was a reasonable assumption, there were several barriers within the platforms – including protocols, best practices, unwritten rules of usage and terms of service – that did not always synchronise well with the expectations and needs of PR practitioners and their clients. However, some PR people did adapt swiftly, both in the way they incorporated social media into their practice and in spotting a new niche of communicative labour from which they could profit. This manifested itself initially through the formation of specialised digital and social media agencies such as the UK's *We Are Social*, which was founded in 2008, before social media capability was more widely integrated into the offerings of mainstream PR firms. PR people's adaption of social media has included using it as a way to better control messages on the owned media sites of their clients on social media platforms such as Facebook, Twitter and others, offering clients the value proposition of high-quality, carefully curated and compelling narratives and content, that are more authentic than the more sales-led material generated for owned social media channels by advertising agencies.

Mediums and messages again

Marshall MacLuhan's explanation of the relationship between the medium and the message has been a mainstay of media and cultural studies for over 50 years. The increased use of social media in society and the decline of consumption of some so-called traditional media, such as newspapers and television, have disrupted the corporatist model of PR in which PR extracted value from the information supply chain by controlling access to types of information, such as the news contained in a press release or access to a celebrity for a photo shoot or a politician for an interview. This classical form of PR was partly about professional skills in the area of written, spoken and sometimes visual communications but was also about relationships. The economic value came from the quality of relationships and trust that existed with a tightly held circle of editors and journalists, in which rents (in the form of fees) were charged to clients, on the basis of access to media and the resulting press coverage. That is to say, the economics of the PR business was driven largely by media access, in a commercial logic that saw PR holding something of value to journalists on the supply side in the form of stories. Control of access to media (through quality of relationships) was used to create value on the buy side in the form of press coverage for clients, who were billed fees relating to the PR peoples' efforts and time, but sometimes with additional bonus payments in return for coverage. In this political economy of media relations, the bargaining chip that PR people were able to bring to the media relations table throughout the classical PR era was information assets that have potential value as media content, whether that original asset was a news story, financial results, survey results or film clip from a video news release (VNR). In the case of social media and important common-pool media such as Wikipedia, this point of value has been undermined by the power of multiple authors contributing freely to a common-pool media resource to generate a richer and more diverse information set than the entire global PR sector could deliver even if it pooled all its content. While acknowledging that a significant proportion of PR activity was not media relations along these rather simplistic lines, this model – in which a PR person was often judged on the basis of contacts and coverage – was reasonably prevalent for much of the classical PR era. In the lobbying or public affairs field, a similar emphasis on the careful cultivation and subsequent exploitation of political contacts was an important source of value creation in terms of client fees.

So while offering opportunities for some, social media also broke some of the boundaries and nodes of value in the system of exchange between media and PR people that was underpinned by classical PR. The erosion of the dominance of print media and replacement of old media boundaries with the free-for-all publishing platforms of Facebook, Instagram, Twitter and others disrupted the economic logic of media relations and undermined the value nexus of press coverage, which was central to the value proposition of many PR agencies. Issues relating to measurement of PR value and impact have been contended for many years within academic circles. There have also been tensions between PR service providers and buyers who continue to favour the simplicity of media coverage. A more effective and appropriate form of measurement would be audience surveys, for example, to assess the persuasive effects before, during and after campaigns, but the market reality is that despite declarations by professional bodies such as the International Association for Measurements and Evaluation of Communication (AMEC), media coverage remains a measurement or more accurately a proxy measure for PR effectiveness for some clients and agencies. Instead of media coverage as a form of measurement and campaign impact – which has been widely criticised as inadequate – PR service providers are subject to micro-measurement and data-driven evaluation of the social media content they produce, using perhaps even more questionable (but cheap and easy to gather) metrics such as how many likes a post has gathered online and how many views an online video has attracted.

In the field of political PR, the widespread use of social media campaigning has led to a dystopian scenario where in "the land of the technically dependent, the savvy political operator is king," (Runciman, 2018, p. 125). For Runciman, there is something about the nature of social media that has led to certain messages prevailing that are inherently harmful to democratic politics:

> Social networks have made representative democracy seem fake. The fake versions that exist online appear more real. For now, we have destroyed something without knowing how to replace it.
>
> –Runciman (2018, p. 151)

Similarly, in mainstream PR practice, social media is not about business as usual, supporting a routine PR system of announcements, launches and good news stories in the commercial world or well-argued, in-depth presentations of policy in the civic sphere. Rather, by around 2010, successful social media campaigns (as judged by levels of user engagement) typically comprised either powerful images or memes that spread swiftly from user to user and/or co-ordinated attacks on either an individual, organisation or issue that one group perceives and presents as an enemy. The second mode of content reflects the unsavoury truth that social media seems to work well in enabling small groups to attack others and affect a form of digital destruction. An early and widely documented example was the 2008 attack on the Church of Scientology by the 4chan hacking community in the United States which focussed on taking down its web sites through denial of service (DoS) attacks. The success of the campaign led one 4chan user to post that "we can destroy whatever we like" and while this may seem hyperbole, the broader "Project Chanology showed how, if you wanted to instigate digital disruption, it was not hard to do – particularly through synchronized collective action" (Moore, 2018, p. 16).

The power of the platforms

Dominant social media applications such as Facebook, Instagram and Twitter provide the platform for the creation, display and distribution of the content and messages generated by post-classical PR workers. With daily users of Facebook alone spending 41 minutes on the platform, according to one study, the potentially transformative effect of these applications was neatly summed up by Nicholas Carr (2010, p. 3): "As our window into the world and onto ourselves, a popular medium moulds what we see and how we see it – and eventually, if we use it enough, it changes who we are, as individuals and as a society." In these conditions of what Giddens (2013) has described as "reflexive modernity," mass media's function as a main provider of information means that media no longer merely reflects the social world but actively shapes it. An element of the significance of post-classical PR is the way it provides inputs to these platforms, with PR content forming a growing component of this information infrastructure.

PR's contribution to the world of mediated content occurs at the local and global level, with space collapsing as both merge in digital media, to create a shared experience of the world for segmented audiences – or at least the ones that are profitable for the social media platforms to segment. But some social media audiences are more powerful than others and despite the early rhetoric of the potential empowerment of users as content producers, platforms have shown little focus on considering the best intentions of small and minority audiences in their quest for measurement and user attention. Post-classical PR has mimicked these priorities and seeks to exploit big data to enable creation and targeting of relevant messages and then exploits the big audiences of the social media platforms in order to maximise distribution. In its embrace of bigness, PR is merely adapting to survive in the big media environment, where the only winning strategy that will enable business survival is scale. Big media and tied audiences are a new reality in the sector, which has already seen owners such as Murdoch-family concluding in 2018 that its Sky subscription TV operations with 23m subscribers and over 30,000 employees were too small to compete in the long term with web-based entrants to the entertainment business such as Amazon, Apple, Facebook and Netflix.

Trust in media and the public relations of distraction

The January 2017 Edelman Trust Barometer reported that trust in traditional media by people around the globe had fallen from 48% to 43% in a year and was mistrusted in 80% of the nations surveyed. In a thoughtful blog post on the findings, Richard Edelman offered his analysis of the change:

> Media is now seen to be politicized, unable to meet its reporting obligations due to economic pressures, and following social media rather than creating the agenda. Donald Trump circumvents mainstream media with his Twitter account, in this way seeming more genuine, approachable and responsive. Technology has allowed the creation of media echo chambers, so that a person can reinforce, rather than debate, viewpoints. In fact, 59 percent of respondents would believe a search engine over a human editor. It is a world of self-reference, as respondents are nearly four times more likely to ignore information that supports a position that they do not believe in.
>
> –Edelman (2017)

A Gallup study tracked a similar decline over a longer time period, concluding that while 40 years ago, almost 75% of Americans trusted the news media to report the news "fully, accurately and fairly" the figure was 32% by 2016. The trend among the Republican voters backing Donald Trump for President was more pronounced:

> Trump's most loyal supporters had already ceased to believe what they read in newspapers or saw on television bulletins. [...] as recently as 2002, nearly half of Republican supporters trusted journalists; in the past year alone, the figure had halved to 14%.
>
> –Rowley (2016, p. 31)

This partisanship among audiences and sense of disdain for the conventional media among Trump supporters meant that they trusted their candidate and their own instincts more than the collective research and analysis capability of the mainstream press. The result was that incidents that would normally be seen as PR disasters – such as a 2005 recording of Trump bragging that he used to grab women "by the pussy," for example – instead confirmed the view of his fervent followers that the press was out to get him (Rowley, 2016, p. 31).

Centrality of media in the public relations of distraction

Exploitation of media is central to the creation of a promotional presence, which can include strategies of post-truth in order to distract audiences from focussing on a lack of substance. A shared characteristic of several political players using this PR approach is their familiarity with the operations of modern media channels either through ownership of a media operation – such as Silvio Berlusconi in Italy – or involvement as performers. In the United Kingdom, Nigel Farage of the Brexit party (and previously leader of the United Kingdom Independence Party (UKIP)) hosted a daily radio show on the LBC news and talk station, Prime Minster Boris Johnson appeared on the BBC TV comedy quiz show *Have I Got News for You* as a contestant and presenter, while in the United States Donald Trump achieved national celebrity status in the United States not through his property empire but as the host of the reality TV show, *The Apprentice*.

In the 1995 film, *To Die For*, Nicole Kidman played a regional TV weather presenter who observes early in the criminal/comedy film that "You're not anyone in America unless you're on TV." This fictional insight was at the heart of the political media relations operation of Silvio Berlusconi, who shrewdly analysed how facts and fabrication interacted in modern media: "Don't you understand that if something is not on TV it doesn't exist? Not a product, not a politician nor an idea!" (Gray, 2017). Berlusconi's existential assumption about modern media effects was coupled by one of his PR aides with theories from Guy Debord's (1994) *The Society of the Spectacle* on how contemporary capitalism and media systems deploy streams of imagery in order to distract audiences from reality. The result of this approach is a focus on subjective views based upon whether something feels right, on sensation and emotions rather than carefully researched facts. The end result for audiences is a sense of emotional entitlement to feel good and not think too hard about the "facts" that are introduced to them in public debate. John Lloyd addressed the informational deficit that results from such emotional audience primacy in his book, *The Power and The Story: the Global Battle for News and Information* (2017), in which he recorded that journalists need fewer facts in order to generate content for modern media "but above all they need to stimulate or imitate emotion." Debord's emphasis on the influence on artificial media spectacles in society has become a dominant feature of the twenty-first century politics, with Berlusconi, Trump and others using emotion, media performance and spectacle rather than policy or facts as their communicative currency with the electorate.

There have also been changes in the attitudes of principal corporate and political actors to the media and how they relate to audiences, with successful politicians from the left and right of the political spectrum sharing communicative characteristics. For example, in their book *Corbynism: A Critical Approach*, Bolton and Pitts

(2018) identified similarities between Jeremy Corbyn and Donald Trump in the way both have projected a conspiratorial view of the world in which elites rig the system against ordinary people while the start point of their media relations approach is that the mainstream media cannot be trusted and is biased against them. For Trump's campaign advisers, delivering a new kind of politics meant media relations with the mainstream media consisted of little more than agitating rather than co-operating with journalists, in a relationship of inverse returns: "What we are witnessing now is the birth of a new political order, and the more frantic a handful of media elites become, the more powerful that new political order becomes" (Danner, 2017). Yet Danner also observed how the first weeks of the Trump Presidency were "an ongoing seminar on where norms end and laws begin." Untroubled by the norms of political communication, the new President's antagonistic statements about Muslims and policy proposals of a travel ban left the propagandists of the Islamic State "nothing short of exultant." Corbyn also brought a combination of fresh ideas and a novel approach to political communications. As John McTiernan (2019), an aide to the UK Prime Minster, Tony Blair, has reflected: "We used to say that political renewal needed new faces, new ideas, new voices, and new channels of communication." He goes on to partly attribute Jeremy Corbyn's success to a combination of the new campaign organisation Momentum and shrewd exploitation of a "digital infrastructure" that in turn "created new channels such as the always interesting NovaraMedia," a left-wing online media organisation that describes itself as "politically committed" and which is largely supportive of Corby's political agenda.

The return of inauthenticity

Towards the end of the classical period of PR, from the 1990s onwards, repeated exposure to the expert but sometimes inauthentic outputs of professionalised communicative labour led to increased public awareness of the presence of PR efforts and the processes of persuasion in daily life that were previously hidden. In the twenty or so years from around 1990 to 2010, more and more people in developed countries became literate in classical PR techniques. As a result of becoming accustomed to the way PR operated (or at least a popular and non-expert view of how it does so), people had an understanding of when they were on the receiving end of PR efforts and began to spot PR techniques when they are deployed. Rather like a disease becoming resistant to antibiotics, so certain audiences became defiant to once reliable modes of communication and civic engagement deployed by politicians, corporates and interest groups, and cynical about the motives for doing so. This new audience literacy led to fatigue and resentment as audiences tired of the sense that they were being manipulated by techniques such as repetition of messages, insincere gestures and avoidance of giving direct answers to questions. The idea that ubiquitous agents were spinning messages through a process of PR seems to have begun to enter general public consciousness from the 1990s onwards. PR people and processes featured in various fictional portrayals, including the portrayal of PR in US politics in the *Primary Colours* book, written by Joe

Klein (but initially published anonymously and widely presumed to be the work of a Bill Clinton campaign insider because of its thinly disguised portrayal of the 1992 Clinton US Presidential Campaign), that was also made into a successful 1998 film. At the same time, corporations, governments, interest groups and others were sometimes said to have made decisions for "public relations reasons" but this was rarely a compliment. When decisions were made in this way, if the resulting solution was insubstantial or a rather showy or phoney course of action, it was referred to as "just a PR exercise" rather than a meaningful resolution. Rather it was a criticism that the decision was superficial, lacking in authentic reasoning and acting to gain favour or even obscure a truth rather than for a more sound set of motivations, such as economic criteria, for example.

Reflecting on the poor performance of the UK's Conservative party in the 2017 election, George Freeman (BBC News, 2017a) chair of the Conservative Party policy forum, concluded that the electorate had rejected the campaign his party had fought, partly because of the artificiality of its classical PR practices of controlled messages repeated regularly across multiple distribution channels to ensure consistency. Voters simply called out the inauthenticity of this type of communication: "People are distrusting of big machine politics, the repeated mantra, the line to take and they want a more authentic, personal form of communication." Freeman's point is a rare recognition by someone in the public realm of the corrosive effect over time of public awareness of the inauthenticity of techniques of professional PR in the public sphere. His comments were recorded after the poor performance of the Conservative party in a campaign that had been based on advice from the political campaign consultant, Lynton Crosby. Crosby's advice on messaging and narrative was for mantra-like repetition by Theresa May and other Conservative leaders of their proposition of "Strong and Stable" government.

Front groups: public relations and inauthenticity in public sphere

As well as the open signs of PR functioning in civil society, front groups created by PR firms and campaign groups have engaged in less-visible forms of persuasion that in some cases amounted to conspiracies to deceive. The deception often starts with a deliberate misrepresentation of the source of finance and membership of the groups themselves which are "designed to persuade in a purportedly open communication context" but operate as "secret persuaders" (Palenchar and Fitzpatrick, 2009, p. 272–273). The public campaign entities that result from these deceptive foundations have a corrosive effect because of the way they represent causes in ways that are not transparent. Moreover, they are based on the false legitimacy of grassroots support or community involvement, giving rise to the term "astroturfing" being coined in 1994 by the US Treasury Secretary at the time, Lloyd Bentsen, who observed that as a rural Texan, he could tell the difference between real grassroots and astroturf. In contrast to the transparency of community interest groups and trade associations, deception is central to the front group, where the purpose is to mislead the public and policy makers and to misrepresent the sources of support. The covert and deceptive nature of front groups' operations – including the use of misleading names that signal grassroots support – means they operate stealth campaigns that seek to influence public opinion through deception.

Front groups have been deployed as a PR tool in various contentious fields of politics such as climate change, tobacco and Middle East wars. Examples in support of smoking include the UK group, Freedom Organisation for the Right to Enjoy Smoking Tobacco (FOREST) which was founded in 1979 and has been largely funded by the tobacco industry as was the US organisation, National Smokers Alliance. In the debate on fossil fuels and climate change, examples include a sophisticated operation created and co-ordinated by the Western States Petroleum Association (WSPA), a lobby group funded by BP, Chevron, ExxonMobil, Shell and others. According to one group critical of the WSPA, the Union of Concerned Scientists (UCSUSA) the operations of the group consisted of using "fabricated organizations to falsely represent grassroots opposition to forward-looking policy on climate change and clean technologies" (UCSUSA). The strategy involved the creation and sponsorship of seemingly genuine campaign groups, such as the California Drivers Alliance and Washington Consumers for Sound Fuel Policy, which were focussed on confronting regulations relating to climate change by exaggerating the level of public opposition to policy changes. The case of the WSPA's regional campaign strategy featured in the UCS's Disinformation Playbook, which lists examples of "how business interests deceive, misinform and buy influence at the expense of public health and safety."

Foreign governments have also used front groups to encourage support for military intervention and to influence war aims. In the case of the first Gulf War after the Iraq's President Saddam Hussein invaded Kuwait in 1990, US Congressman Jimmy Hayes – a Democrat who supported the war – would later claim that the Kuwait government funded "as many as 20 PR, law and lobbying firms in its campaign to mobilize US opinion and force against Saddam Hussein" (Stauber and Rampton, 1995, p. 73) with Hill and Knowlton taking the role of lead agency or "mastermind." Hill and Knowlton's work included the creation of the front group, Citizens for a Free Kuwait. The Kuwaiti government provided $11.9m of funding to the group, with $10.8m going to Hill and Knowlton as fees and just $17,861 coming from 78 private individuals. Hill and Knowlton's work extended to arranging for a young witness, Nayirah al-Sabah, to testify before the US Congressional Human Rights Caucus on atrocities she had observed while in a Kuwaiti hospital, which she claimed had included Iraqi soldiers removing babies from incubators and leaving them to die on the floor. This testimony was widely cited in the media and by politicians, including President George Bush, in the run up to the deployment of US troops in an invasion force to liberate Kuwait. However, an investigation by the US's ABC News which included interviews with hospital doctors suggested that this story was false. Moreover, the young girl giving evidence was in fact the daughter of Kuwait's US ambassador, Saud bin Nasir Al-Sabah.

The end of the classical PR era was marked by deliberate moves by some corporations away from public conformance with civic, economic norms (on tax and regulation matters, for example) and consensus politics. In some cases, the move was an expression of corporate and political power and in others part of a strategy for differentiated communication. The PR approach of the large technology companies known by the acronym FANGs, for Facebook, Apple, Netflix and Google, have provided several examples of this low conformance approach in practice. In September 2016, for example, Apple CEO Tim Cook publicly condemned the European Union for imposing a $13bn back tax bill on Apple and described the action as "political crap." Rather than showing the conformance that might be expected from one of the largest companies in the world when dealing with political and regulatory representatives of a European Union of over 600m citizens – or even apologising and undertaking to ensure compliance in future – Tim Cook instead complained about being picked on and "targeted" as a result of anti-American bias and showed limited awareness of his civil society obligations to ensure that the company he leads pays a fair amount of tax in the countries in which it operates.

The interchange of campaign, policy and communications staff from the Obama administration to the big technology companies once the President left office in 2017, was so noticeable that for *the Financial Times* West Coast correspondent, Hannah Kuchler, (2018), "it felt like every new communications or policy person I met in Silicon Valley was an Obama refugee" and by 2018, "The Bay Area Obama alumni network" had 700 members, who were now in jobs at Facebook, Google or start-ups, who "saw it as a way to bolster public policy and communications departments." This transfer of political staffers from the Obama administration "to the PR departments of the West Coast tech monopolies" was not universally popular, with one critic claiming that the deployment of talent "to defend an industry that is monopolistic and gives rise to income inequality" debased President Obama's legacy (Clarke, 2018).

The rise of the political technologists

The template for delivery of the post-truth style of state PR has been developed most completely in Russia. The term political technology is used to describe the way a mix of messaging, entertainment, media technology and data is used to create and support political propositions. Although largely confined to recent Russian political history, the term was used by the fascist historian Julie Gottlieb (2006) to describe the aspects of cultural and media production associated with the British Union of Fascists (BUF) in the 1930s. In particular, she used it to describe the blend of the written words for political ideas, revolutionary rhetoric delivered in an evangelical style, meetings that deployed the visual lexicon of cinema (as well as using cinemas for meetings) and the elements of political celebrity used in the promotion of Oswald Mosely as leader. The BUF of 1930s Britain moved forward various aspects of political technology in what Gottlieb (2006, p. 50) suggested was a "propaganda arms race" of the time, that included creating its own "information technology" to channel its propaganda as a way of overcoming marginalisation of its leaders and messages by mainstream media.

In post-Soviet Russia, the PR techniques of creating and sticking to messages plus creating diverting theatrical stunts are mixed with the efforts of system designers, decision makers and political controllers all combining to apply "whatever technology they can to the construction of politics as a whole" in the form of a "virtual politics," according to Andrew Wilson (2005, p. 49). Wilson makes a useful distinction between the spin doctor and the political technologist, emphasising that the press secretary or spin doctor is situated "at the point where politics and media intersect." For political technologists, "the manipulation of the media is central to their work" but also extends to the construction of parties, the destruction of others, the framing of general campaign dynamics and the manipulation of results. The first wave of political technologists emerged during Boris Yeltsin's Presidency from 1991 to 1999, when actors with business, political and media interests – including oligarchs Mikhail Khodorkovsky, Vladimir Gusinsky and Boris Berezovsky who controlled TV channels – were often fighting amongst each other. In contrast, when Putin became President in 2000, a new discipline was imposed and "the Kremlin established a monopoly of manipulation" in which the Presidential Administration became the dominant political technologist (Shekhovtsov, 2018, p. 72). Vladislav Surkov served as Putin's First Deputy Chief of the Russian Presidential Administration from 1999 to 2011 where he put disinformation (*dezinformtsiya*) at the centre the international relations and state-level PR playbook during several geopolitical upsets. In his filmic explication of how fake and simplistic presentations of our complex world are accepted as routine in a world of "*Hypernormalisation*," to use the title to the film, Adam Curtis (2016) suggests that Surkov's mixed repertoire of theatricality, sleight of hand with truth, the creation of multiple narratives for media have helped to manipulate public opinion and weaken any opposition in ways that have enabled Putin and his appointees to retain power. Surkov studied theatre and it is also claimed that he writes novels under the pseudonym of Natan Dubovitsky, giving him the skills of narrative making and political choreography. During Russia's annexation of Crimea in 2014, the disinformation campaign laid on by Surkov and the Kremlin "orchestrated an elaborate political spectacle to create the appearance of strong support for the annexation" (Mariani, 2017). The word in Russian for such a theatrical spectacle is *dramaturgia* or theatre craft, and in the case of Crimea, it included the appearance at key border points and strategic sites of what Putin claimed were "little green men" who had spontaneously formed local defence units, but who were in fact well-equipped and well-armed members of Russian special forces in an invasion mode. The PR messaging and statements from Putin and the political technologists at the Kremlin to support the annexation of Crimea were typical of the alternative reality that Russia has become skilled at generating support for its often aggressive foreign policy. The state is then able to use the media channels it controls, such as RT, to control the images and influence the lines of argument that are inserted into public discourse. In a lengthy article published in 2019, Surkov reflected with some satisfaction that as a result of Russia "playing with the West's minds […] they don't know how to deal with their own changed consciousness" (Carroll, 2019). The tactic of conflict and breaching norms has been used by the Kremlin to generate the perception among audiences at home and abroad that anything may happen next. This volatility of perception is used by the Russian state to justify the need for more power to be exercised by Putin, as well as more control being exercised over messaging by the Kremlin's sophisticated post-modern state PR operation.

Russia's use of post-truth public relations to project power

Russia's confidence in its post-truth PR approach is so strong that it ignores the communicative norms of international relations and deploys it even in incidents where video evidence is available that contradicts its case. In March 2018, Russian state operatives engaged in the Novichok poisoning of a Russian double agent, Sergai Skripal, and his daughter Yulia in Salisbury. The incident led to the death of a passer-by Dawn Sturgess, who was exposed to the poison. Despite convincing video evidence and intelligence placing the two Russian operatives at the scene, the incident was denied with a series of almost comical lies. In explaining the movements of two alleged Russian agents after a dossier of compelling evidence showing their visit to Salisbury was made public by the UK government, the two men appeared in a television interview to explain that they had made the journey from Russia to see Salisbury's "123 metre spire" and for no other reason. To counter the British evidence, an interview with the two Russian intelligence operatives was aired on the RT (Russia Today) television network, which is funded by the Russian government. RT was used as a media platform for Russian propaganda on the incident to be inserted into global news coverage, with the RT twitter feed and other social media deployed to further influence public discourse on the topic, using both overt posts and more covert fake news accounts and bots to amplify the messages.

A report entitled *Weaponising news: RT Sputnik and targeted disinformation* from researchers at King's College London found that Russian state outlets had published 138 sometimes contradictory narratives of the Novichok incident in Salisbury across 735 articles in the four weeks after the March 2018 poisoning (Ramsay and Robertshaw, 2019). Of these, 32 narratives focussed on the response by the United Kingdom and its allies in the aftermath of the events in Salisbury, which included Russian PR argumentation that the response was based on an unfair "Russiaphobia," that the investigation into the matter was an illegal "witch hunt" against Russia. The next line of argumentation was to create doubt around the source of the Novichok poison, which the Russian PR narratives suggested could have come from laboratories in Iran, Ukraine, several other post-Soviet states, the United States and even the United Kingdom. There were 16 narratives focussed on the Skripals, which made varied allegations, including that the family was involved in organised crime and this was the reason for their poisoning, that Yulia Skripal had carried the poison to the United Kingdom herself and finally that the event had been staged and the reason the United Kingdom would not reveal the location of the Skripals after the incident was because they had not been poisoned at all. Finally, seven conspiracy theories put forward the proposition that the poisoning had been staged by the intelligence agencies of United Kingdom or another country in order to damage Russia. This content was distributed through publication of news stories and features in RT and Sputnik, which was then picked up and used sometimes without attribution – by other news outlets. In the case of the UK media alone, content from these sources was detected in four high circulation tabloids – the *Daily Mail, Daily Express, The Sun* and *Daily Star* – as well as numerous online channels. Russia's response to the Salisbury incident showed how it is using owned media channels to insert messages into global news flow, by making news itself a weapon of post-truth PR. Lead researcher, Dr Gordon Ramsay, summed up how this new style of post-truth news flow works in practice:

> RT's and Sputnik's coverage of the Skripal incident had all the features of a disinformation campaign; they sought to sow confusion and uncertainty through a vast array of contradictory narratives and unchallenged conspiracy theories. Understanding the extent to which these techniques can exist within state-linked outlets like RT is an important step towards preventing the spread of disinformation and its damaging effect on journalism and public discourse.
>
> –Ramsay (2019)

Owned media, weaponing news and other digital mischiefs

In 2017, the UK Prime Minister Theresa May publicly hit back at the way news was being used as a weapon in Russia's state PR efforts. She accused the Russian government of "planting fake stories" in news media in order to "sow discord in the West" (*The Economist*, 2017a). The same article recorded that when executives from Twitter were summoned to appear before the Congress in October 2017, they published a list of 2,700 accounts run by the Saint Petersburg based internet troll farm, the Internet Research Agency, which has links to the Kremlin. Analysis of this list by British researchers uncovered that messages, content and campaign material had been pushed out from these accounts during the Brexit referendum. While claims that this interference through a covert digital PR campaign affected the outcome remain unproven, the evidence combined to confirm that meddling in elections through social media influence campaigns had become a pre-eminent component in the Russian repertoire of disinformation. As *The Economist* reported, the discovery confirmed the beginning of a new era of digital disinformation:

> Trolls, bots, hackers, propagandists and provocateurs of Russian origin have lately descended on the Western democracies. The tentacles of the disinformation apparatus, thought to be rooted in the Kremlin, have been found fiddling in elections everywhere from Ukraine and Bulgaria to France and America.
>
> –*The Economist* (2017a)

In June 2019, a report from the European Commission and the European Union's foreign policy organisation gave a detailed account of how Russian digital propaganda operatives had undertaken a "continued and sustained" campaign of disinformation aimed at both suppressing turnout and influencing voter preferences in the May 2019 elections for the European Parliament (Peel, 2019). Despite Russian denials of involvement in election manipulation, the report detected evidence of continued and co-ordinated disinformation work, although it was noted that the nature of the operations had been re-calibrated, perhaps in response to the increased monitoring of online content and advertising by social media platforms: "Instead of conducting large-scale operations on digital platforms…actors, in particular linked to Russian sources, now appeared to be opting for smaller-scale, localised operations that are harder to detect and expose."

In the political and communicative turbulence of recent years, Russia has embraced post-truth PR as an arm of its foreign policy efforts. RT and other media channels have been put to work on behalf of the state and have swiftly evolved their tactics to evade the countermeasures being put in place by nation states and technology companies. In addition, Russia also funds *Sputnik*, a news web site and online radio platform that had previously existed as *The Voice of Russia* radio station. President Macron of France banned *Sputnik* from campaign press conferences in 2017 after concluding it was an agent of influence and propaganda. Governments in most of Europe and the United States concur that *Sputnik* has a "richly earned reputation as a Kremlin mouthpiece" (*The Economist*, 2019) with a track record of attempting to set up multiple fake accounts on Facebook in order to "spread disinformation."

On 5 December 2017, the Australian government announced proposals for a range of measures aimed at preventing China and other nations from influencing its domestic politics through what Prime Minister Malcolm Turnbull called "unprecedented and increasingly sophisticated attempts" through sometimes "covert and coercive" methods to influence the political process and public opinion on issues (BBC News, 2017b). The methods used include overt and covert lobbying of politicians, alongside donations to political actors and think tanks. The more covert tools in this repertoire of influence included attempts to engage with Australian universities and publishing, as well as politicians and government officials. On 10 December 2017, Germany accused China of "trying to groom politicians and bureaucrats" using what the National Endowment for democracy has labelled sharp power "to manipulate opinion abroad" (*The Economist*, 2017b). This repertoire of sharp power is a hardening development from the soft power approach that has used language, culture and values to promote a nation's interests and influence, often alongside diplomacy. For example, the UK's soft power agency, the British Council describes itself as the UK's "organisation for international cultural relations and educational opportunities," and continues to promote the United Kingdom through a cultural diplomacy, using the arts, literature and science as vehicles for engagement, through supporting exhibitions and lecture tours by British authors, for example, as well as offering English language courses. Founded in 1934, The British Council was arguably a successor in several ways to the Empire Marketing Board, which had been run by Sir Stephen Tallents (who would go on to become founder President of the UK's Institute of Public Relations in 1948) although it was more explicitly focussed on the promotion of trade relations. Also in December 2017, the US Congress held hearings on "China's growing influence" and the mix of espionage, deception and sponsorship that it was using to achieve its goals. In one case, according to German intelligence, the online deception included using the LinkedIn business contacts application to pose as think tanks and recruiters in order to entrap politicians and government officials into accepting free trips.

Case Study 3.1

Think tanks: facts and influence in the post-truth era

China's use of think tanks in order to reach out to new contacts, affect policy in another country and to promote a point of view is a useful reminder of their role as both connectors of people and conduits of an almost invisible form of influence. In the United States, after inheriting from their father, the billionaire Koch brothers began what Jane Meyer has described as "a life-long, tax deductible sponsorship of libertarianism in America" in which they "weaponised philanthropy" on behalf of right-wing causes, through sponsorship of think tanks, alongside spending on education projects, advertisements and acquiring data on voters (Meyer, 2016). A think tank is simply a non-government organisation that usually operates not-for-profit which seeks to inform public policy decisions through the presentation of policy ideas and relevant research in support of policy proposals. In the United Kingdom, the status of think tanks as charities means they cannot operate in party political interests, yet there is widespread evidence that several organisations breach this regulation. For example, in February 2019, the UK's Charity Commission gave an official warning to the Institute of Economic Affairs (IEA) think tank (which is registered with the Commission as an educational charity) and sought assurances that the organisation would not "engage in campaigning and/or political activity that contravenes legal or regulatory requirements as set out in CC9" which is the Commission's guidance on campaigning (Weakley, 2019). The warning came after a politically biased pro-Brexit report entitled "Plan A+" was published by the IEA in September 2018, which the Charity Commission considered to have been a breach of charity law.

That so many are called institutes gives think tanks the surface appearance of independence and academic underpinnings, yet they often have close links to specific political positions and parties. Indeed, the attraction of think tanks for corporations and wealthy individuals such as the Koch brothers is the way they are able to exert influence by setting the boundaries for public policy debates to suit their own political agenda. Barros and Taylor offered this useful summary of the development of think tanks in their consideration of the ethics of their promotion of pro-corporate ideology:

> Think tanks became key political and economic actors during the twentieth century, creating and occupying an intellectual and political position between academic institutions, the state, civil society, and public debate on organization and management. Think tanks are especially active in setting frames for what constitutes politically and socially acceptable ways of thinking about economic activity and the rights or obligations of corporations.
>
> —Barros and Taylor (2018, p. 1)

The subtlety of the influence of think tanks comes from the way they are one step removed from the formal – and often more tightly regulated – institutions and structures of politics, such as political parties. Instead, they seek to affect public policy by introducing ideas to the political sphere, most often through links to individual policy makers, and then mobilising their ideas more broadly within parties and the wider political sphere, in order that they become adopted as policy proposals. In promoting policy ideas, think tanks engage constantly in PR work, offering papers, opinion articles and research reports to the media, alongside frequent appearances on the media as spokespeople, reviewers of the daily news and even appearing alongside politicians on political panels such as the BBC's *Question Time.* In addition to the realm of PR, Philip Schlesinger has written on the emergence of what has been named the "creative economy" and how think tanks in the United Kingdom played a role in the propagation of this idea as producers of mediated discourse as "part of a wider communications industry" (Schlesinger, 2009).

In the United Kingdom alone, there are 120 registered think tanks, with several registered at the same address, 55 Tufton Street, SW1, close to the Houses of Parliament in Westminster. While policy organisations have been present in politics for 50 years or more, the growth in numbers in the past 20 years marks an increase in the volume of their activity, their increased visibility as policy actors and their use by organisations and individuals in wider campaigns of influence. A salient indicator of the relative influence of elected policy makers and the more opaque think tanks was the reason South Carolina Senator James DeMint gave for his decision to leave the Senate in order to lead the conservative think tank, The Heritage Foundation, when he claimed he would have greater influence policy making in the think tank (Bruckner, 2017). For PR people with deep pockets, think tanks can be a source of special capabilities and influence when running campaigns on policy issues or controversial sectors, which are affected by public policy and regulation. This section concludes with summaries of interviews conducted with two London-based corporate PR executives in 2018, who described how they have worked with think tanks on campaigns on behalf of clients.

How think tanks fit with PR work

Think tanks can play a very useful role in complex or controversial campaigns and issues. Yes they are charities, yes they are one step removed from individual politicians, political parties and government on paper, but the reality is different. They operate as a space for like minds to meet up and exchange ideas across the spectrum, from left to right to the middle. The means members of the House of Commons, House of Lords, donors, political journalists and other policy wonks come together at their meetings. They tend to be out of bounds to Ministers, but it is not unknown for special advisers and other staff members to come along to a session on a relevant policy issue or just to stay in touch with what is going on.

It can be convivial and quite easy going rather than the ultra-pressured selling of ideas, which just would not work in that setting. That is where the PR and lobbying firms and their clients come in with funding for think tanks as members or as sponsors of special events such as lunches and dinners and publications.

–Director at corporate PR Firm, London

Think tanks can work well on PR campaigns where we have a client who is involved with a controversial or polarising policy issue. For example, I worked for a long time with a client on a tax matter that would have benefitted from reform and a better – i.e., more sympathetic -political climate. So alongside supporting the court case and legal work through media relations, we worked with a couple of think tanks that were sympathetic to the issue. The first step was getting involved through an annual donation or corporate membership for general funding. Next, there was a lunch at the think tank's offices to discuss several themes related to tax, with the client issue I was handling as one of the case studies. The think tank was able to get a Select Committee Chair along, a couple of members of the House of Lords who were interested in the area and a couple of MPs, as well as some people from the other two think tanks who operated in the field. We had an agreeable lunch, a good discussion and the client was happy to be able to explain his case, answer questions and so on.

–Director, reputation management firm, London

A platform for influence on controversial issues

One thing that surprised me when engaging with think tanks was the way the more politically-aligned think tanks – the ones on the right such as Adam Smith Institute, IEA and Taxpayers Alliance, for example – will actually act in concert sometimes, as well as competing for support. The result on one project for us was that some policy makers got to hear our case, or our client's case, who would not otherwise have done so, which was useful and impressive from the client's point of view. We also had the option to sponsor a white paper or research monograph on a related theme to back up the lunch, alongside some blog posts on the issue on the think tank's web site, which the media sometimes pick up on. The cost of all this was around £12,000 plus around £8,000 more for the publication and accompanying launch party. So not cheap but not too expensive either when the issues are difficult and you are struggling to get a hearing in the media because of a combination of complexity and controversy, which also makes overt lobbying difficult.

These types of reports, research or policy papers are handy as they can become a good basis for proposing a thought-through policy change that can go to relevant MPs, select committees and others. The publications and media relations side is also important. If you want to reach the Labour Party, for example, for years now *The New Statesman* has offered inserted special reports and roundtables on policy issues that they write up and publish in the magazine. That can be tied in with asking a think tank along too, as they are very well connected in that world.

–Director, reputation management firm, London

PR and think tanks: "a neat package of influence"

Think tanks are primarily policy outfits and that is their core area. But their special place at the heart of Westminster means that alongside that, they can offer a very neat package of influence that suits certain projects at certain times. It is not right for every case as it is often off the public radar, but when it works, it can work well. Think tanks are in the business of selling ideas and nothing else and so their own PR operations are normally very good and they work well with the media to get the ideas shared more broadly through news items and op-eds.

PR firms like ours get involved because it makes us look in touch, connected and able to influence at the right level, as well as providing some useful intelligence on policy matters. I've taken clients along to think tank meetings, for example, and for some it was a buzz to be at the centre of things with MPs, advisers and others. Going along to the donor dinners, the book launches and Christmas drinks and so on is also useful for networking. It is a pretty agreeable way to spend time with interesting people you would not otherwise get close to. For example, at one private donor dinner for a think tank I was involved with during the Cameron era, the guest was the head of policy at 10 Downing Street. The interesting thing was how eager he was to learn from those of us round the table and get some views from business, about start-ups and tax policy, for example, from outside the close confines of Whitehall. So it is a two-way street and not just about corporate influence. I was able to make a point about start-ups to him directly that he found quite helpful and mentioned in his summing up of points he was taking away.

–Director at corporate PR Firm, London

A point I would like to make is that the think tank world is not as sinister as it sounds or can look once investigative journalists start setting up stings. While they do attract money from wealthy individuals, think tanks need funding and individual donors do not pay all the bills, which opens the door to corporate involvement and PR and lobbying firms. That's when it can also look a little more sinister than it actually is when investigative reporters have run stories about think tanks selling access and so on.

–Managing director, reputation management firm, London

References

Barros, A. and Taylor, S. (2018) Think tanks, business and civil society: the ethics of promoting corporate ideologies. *Journal of Business Ethics*, 1–13. Available at: https://link.springer .com/article/10.1007/s10551-018-4007-y

BBC. (2017a) How are the Tories going after young people? *BBC News*, 31 August. Available at: https://www.bbc.co.uk/news/uk-politics-41101480

BBC News. (2017b) Australia unveils laws to prevent foreign interference, BBC News, 5 December. Available at: https://www.bbc.co.uk/news/world-australia-42232178

Bolton, M. and Pitts, F. (2018) *Corbynism: A Critical Approach*. Bingley: Emerald Publishing.

Bruckner, T. (2017) Think tanks, evidence and policy: democratic players or clandestine lobbyists. *LSE Impact Blog*, 8 February. Available at: https:// blogs.lse.ac.uk/impactofsocialsciences/2017/02/08/think-tanks-evidence-and-policy/

Carr, N. (2010) *The Shallows: How the Internet is Changing the Way We Think, Read and Remember*. London: Atlantic Books.

Carroll, O. (2019) Russia is 'playing with the West's minds' says Putin advisor. *The Independent*, 12 February. Available at: https://www.independent.co.uk/news/world/europe/putin-russia-kremlin-vladislav-surkov-grey-cardinal-moscow-a8773661.html

Clarke, P. (2018) Transfer of brain power debases Obama's legacy. *Financial Times*, (letters) 20 January, p. 16.

Curtis, A. (2016) *HyperNormalisation*. London: BBC. Available at: https://www.bbc.co.uk/programmes/p04b183c

Danner, M. (2017) What He Could Do. *The New York Review of Books*, 23 March–5 April, pp. 4–7.

Debord, G. (1994) *The Society of the Spectacle*. Translated by D. Nicholson-Smith. New York: Zone Books.

The Economist (2017a) Russian Twitter trolls meddled in the Brexit vote. Did they swing it? 23 November. Available at: https://www.economist.com/britain/2017/11/23/russian-twitter-trolls-meddled-in-the-brexit-vote-did-they-swing-it

The Economist (2017b) How China's "sharp power" is muting criticism abroad. 14 December. Available at: https://www.economist.com/briefing/2017/12/14/how-chinas-sharp-power-is-muting-criticism-abroad

The Economist (2019) In Sputnik's orbit. 2 March, p. 30.

Edelman, R. (2017) An implosion of trust. *Edelman*, 7 March. Available at: https://www.edelman.com/post/an-implosion-of-trust

Giddens, A. (2013) *The Consequences of Modernity*. London: John Wiley & Sons.

Gottleib, J. (2006) The marketing of megalomania: celebrity, consumption and the development of political technology in the British Union of Fascists. *Journal of Contemporary History* 41 (1), 35–55.

Gray, J. (2017) Distraction stations. *New Statesman*, 11–17 August, p. 36.

Grunig, J. and Hunt, T. (1984) *Managing Public Relations*. New York: Holt, Rinehart and Winston.

Jenkins, H. (2006) *Convergence Culture*. New York: New York University Press.

Klein, J. (1996) *Primary Colours*. New York: Random House.

Kuchler, H. (2018) Why Obama's West Wingers went west. *Financial Times Magazine*, 13 January. Available at: https://www.ft.com/content/56712806-f58f-11e7-88f7-5465a6ce1a00

Lloyd, J. (2017) *The Power and the Story: The Global Battle for News and Information*. London: Atlantic Books.

Mariani, M. (2017). In Trump's Amerika. *Vanity Fair*, November, pp. 86–89.

McTiernan, J. (2019) Left to their devices. *Financial Times* (*Life and Arts Section*), 18/19 May, p. 9.

Meyer, J. (2016) *Dark Money: The Hidden History of the Billionaires Behind the Rise of the Radical Right*. New York: Doubleday.

Moore, M. (2018) *Democracy Hacked: Political Turmoil and Information Warfare in the Digital Age*. London: OneWorld.

Palenchar M. and Fitzpatrick, K. (2009) Secret persuaders: ethical and rhetorical perspectives on the use of public relations front groups. In: Heath, R., Toth, E. and Waymer, D. (Eds.) *Rhetorical and Critical Approaches to Public Relations II*. New York: Routledge, pp. 272–289.

Peel, M. (2019) EU poll hit by Russian 'disinformation'. *Financial Times*, 15/16 June, p. 4.

Phillips, D. and Young, P. (2009) *Online Public Relations: A Practical Guide to Developing an Online Strategy in the World of Social Media*. London: Kogan Page Limited.

Phillips, R. (2015) *Trust me, PR is dead*. London: Random House.

Ramsay, G. (2019) Russian state media weaponises news to sow confusion and division. King's College London, 1 March. Available at: https://www.kcl.ac.uk/news/how-russian-state-media-weaponises-news

Ramsay, G. and Robertshaw, S. (2019) Weaponising news: RT, Sputnik and targeted disinformation. King's College London, January. Available at: https://www.kcl.ac.uk/policy-institute/assets/weaponising-news.pdf

Rowley. T. (2016) Meet the Trump superfans – on the road with The Donald's most loyal supporters. *Telegraph Magazine*, 4 November, pp. 28–34.

Runciman, D. (2018) *How Democracy Ends*. London: Profile Books.

Schlesinger, P. (2009) Creativity and the experts. New labour, think tanks, and the policy Process. *The International Journal of Press/Politics*, 14 (3), 3–20.

Shekhovtsov, A. (2018) *Russia and the Far Right*. London: Routledge.

Stauber, J. and Rampton, S. (1995) *Toxic Sludge is Good for You!: Lies, Damn Lies and the Public Relations Industry*. Monroe, Maine: Common Courage Press.

Valentini, C. (2014) Is using social media "good" for the public relations profession? A critical reflection. *Public Relations Review*, 41(2), 170–177.

Weakley, K. (2019) Official warning to Institute of Economic Affairs is withdrawn by Charity Commission. *Civil Society*, 28 June. Available at: https://www.civilsociety.co.uk/news/charity-commission-withdraws-official-warning-to-institute-of-economic-affairs.html#sthash.tFTQ3voJ.dpuf

Wilson, A. (2005) *Virtual Politics: Faking democracy in the Post-Soviet World*. New Haven: Yale University Press.

4 The mixed public relations repertoire for the age of disruption

As we live through what journalists and commentators commonly call an "age of disruption," (with the term appearing in over 100 headlines in English language newspapers in 2018), it is unsurprising that rather than seeking balance and consensus through persuasion, the objective of some post-classical public relations (PR) approaches is to disrupt and to support a process of wider dislocation in society. For example, President Trump's disruptive approach to communications during the 2016 US Presidential election campaign was soon enacted in the form of policy choices that were equally non-conformist and unsettling to the world order. The post-classical style of PR for these times of disruption and post-truth involves use of a mixed communicative repertoire. It is a diverse cocktail of approaches that sometimes combines all four of Grung and Hunt's (1984) typologies of PR practice, of press agentry/publicity, public information, two-way asymmetrical and two-way symmetrical. Online, it is a digital mixology of tools, techniques and trickery that takes advantage of the media logic and functionality of social media in order to achieve maximum influence on audiences. PR campaigns are often run with a determination to prevail at all costs, even if that sometimes includes paying little attention to truthfulness in the content of messages and processes by which they are distributed.

In the case of the disruptive terrorist group, Islamic State (IS) from 2012 onwards, the mix of the four Grunigian communicative approaches is supplemented with variants and additions which brought modernity and efficacy to the group's PR effort. The classical elements included the propaganda of the press agentry in one-way distribution of public information, persuasion plus manipulation in the two-way asymmetrical communications and then the mutual understanding shown in the symmetric recruitment outreach. All levels of this classically derived communication show a PR approach in the segmentation of messages for different stakeholders. The divisive rhetoric of IS was also post-classical in the way it was unconcerned with promoting dialogue or contributing to a fully functioning society as envisioned by Heath (2006). Instead, rhetoric was used to dominate, to convey certainty about the cause and to divide society. In particular, the rhetoric of IS sought to divide the Middle East from the West, Shia Muslims from Sunni Muslims, Muslims living in the West from non-Muslims, in a way that undermines what IS has called the "grey zone" of multiculturalism.

Despite the IS's outlier status as a violent extremist group, the five common elements of post-classical PR can be observed beyond terrorism settings in aspects of public communication in Western society. Although the context was different and there was no terrorist action involved, some nationalistic political communicators have deployed elements of post-classical public relations. For example, the level of certainty and conviction in the rhetoric of Donald Trump of the Republican Party, Nigel Farage of the United Kingdom Independence Party (UKIP), Geert Wilders of the Dutch Party for Freedom and Marine Le Pen of the French National Front is closer to the high-conviction rhetoric of IS than many conventional political parties. One long-time Trump watcher, the US journalist Graydon Carter has described the President's communications style as combining "ignorance and certitude" (Carter, 2017, p. 53). Social media posts that seemed designed to cause outrage were a feature of what the head of the Leave.EU campaign Aaron Banks described as the "guerrilla war" he fought using "the power of social media" (Banks, 2017, p. xxvi). In considering the performative element, it is significant that several of the political entrepreneurs to emerge in the past two years share experience of mass media, as performers either in reality television (Donald Trump), talk radio (Nigel Farage) or television comedy (Brexit campaigner Boris Johnson and Italian Beppe Grillo of the Five Star Movement), which helps explain why they are skilled at the performance of politics in ways that sustain media attention.

Incivility as public relations campaign tactic

In something of a reversal of normal campaign planning, Donald Trump's Presidential 2016 election team spent more during 2015–2016 on *Make America Great Again* baseball caps than on research and polling. While political elites were sneering at the focus on leisurewear, the "silly red hats proved a PR masterstroke" according to Freddy Gray (2016), who observed how Trump also managed to turn his unpleasant personality of "almost psychotic aggression" and "thuggishness" into a PR asset:

> By not caring about his own popularity and insulting as many people as he could – he made himself more popular. Through the sheer force of his obnoxious personality, he has pulled off the most extraordinary election victory in US history.
>
> –Gray (2016)

According to Gray, despite this disregard for the norms of political campaigning – or perhaps because of this approach – Trump has emerged as "the greatest political entrepreneur of our time" with a PR style and messages that reach out to the audience that exists in the "huge gap in the disgruntlement market" that Trump spotted ahead of his campaign. When Steve Bannon joined the operation as a campaign director, he bought clarity and consistency to Trump's positioning as the outsider candidate who would look after the interests of ordinary voters against the privileged elite. While not a PR person, Bannon had a well-developed understanding of varied channels of media, including the community of online video gamers in which he invested, the right-wing *Breitbart News* site of which he was a founder director and the use of film, through his experience as a producer of documentaries on political topics. He used this background to get Trump's outsider message and other campaign themes directly to voters using online channels that bypassed the traditional media. Messages, channels and the candidate were all synchronised in a mixed repertoire of political PR that contributed to one of the most powerful and effective campaign strategies in modern politics.

At the Dublin-based discount airline, Ryanair, chief executive Michael O'Reilly spotted a similar gap in the airline market for flights at the lowest cost possible, provided by an airline focussed on cost-cutting with no meaningful regard for customer service. Up until a change of strategy in September 2013, when O'Reilly seemed to acknowledge the need to be civil to passengers, he had routinely referred to them as idiots in public and much worse in private correspondence. The entire approach to PR and customer relationships was a reversal of the orthodoxy of good practice. At the core of this PR strategy of offence were O'Reilly's frequent, loud and deliberately provocative public statements such as his regular expletive-ridden rants against regulators and governments. In 2006, he described plans for taxes on air travel to combat climate change as "the usual horses**t" and pursued a strategy of non-conformance to customer service norms and even to air travel regulations such as the European Union's directives on passenger compensation.

Donald Trump as a political entrepreneur and Michael O'Reilly as a business entrepreneur are examples of disruptive actors in their sectors who have harnessed the communicative power of incivility as a tool of post-classical public relations. Using offensive performances in press conferences, abusing competitors, mocking regulators and even posing with a model Ryanair aircraft between your legs in a phallic pose for a press photo are all examples of a planned approach to PR that is deliberately uncivil in its style. As Professor Jon White (2018) has written, "questions of tone and civility bear on the likely quality of relationships" which is an area where PR advisors should be advising clients. He acknowledged in a piece for the UK's CIPR publication, *Influence*, entitled "Politics, incivility and public relations," that despite 30 years of research and teaching suggesting that PR works best in promoting collaboration and symmetry in relationships, we may be moving towards a more asymmetric approach to problem solving in politics and other fields. Certainly, the uncivil, aggressive and uncaring approach of Michael O'Reilly seemed to work well for Ryanair in terms of growth. The airline was ranked as Europe's largest in 2019 by passenger numbers and was also the most profitable, yet simultaneously was ranked as the worst short haul airline in Europe for the sixth year in a row by *Which* magazine. While a typical response from an airline's PR team to such a negative results would be that they are trying to improve, Ryanair, in keeping with its aggressive and uncivil style of communication, simply dismissed the survey as "unrepresentative and worthless" (Topham, 2019). Even after the 2013 refocus on customer service, Ryanair and its CEO continued to pursue a PR style that had little regard for customer care, relationships with regulators or suppliers. Yet despite going against many norms of public relations, O'Reilly's style did succeed in gaining media attention in a way that was consistent with the airline's proposition to pile high and sell cheap with little regard for customer service.

The new entrepreneurs of political communication

A week after the Brexit referendum had resulted in a majority of UK voters opting to leave the European Union, co-founder of the Leave.EU campaign, Aaron Banks reflected on the nature of the messages that had featured in the election as a result of advice from the US political consultancy, Goddard Gunster:

> What they said early on was "Facts don't work" and that's it. The Remain campaign featured fact, fact, fact, fact. It just doesn't work. You have got to connect with people emotionally. It's the Trump success.
>
> –Fletcher (2016)

Banks went on to explain how meetings with the media team on the Trump Presidential campaign led to Leave.EU following advice not to advertise but to use social media as the main tool of promotion and get noticed on there through outrageous posts. Banks' PR adviser, Leave.EU PR chief and self-described "worst head of communications in the world," Andrew Wigmore described the messaging strategy in simple terms: "The more outrageous you are, the more attention you get." Banks himself has also described the way their campaign used confrontation and outrage as a strategic communications device that helped establish a distinct positioning for Leave.EU and reach a larger audience:

> We picked fights with just about everyone. We learned how to use and abuse the mainstream media with their phoney outrage. We fed off that fake outrage. All they were doing was giving us more oxygen…The mainstream media did more to grow our reach than anything else.
>
> –Fletcher (2016)

Having decided not to spend on advertising, the Leave.EU campaign relied instead upon a combination of classical PR in the form of press conferences, press releases and rallies, alongside a social media operation that was creating content in the form of text posts, videos, memes and news clips that were posted on the various platforms, most predominantly on Facebook, Twitter and YouTube. As Fletcher (2016) concluded in a lengthy article based on interviews with Banks "Much of the comment was inflammatory, if not downright xenophobic," with one typical video news story concluding with the question "Are you concerned about the amount of crime being committed in the UK and foreign criminals?"

The right messages to the right people: technology and targeting

In a post in the news section of its web site on 20 November 2015, which has since been deleted, the Leave.EU campaign group offered some additional details for media following a press conference held on Wednesday 18 November in Westminster. Gerry Gunster from the US political and referendum consulting firm Goddard Gunster presented alongside Brittany Kaiser from Cambridge Analytica. Headlined, "The Science Behind Our Strategy," Leave.EU laid out its plan of campaign, boasting that it had hired "the best people on the world to help us make sure those messages are delivered by the right messenger and to the right voters" (Leave.EU, 2015). The post in the news section of the web site then laid out how its targeting operation would be undertaken:

> Cambridge Analytica are world leaders in target voter messaging. They will be helping us map the British electorate and what they believe in, enabling us to better engage with voters. [...] While Cambridge Analytica will be helping with the data, Goddard Gunster, who have fought some of the most contentious Referendum campaigns all over the world (with a success rate of over 90%) will be helping us turn that data into a comprehensive strategy.
>
> –Leave.EU (2015)

This mix of specialists on the Leave.EU campaign and the functions they offered was by no means revolutionary. Cambridge Analytica was offering in-depth audience research, while Goddard Gunster was providing advice on campaign strategy and messaging. What was potent in this digital mixology was the way that data were gathered from voters as the campaign progressed and used to create messages for distribution via social media and other online channels that the data models predicted would be effective. Leave.EU itself described the approach as a "psychographic methodology" that was "on another level of sophistication." The emphasis on accurate targeting was emphasised by Cambridge Analytica itself, with CEO Alexander Nix telling Campaign magazine:

> Recently, Cambridge Analytica has teamed up with Leave.EU [...] to help them better understand and communicate with UK voters, We have already helped supercharge Leave.EU's social media campaign by ensuring the right messages are getting to the right voters online and the campaign's Facebook page is growing in support to the tune of about 3,000 people per day.
>
> –Cadwalladr (2019)

The mix of data on audiences and their preferences allowed PR messages to be trialled and tested in real time through social media posts and advertising on platforms such as Facebook, with feedback gathered almost in real time. The ability to try out multiple messages with audiences is perhaps the capability that Leave.EU co-chair, Richard Tice, was referring to in a comment posted on the campaigns news section: "This is a campaign with lots of different messages. It's not about politicians, it's about the people." Provocative posts were used by Leave.EU to generate argument online and identify potential supporters as the debate polarised. Examples of this tactic included the use of photographs of controversial campaign posters, such as the June 2016 Leave.EU poster headlined "Breaking Point," illustrated with a queue of refugees at a border crossing.

This tactic and similar efforts by populist political campaigns illustrate a sound level of understanding of the network and communicative logic of social media alongside a serendipitous synchronicity between the way social media works and the messages and distribution approaches that suit upstart campaigners, who can present themselves as rebels and outsiders. Moreover, it also shows how messages and delivery systems are selected not for their capacity to appeal to as wide an audience as possible and achieve balance, but optimised to appeal to multiple segmented and partisan audiences within a divided public.

Emotion, promotion and "truthful hyperbole"

Social media rewards engagement and digital campaign planners were swift to recognise that emotions in general and anger in particular, are potent accelerators of engagement. This insight has encouraged the use of memes and social media content that establish clear positions, polarise opinion and get attention because they are out of the ordinary or even outrageous. In his book *The Art of the Deal*, Donald Trump showed his own understanding of this type of exaggerated messaging and how it appealed to traditional media: "I call it truthful hyperbole. It's an innocent form of exaggeration, and a very effective form of promotion." In the environment of online media, these polarising messages can be tried and used again if they find favour in the digital feedback loop of Facebook likes, retweets on Twitter and so on, or dropped while another message is tried if they fail to engage. In the case of successful campaigns, messages appeal to audiences, who in turn engage and reveal more data about themselves and their preferences, which in turn can be used to predict what type of person might best respond in future. In his account of Leave.EU's campaign in the Brexit referendum, the co-chairman Aaron Banks described the publicity episode that resulted from one emotionally provocative tweet, posted by his PR adviser Andrew Wigmore on Remembrance Sunday:

> "Freedom and democracy: Let's not give up on the values for which our ancestors paid the ultimate sacrifice" was his message of the day. We'd posted it along with a picture of an old Chelsea pensioner whose views I admit, we had no idea about. At least Wiggy had the sense to wait until after the two minutes silence, but predictably, everyone kicked off anyway, accusing us of "shameful opportunism" etc.

After criticism and complaints from multiple sources, including doubters from within their own campaign, Wigmore took the tweet down, resulting in an instructive response from Banks:

> "Put it back up!" I instructed. We were getting a load of supportive emails form ex-servicemen. So he did. That made three stories for the price of one. First for the original tweet; then a story about how we'd taken it down in shame; and

then another story about how we'd brazenly put it back up again. OK, it was probably all a bit crass, but I stand by the sentiments of the message, and we got loads of publicity. We're slowly beginning to understand how the media works.

The digital media feedback loop illustrated in this example generated absolute growth in support for the campaign (as measured by engagement) while also gathering more detailed data on the audience. This in turn enabled more precise targeting of micro-messages that can be delivered directly to the enlarged audience, who have identified themselves online through affinity behaviours and actions such as liking the post or related material. Similarly, populist politicians can use the same tactic in order to test out policy ideas to see if they meet voter approval.

The language and style of populist campaigns such as Leave.EU are vibrant, contemporary and at ease with social media. By contrast, the evasive, indirect language used by many politicians in traditional parties can appear to voters as lacking in vision, tired and outdated. Davide Casaleggio, whose father helped found Italy's Five Star Movement (*M5S or Movimento Cinque Stelle*), captured this difference with his comment that established political parties were like the high-street video chain Blockbuster while his upstart online party was like Netflix ("*La vecchia partitocrazia è come Blockbuster, noi siamo come Netflix*"). His father was the entrepreneur, Gianroberto Casaleggio, who created a substantial Italian web marketing and internet consulting business, Casaleggio Associati, which specialised in online positioning and messaging services. The experience of the Casaleggios in digital messaging and the confection of complete online identities for organisations appeared to be a more significant influence on the resulting party formation than any ideological priorities. Instead, canny political positioning and policy messaging was crafted and distributed through online channels in order to appeal to supporters on the left and right of Italian politics, in ways that enabled all to see their policy reflected in an ambiguous political mirror. According to a former head of communications for Five Star, Nicola Biondo, the policy ambiguity is not an oversight but central to the party's political PR strategy. "It was conceived as a marketing product. Its only aim is to get power and consensus. Once it takes power, it has no ideology so it immediately becomes a tool for other structures, business or even states" (Roberts, 2018). Hannah Roberts goes on to say that Five Star's support for Russia since 2014 is one sign of its engagement with third parties that could potentially be harmful to Italy's interests:

Opponents say Five Star is ideologically bankrupt, with opaque backing, and an Orwellian power structure. Its websites have been accused of social conditioning and spreading disinformation via a digital army of supporters.

Beyond the strengths of their online offering, the PR repertoire of the upstart parties also included a recognition of the need to entertain and bring vibrancy and performance to their campaigning. In Italy, the frontman for the Five Star Movement was Beppe Grillo, an established stand-up comic as well as political activist, who was enlisted as both performative frontman for rallies and videos, as well as online influencer.

Dossier-based public relations: weigh the facts, don't analyse them

In 2003, in justifying the case to go to war in Iraq, the UK and US governments employed a PR approach based on publishing almost overwhelming amounts of information in dossiers. In the case of the United Kingdom, Prime Minister Tony Blair published a summary of intelligence assessments in what became known as a "dodgy dossier" entitled *Iraq – Its Infrastructure of Concealment, Deception and Intimidation*, which was issued to journalists on 3 February 2003 by Alistair Campbell, Blair's director of communications and strategy. In what seemed like a tightly co-ordinated transatlantic plan, in the United States, two days later on 5 February 2003, the US Secretary of State gave a briefing speech to the United Nations Security Council supported by a visual dossier of intelligence information. In both cases, dossiers were used as a tool of public information to support a position and were unusual in that they made public types and amounts of information on a proposed foreign war that would normally not be shared with public audiences in this level of detail. While very few citizens beyond interested specialists appear to have read the material in full if at all, audiences were exposed to news reports and saw the analysis, graphics and the mass of material gathered. The resulting persuasive effect was that the length of the dossier coupled with authoritative presentation built credibility for the general argument. The sense that there were many pages was enough to satisfy the majority of media audiences of the substance of the dossier's content. More recently, the carefully curated January 2017 publication of the 35-page Donald Trump-Russia dossier provided a contemporary example of the impact of dossier-based public information campaigning, apparently by a coalition of anti-Trump Republican and Democratic supporters (Buncombe and Garcia, 2017).

In financial public relations, this "weigh the facts" approach using weighty dossiers to overwhelm audiences has been used in shareholder campaigns. In 2012, as part of a five-year investor relations campaign against the US health products firm, Herbalife, the CEO of hedge fund Pershing Square, Bill Ackman, gave a lengthy presentation backed by a 300-page dossier of research material gathered by the firm's analysts, as well as external corporate investigators and law firms. Ackman himself repeatedly stressed the dimensions involved in this work, whether it was the number of pages (330 for the first December 2012 presentation in New York), the time spent by Pershing Square (50 people for 18 months), the budget (around $50m) or the range and calibre of advisers involved (New York law firms, several research specialists). This explanatory effort appeared to be aimed at building credibility based on the time and cost of preparing the dossiers as information assets and campaign artefacts as much as their contents. Pershing Square's PR campaign used several PR agencies as well as in-house resources and was interesting for its use of research/dossier-based campaigning in enacting a voice that supports the financial interests of the position it held. Although it is common practice in issues-based campaigning to deploy research and the third-party endorsements, the sheer volume, scope and depth of information in this case was unusual. Moreover, the campaign was not built around one report but rather a series of detailed dossiers from various third parties on different aspects of Herbalife's operations that were issued at intervals over the course of the multi-year campaign. It also appeared to be building depth to the investment arguments as well as defining the tone of voice as solid, dependable and well-grounded in facts.

The role of race in reputation laundering

In its final destructive campaign of reputation laundering, the London-based PR firm Bell Pottinger chaired by Lord Bell, who *The New Yorker* magazine judged in its report on the matter to be "perhaps the best-known figure in British public relations," deployed a mixed repertoire of distasteful post-truth PR tactics in its campaign on behalf of the Gupta family and its businesses in South Africa. While at one level Tim Bell claimed to have accomplished the transformation of PR advisers from being "senders of press releases and lunchers with journalists into serious strategists," the new strategic value proposition also included offering clients services that extended to the dark arts of optimising Google searches, surreptitiously editing relevant Wikipedia pages and creating online content to divert online searches. In reputation management, Wikipedia has become a critical nexus of online information because of the way Google searches will typically rank Wikipedia content on a person, company or issue highly, with journalists then sourcing background from the site, which means that material then appears many times in different stories. The programme of work undertaken by the firm in early 2016 included the "covert dissemination of articles, cartoons, blog posts, and tweets implying that the Guptas' opponents were upholding a racist system" (Caesar, 2018).

While often risky and almost always unethical, the introduction of racial and cultural messaging in planned PR and lobbying campaigns has apparently become an option that is seen as useful in amplifying emotional appeal. In political messaging, John Gray (2018) has written how the disturbances of contemporary politics include "political poisons from the past being recycled in new and virulent forms" with the "re-normalisation of anti-Semitism" at the heart of this process. Examples include public statements by Marine Le Pen during her 2017 campaign during the run-off in the French Presidential election, in which she denied French involvement in the arrest of 13,000 Jews, many of whom were confined in the Paris *Velodrome d'Hiver* sports arena before being sent to Nazi death camps, against accepted historical evidence on this notorious round-up known as the *Vel D'Hiv* case.

Race also appeared to have been deployed somewhat cynically in a 2019 PR effort against proposals to ban the sale of fur in New York, following on from similar statutes being enacted in Los Angeles and San Francisco. Speaker of the New York City Council, Cory Johnson, proposed the prohibition which had been campaigned for over many years by animal rights activists. However, he came under pressure to drop the proposal after several African Americans mounted a campaign against the proposed ban. Harlem pastor Johnnie Green of Mount Neboh Baptist Church and also as President of Mobilising Preachers and Communities (or "MPAC"), which is a non-profit civil right and faith-based organisation with a membership of over 300 churches through the New York, wrote an open letter to Cory Johnson in which he criticised the "discriminatory fur ban proposal" that would strip black people of their right and long-established history of wearing fur "as a symbol of achievement" going on to conclude that "a ban on fur is a ban on black culture" (Green, 2019). According to the *Financial Times*, it was not clear whether this letter and other elements in the wider energetic lobbying effort were "a sincere expression of cultural injury or the handiwork of cunning lobbyists – or a bit of both" (Chaffin, 2019) but either way, the argument appears to have been deployed in a deliberately emotive move. One of the three lobbying firms hired by the fur trade on the campaign, Mercury Consulting, describes itself as "a high stakes public strategy firm" employing "exceptional, proven talent from media, government, business, politics, and technology" to deliver its brand of "bipartisan consultancy" (Mercury, 2019). The firm's services include "strategic media relations," "public affairs campaign management" and "grassroots coalition building." The firm has explained that its grassroots capability involves the development and execution of "comprehensive 'outside games' that elevate our clients' issues and enhance their brands in D.C. and across the U.S." (Mercury, 2019). The delivery of these "outside games" of grassroots campaigning is co-ordinated by the firm's "Strategic Media, Digital Communications, and Government Relations teams" and draws upon "an unmatched network of over 500 leading bipartisan political operatives in every congressional district in all 50 states."

One of Mercury's partners working on the project, Charlie King, described how the grassroots campaign was developed, seeming to anticipate and counter claims of cynicism about the campaign approach:

> When we were talking about strategy, people were saying, "we're going to lose jobs" and I would say, "the jobs are important but for someone like me, this is about emotion." Tying fur to race was not a cynical ploy ginned up by a hired hand like myself; it is a heartfelt issue.
>
> –Chaffin (2019)

The focus of the campaign on emotion rather than economic factors such as job losses in this case is notable, as is the surprising turn in the campaign's decision to link its messaging to racial and cultural themes, especially so as the fur ban proposal came from the progressive Speaker Johnson as he sought mayoral office. Ashley Byrne, associated director of the animal rights group, People for the Ethical Treatment of Animals (PETA), was swift to point out the many prominent African Americans who have supported the move against fur and insisting that:

> There is absolutely not a genuine grassroots movement opposing the bill. [...] The fur industry has been spending millions of dollars on lobbyists to try and fight this bill.
>
> –Chaffin (2019)

Undermining mainstream media

The mixed repertoire of post-classical PR can include an unusual approach to media relations that seeks to undermine the media rather than cultivate a productive working relationship. For example, at Donald Trump's campaign rallies even once he had become President, he encouraged the crowd to chant and boo the reporters in the media area and led them in mocking specific channels with shouts such as "CNN sucks." Online, Trump uses his Twitter feed to put out the message that mainstream journalists are "sick," enemies of the people" who spread "fake news" about him and his campaign, in smears that echo the tactics of media suppression used by Goebbels on behalf of the Nazi party, Mao in China and Stalin in Soviet Russia.

These sinister and oppressive media relations tactics are focussed on undermining mainstream media and form part of a broader and aggressive PR strategy that prioritises winning at all costs. As will be discussed in Chapter 6, the approach involves simultaneously waging war on the mainstream media for running fake news stories, while putting statements that contain outright falsehoods. In the case of Trump, this has included undermining the legitimacy of the US electoral system with his claim that his victory over Hilary Clinton would have been even more decisive if millions of people had not voted illegally in the 2016 election. This win at all costs mentality was in evidence when *Financial Times* editor, Lionel Barber, called at the White House to interview the President in 2017. After thanking President Trump for finding time to see his paper, Barber reported Trump's reply: "That's OK, you lost I won" (Barber, 2017). A win at all costs approach to media relations was adopted by Trump early in his property developer career, apparently on the advice of his long time New York lawyer, Roy Cohn. Cohn was renowned for his ruthless approach and his name remains "synonymous with the rise of McCarthyism and its dark political arts" (Brenner, 2017). His advice to Trump was that of a "master of situational immorality" and involved a three-dimensional strategy for handling business and media situations:

1. Never settle, never surrender
2. Counterattack, countersue immediately
3. No matter what happens, no matter how deeply into the muck you get, claim victory and never admit defeat

It was an aggressive approach that Trump (1987) applied to all business dealings, as well as to handling bad press, as he outlined in *The Art of the Deal:*

> One thing I've learned about the press is that they're always hungry for a good story, and the more sensational the better. It's in the nature of the job, and I understand that. The point is that if you are a little different, or a little outrageous, or if you do things that are bold or controversial, the press is going to write about you. [...] The benefits of being written about have far outweighed the drawbacks. It's really quite simple ... The funny thing is that even a critical story, which may be hurtful personally, can be very valuable to your business.

The result of this approach over 30 years or so was that Trump created "a brand that is entirely amoral" according to Naomi Klein (2017, p. 34), who extended the critique of a branded world first developed in her book *No Logo* (1999) and applied this to the Trump family, in a chapter entitled "The First Family of Brands" in her 2017 book, *No is Not Enough*. So while Trump's approach to PR may have appeared chaotic and almost as an anti-PR effort that went against all political PR norms, the result was that the campaign established a personal amoral brand for Trump, that in turn allowed him to get away with numerous misdemeanours that would have felled more conventional candidates for President, such as failing to reveal tax returns and multiple allegations of sexual misconduct from various women.

Owned media and post-truth public relations on behalf of the nation state

Ownership of media has been a mainstay of state efforts to project power and distribute messages widely. While there has been attention on Russian media channels such as RT in recent years, the use of owned media to project political power and ideology is not only a Russian preference. Media as a tool of soft influence has been deployed prominently by countries and services, such as the UK's *BBC World Service* which was for many years funded by the UK's Foreign Office and provided a radio service since 1932. Similarly, *Voice of America*, was originally a radio station funded by the American government but describes itself today as "an international news and broadcast organization serving Central and Eastern Europe, the Caucasus, Central Asia, Russia, Middle East" with the news items on its website appearing under the banner "Telling America's Story" (Voice of America, 2019). The technique has been appropriated by political campaigns. In the Brexit referendum, for example, various staff from the official Vote Leave campaign were involved in the setting up and running of the news web site, *Brexit Central* that describes its mission as "Promoting a positive and optimistic vision of Britain after Brexit." After journalists from *Brexit Central* were given official journalists' passes to the Houses of Parliament in 2017, the *Buzzfeed* news web site suggested that the organisation had provided a textbook example of "How to turn a campaign into a journalistic outlet approved by parliament" (Waterson, 2017).

In November 2017, Crown Prince Mohammed bin Salman launched a highly publicised crackdown on corruption in Saudi Arabia. While the crackdown was lauded in some quarters, according to the *Financial Times*, it also hinted at "a desire by Prince Mohammed to tighten the government's grip on the media as he pushed ahead with ambitious reform and an increasingly assertive foreign policy" and included a demand that the founder of the largest free to air Arab TV network, the Middle Eastern Broadcasting Center (MBC) hands over a controlling stake to the Saudi authorities to secure his release (Kerr, 2018). As the report goes on to comment, Mohammed bin Salman "would not be the first Saudi leader to move to take charge of private media assets to use them to promote the state's message" recalling that the Saudi satellite news channel, Al Arabiya, part of the MBC group, was secretly taken over by the regime in 2015. In the shadow of the October 2018 death of the dissident Saudi journalist Jamal Khashoggi, apparently at the hands of an assassination squad operating on behalf of Saudi Arabia's Crown Prince Mohammed bin Salman and other Saudi officials, in June 2019 a banker, Sultan Muhammad Abuljadayel, who is "believed to have connections to the Saudi government" according to *The Economist*, (2019) took a 30% stake in the parent firm of the London *Evening Standard* newspaper. The investment in the London paper followed Mr Abuljadayel taking a similar 30% stake in the ownership of all-digital news site, *The Independent*, in 2017. After the investment in Independent Digital News and Media, in 2018, *The Independent* announced the launch of four new web sites in Arabic, Urdu, Farsi and Turkish, which would be published in partnership with the Saudi Research and Marketing Group (SRMG). SRMG is based in Riyadh and is one of the largest publishers in the Middle East, while also offering PR and advertising services. *The Economist* report claimed that the company has links to the Saudi royal family and is "viewed as an organ of soft power" for Saudi Arabia. Quoted in the same piece, David Yelland, ex-editor of *The Sun* newspaper and now a PR consultant, commented that "chapter one in a dictator's playbook is controlling the media," leading to concern about Saudi investment in UK news outlets.

During the 2019 Indian general election, a mysterious "propaganda channel" entitled *Na Mo TV*, began non-stop TV broadcasts about Prime Minister Narendra Modi (Kazmin, 2019). The channel featured an endless loop of Modi's past speeches, uninterrupted coverage of his live rallies and displayed his face as its logo. Although opposition parties and media observers complained that the channel breached election rules, and its precise ownership is not clear, it became clear that the ruling BJP party and government officials had simply began broadcasting under their claim that "NaAmo TV is a promotional channel and thus not subject to the same strict laws applied to those who wish to establish news or entertainment channels" (Kazmin, 2019). While critics deplored the cynicism of the BJP in launching the channel without the appropriate clearances, veteran political analyst and campaigner for electoral transparency, Yogendra Yadav acknowledged the modernity of this approach in an interview with Amy Kazmin (2019): "The BJP is the first twenty-first century party in India – they understand the importance of communicating."

In the US media sector, *Fox News* has always been acknowledged as partisan, but in a lengthy cover article in *The New Yorker* entitled, "The Fox News White House," Jane Mayer asked the question "has it become propaganda?" (2019). As well as addressing the question directly through interviews with ex-contributors to *Fox News*, with one stating: "It's changed a lot. Before it was conservative but it wasn't crazy. Now it is just propaganda." Joe Peyronnin, an ex-President of *Fox News* and now a professor of journalism at New York University was also cited: "I've never seen anything like it before. It's as if the President had his own press organization. It's not healthy." There has also been a casual exchange of staff between *Fox News* and the Trump administration, with the former co-President of *Fox News*, Bill Shine, joining as director of communications and deputy chief of staff for communications in July 2018. Meanwhile, PR personnel were also moving in the other direction, with Shiner's predecessor as White House director of communications, Hope Hicks, moving to 21st Century Fox as chief communications officer in October 2018. On 22 August 2019 Fox News announced that Trump's White House Press Secretary from July 2017 to July 2019, Sarah Sanders, would be joining Fox News as a contributor.

The claim that while partisanship in political opinion and media may be undesirable, at least there is some parity between left and right, was debunked by Benkler *et al.* (2018) in their book, *Network Propaganda: Manipulation, Disinformation, and Radicalization in American Politics*. The book is based on the authors' tracking of how misinformation was propagated during the 2016 Presidential election campaign by conservative interests – specifically operators such as *Fox News* and Steve Bannon's *Breitbart News*, which in turn was funded by Robert Mercer and others – by pushing content and narratives into the mainstream news flow. In the 2016 election campaign, this material included damaging but unsubstantiated allegations of corruption against the Clintons, alongside hyberpole and counterclaims to deflect negative news on Trump. The central proposition of the book is that the misinformation was enabled by these polarising right-wing news sources that were able to take advantage of weaknesses in the media infrastructure – which they describe as the asymmetric media system in order to create a "propaganda feedback loop" for their content in all media channels (2018, p. 75).

The revival of religion in public communication

The revival of religion in populist politics has manifested itself on both sides of the Atlantic in the form of campaign rhetoric that places religion at the centre of a culture war between Christianity, Islam and secularism. IS's core message of creating a new national stronghold based on religion and then defending and expanding the same through a holy war (or *jihad*) is perhaps one of the more extreme examples of religiously oriented communications outreach. As Chris Galloway (2016) has suggested, the IS PR operation, while predominantly described as propaganda, is more accurately a "propagation of a minoritarian 'take' on Islam" using owned media channels as "venues for rational, strategic communication designed mainly for regional consumption." Beyond the Middle East, IS became notorious globally, partly because of an online PR effort that deployed digital artefacts of visual terror in order to cause outrage, such as the videos of Western IS fighters beheading Western hostages, including the murder of James Foley in August 2014 and the burning alive of Jordanian airline pilot, Moaz al-Kasabeh in February 2015. There was careful choreography and attention to visual detail in these incidents, which featured Orange jumpsuits as a reminder of the humiliation of Muslims in Guantanemo Bay, along with the soundtracks of Islamic chants and rhetorical declarations or war on the West. While this media-aware performative dimension to IS's visual communications is evidence of literacy in the tactics of PR, in the field of communications strategy, IS combined message control with a digital liberalism in encouraging freedom in the use of social media that goes beyond two-way communication and embraces advocacy by its supporters. This mix of control of the core message (based on the strong ideological message structure) was balanced with freedom for a fragmented network of supporters to distribute existing material (through re-tweeting, for example). For fighters in the IS itself, there was the opportunity to create their own digital content that communicated their personal experience of IS in their own national register and language, creating high impact recruitment communications with a global reach.

Populist campaign rhetoric in Europe and the United States has included messages that position its politicians as protectors of Christian values and way of life against threats such as Islam and secular liberalism. Steve Bannon, who acted as adviser to the Trump Presidential campaign in 2016, emphasised this combined religious and political purpose in the campaign and again in a speech to a rally in Budapest in May 2018: "What matters is the survival of the Judaeo-Christian West. The West does not have to decline. This is not a law of physics. It can be reversed." (Lloyd, 2018). The same article reported how in Hungary, following his 2018 election victory, Viktor Orban announced his plans to build "an old-school Christian democracy" which would not "yield ground to any supranational business or political empire." In Italy, Matteo Salvini's invocation of Christianity at a 2019 European election rally was criticised by the Catholic Church as cynical exploitation. According to an Associated Press report (Winfield, 2019) of the event that featured several invited right-wing political leaders, Salvini brandished a rosary and acknowledged the work of St. John Paul II and retired Pope Benedict XVI in "reminding Europe of its Christian roots."

In Russia, President Vladimir Putin's introduction of laws protecting the feelings of religious believers has been described as part of "Putin's holy war" to enforce Orthodox Christianity in the country (Bennett, 2017). In 2016, a draft resolution in the European Parliament accused Russia of using the Russian Orthodox Church as a propaganda channel and "agent of government messages" alongside more conventional channels of distribution such as the RT television and online news service (Walton, 2016).

Contesting the facts: the booming industry of public relations, law and investigation

The need to win at all costs in post-classical PR has led to the intersection of PR with private investigators and lawyers in a triumvirate of influence services. A lengthy investigation by Tom Burgis (2017) for the *Financial Times* described the new service combination as "the information wars" or the "west's booming secrets industry" in which "spies, moneymen, lobbyists and PR firms jostle to serve the world's kleptocrats and their rivals." This new industry blends the PR work of reputation management with the legal remedies of injunctions, defamation and other court actions, with the risk and investigative work of private security specialists. It is a high performance and high-cost niche of the PR business, serving corporate and individual clients who come with high expectations. The outcome these clients are seeking and which the PR, legal and security triumvirate collaborate on delivering is increased control over the facts about them that are in the public domain already and influencing the information flow that will emerge in future. In delivering such campaigns, boundaries between the fields of risk management and security, law and public relations, which often positions its services as reputation management in this sector, become fuzzy. The scope of the risk management work can include enforcing military-levels of privacy and data security protocols, while also undertaking investigations into the background of counterparties. This intersects with the legal side of privacy, where law firms advise on legal strategies, including the use of injunctions and the handling of cyber defamation matters. At the heart of many of the reputational issues faced by clients, are the aspects of press coverage which requires the media relations, crisis management and overall reputation management expertise which is offered by the PR firms.

The development of PR services and propositions to serve clients seeking this sophisticated and often highly aggressive mode of reputation management has developed in an accelerated way since around 2005. In major global centres such as New York and London, wealthy individual business people and other high net worth individuals have got used to using security firms as part of their day-to-day business life for personal security, managing property and for investigating and undertaking due diligence research into counterparties such as potential business partners, investors and also competitors, in the mode of a private intelligence service. From this engagement, it was a small step for these clients to seek the same level of investigatory expertise they used in their core business activity when confronted with both personal privacy and defamation threats, as well as threats from activists against their business and lifestyle. An additional driver of demand was the increased adoption of social media and the unruly way it enabled more people to publish stories and gossip online, while also enabling international distribution of the same with no regard to national boundaries or legal systems on privacy. The net effect was that social media not only disturbed the print media industry, it also upturned the mechanisms for controlling negative stories in the press that PR people and lawyers had developed and worked on in the previous two or three decades. *Spears* magazine launched in London in 2005 around the time reputation-management market was accelerating its growth and describes itself as "a wealth management and luxury lifestyle media brand whose flagship magazine has become a must-read for the ultra-high-net-worth (UHNW) community." *Spears* publishes an annual Reputation Management Index of professional advisers and in the introduction to the 2018 Reputation Management Index, Matthew Hardeman (2018) wrote that demand for this "secretive set of the best lawyers, PRs and digital gurus money can buy" was high because "the social media age has left high-profile figures more in need of expert reputational advice than ever." Hardeman went on to give an indication of the type of work that London's reputation management experts had been up to over the past busy year:

> Advising the likes of the Royal Family, Hollywood A-listers, City bigwigs and sports stars has certainly kept them busy – busier than ever, in fact, after a year marked by cyber threats, sexual assault allegations and self-immolation on Twitter. In fact, many of the advisers we spoke to said they had witnessed a year of record enquiries, despite their fields swelling with upstart talent, new firms and plenty of old firms looking to cash in with new departments.

While mainstream PR firms were often involved in the early stages of development of the global reputation management market, it was also being served by boutiques and specialist sole traders, on both the legal and PR side, with the growth and service expansion of Schillings in London and New York perhaps the best example of this on the legal side. Some overlap and referral of work has occurred routinely between PR firms and lawyers working on projects, but a significant development in the past ten years is the prominence of new firms or divisions within old firms, for which the service proposition is a hybrid form of legal and communications management in relation to reputation. One firm that has developed this model is the London-based law firm Schillings (with an office in New York), which has worked on many high-profile cases, including the 2019 attempts by Sir Philip Green to avoid his name being linked to reports of alleged sexual misconduct, the use of a super injunction in a case to prevent *The Sun* newspaper reporting on the private life of footballer Ryan Giggs in 2011 and a 2004 defamation suit on behalf of cyclist Lance Armstrong against *The Sunday Times* regarding doping allegations. Besides the need for a specialist service driving the boutique approach, the confidential and personal nature of some of the issues involved in reputation management matters also influenced clients who often appeared more comfortable going to a fresh but recommended set of advisers rather than, say, the PR firm they had used for corporate work or the law firm engaged for corporate transactions. However, the importance and growth of the sector meant that by 2018, mainstream PR agencies were either hiring in people with experience in high-profile privacy, media and reputation management – such as Weber Shandwick's hire of Patrick Harrison as director of reputation management and strategic media relations in 2014. Harrison worked for several years as press secretary for the Prince of Wales, where in addition to work for the Prince, he also advised the Duchess of Cornwall on reputation management as well as securing privacy agreements on behalf of Prince William at St Andrews University and also for Prince Harry while serving in the Army.

The early growth of the field saw much cross-referral work between lawyers, PR specialists and security firms, and loose alliances developed too as the result of working together on client work. While this system of alliances, preferred working partners and mutual referral continues, recent developments in the sector have included some of the specialist firms expanding their scope of services. For example, as well as a cyber-security capability, Schillings now has its own in-house investigations unit, with experienced individuals from Kroll and other risk firms hired, who use "open source research techniques and investigative methods and help clients mitigate risks to their privacy and reputation" (to quote from one staff profile). The aim of this work and the role it plays in reputation management are explained well in the profile Schillings published on a web site of its partner in the investigations team:

> Juliet knows where to look for information across multiple jurisdictions that may be of interest to journalists and third party detractors, and how it may be used. She also helps to design strategies for dealing with reputation management problems, both identifying areas of reputational risk as well as proactively gathering information that may undermine an assertion by a third party.
>
> –Schillings (2019)

Perhaps the most impressive and also slightly sinister indication of Schillings commitment as a law firm to expanding the scope of its reputation management service in the field of security is its 2017 hiring of Sir Robert Hannigan, who has run the UK's Government Communications Headquarters (GCHQ) and also served as the Prime Minister's adviser on security, to its advisory board. While Schillings expands from law into security, some private security firms are offering campaigning and influence capabilities alongside investigative and intelligence gathering services, with the more aggressive of these firms apparently willing to do just about anything it takes for their clients to win. In a February 2019 edition of *The New Yorker*, under the title "Deception Inc.," Adam Entous and Ronan Farow (2019) described how a consultation with a Washington law firm by a private hospital management company on how to respond to a hostile community campaign led to a referral to a group of ex-Mossad agents who "offered avatars for influence campaigns" and used "elaborate false identities to manipulate its targets." While Bell-Pottinger and several other PR firms employed military personnel and cited their experience in a low key way, the service proposition of Psy-Group was rooted in the experience of its key people in the Israeli defence and security services. Until it was closed in 2018 after it was made public that the firm was under investigation by US Special Counsel Robert Mueller, as part of the probe into the 2016 Presidential election, Psy Group's slogan was "Shape Reality," and while it did offer traditional on-the-ground investigations, the firm's specialism was the digital sphere, starting with online perception management and leading to social media influencing campaigns and manipulation. Its marketing literature boasted that "Reality is a matter of perception" and in the case of the hospital company, their proposal was for a combination of "a coordinated intelligence operation and influence campaign." This proposition of a combination of intelligence and influence in the world of social media campaigning was apparently offered to Donald Trump's son in law, Jared Kushner during the 2016 campaign, during a pitch which included "brash claims about Psy-Group's skills in online deception" (Entous and Farrow, 2019). The same article summed up the firm's mode of operating as combining defensive security work with proactive intelligence gathering, leading to a messaging campaign based on that information: "Psy-Group stood out from many of its rivals because it didn't just gather intelligence; it specialised in covertly spreading messages to influence what people believed and how they behaved."

In 2015, Max Clifford, the late PR executive and convicted sex offender, used a security firm to investigate counterparties as he faced fresh allegations – and the prospect of related civil claims and criminal investigations – from 20 new claimants. Responding to a media report that Clifford was using private detectives to probe the lives of alleged victims, a spokesperson for Clifford said: "Max is not prepared to leave any stone unturned in trying to defend himself" (Wright and Drake, 2015). The same report quoted a source from the family of Rolf Harris, who had also instructed a private detective to investigate claimants, describing the scope of work and defending the decision to use the firm: "The detective has been instructed to build a dossier to robustly rebut any future allegations. That includes any future criminal charges as well as claims for compensation by victims he has already been convicted of assaulting. It's all very under the radar. They want the enquiries dealt with discreetly."

Despite their status as a law firm regulated by the Solicitors Regulatory Authority in the United Kingdom, Schillings' marketing material and service proposition reads like that of a PR firm. The headline offer is that Schillings will help you "find the fix" and "control, the crisis" whether you are an individual or organisation, "because privacy is vulnerable and reputations are under attack" (Schillings, 2019). The firm offers a long list of situations, in which its reputation management services can help, including litigation proceedings, media intrusion, privacy threats, cyber-attacks/data theft, fake news, smear campaigns, bad leavers, insider threats, inaccurate reporting, regulatory enquiries, blackmail and extortion. While the issues arising from smear campaigns, media intrusion, fake news and inaccurate reporting could be handled by a PR firm, the other aspects move into the realm of private security. To that end, Schillings explains that it is able to offer those services through its own resources, as well as external specialists: "We are the only business in the world to deploy – under one roof – intelligence experts, investigators, cyber specialists, risk consultants, lawyers and top people from the military, banking and government." Alongside specialists with an intelligence and investigative background – often ex-police staff – to give in-house capability in that area, there are many instances of ex-military personnel working at the sharp end of reputation management and international political public relations. Bell Pottinger, for example, employed several seasoned UK military communicators who had served as officers in the Army and Royal Navy, in its geopolitical business. The intelligence and investigative capability that Schillings describes is typical of that offered to the PR and legal sector by the private security and investigative firms, and is focussed on countermeasures and investigating the other side of any reputation management battle. Also on the defensive and counter investigative side, Schillings has owned the data and cyber security firm Vigilante Bespoke since 2012 in a move that *The Lawyer* (Griffiths, 2017) magazine described as marking the firm's transformation from "defamation defender to reputation bodyguard."

When the fugitive Kazakh oligarch Mukhtar Ablyazov faced threats from his opponents when he was accused of embezzlement from BTA Bank, he enlisted help from the combined services of London security firms, lawyers, lobbyists and PR companies: "I saw the spies all around me and wanted to hire a group to counter what they were doing" Burgis (2017). Facing charges of embezzlement and with the Kazakh authorities from President Nazarbeyev downwards attacking him for his support of opposition politicians, Ablyazov also attracted attention from London-based PR firms. In 2015, Patrick Robertson of World PR, messaged Ablyazov's lawyer, Peter Sahlas: "Dear Peter Sahlas, please tell that bald-headed c★★★ that you work for that we are bringing him down and all his criminal S★★★ down around his ears. [… And just to be clear, you Quebec piece of s★★★, you're going to loose your shirt along the way." The note was signed "PR" by Patrick Robertson, who is an establishment PR operator in London, Fellow of the Royal Society of Arts (FRSA) who founded his firm alongside the Conservative peer Lord Parkinson and who has extensive experience in the Conservative Party as well as working for the World Economic Form as a special adviser. In all, this combines to confirm World PR's claim that Robertson runs "a respected PR business whose reputation was built upon successfully resolving seemingly intractable challenges in the international corporate and political arena" with a particular focus since 2003 on Kazakhstan, where the firm appears to provide PR advice to the President and represent some of its interests overseas. Robertson's World PR (2019) firm describes itself on its web site as providing "corporate and government communications." As Burgis writes in his report on the case, "Kazakhstan under Narbayez has hired a long line of propagandists to tend its image." In what Burgis describes as the "battle of perception" in London over the Ablyazov case, Kazakhstan hired Portland Communications, a firm founded and headed by Tim Allan, who served as deputy press secretary to Tony Blair, when he was UK Prime Minister. In 2011, when Ablyazov was granted asylum in the United Kingdom, one of Portland's first ideas for the campaign was the hardly original step of surreptitiously making changes to Mukhtar Ablyazov's Wikipedia page, which a moderator soon spotted and identified as coming from an IP (Internet Protocol) address that was registered to Portland. Alongside other London PR firms operating in the reputation management space for oligarchs, foreign governments and high net worth individuals – including Bell Pottinger and Finsbury – after the embarrassment of discovery, Portland undertook training for its staff on conforming with what it described to Burgis (2017) as "the most up-to-date standards," alongside hosting a visit from Jimmy Wales, founder of Wikipedia to talk to staff about the operating protocols of the online encyclopaedia. The visit from Wales formed part of the ritual of public apology that Bell Pottinger also undertook around the same time.

Clandestine editing of Wikipedia was apparently one of the milder practices so-called black PR deployed in this case, which is a phrase widely used in the Mayfair offices of reputation specialists. It is the PR tactic of stealthily creating and distributing narratives with the aim of blackening an opponent's name in the media or public sphere. A PR executive described the practice to Tom Burgis as "putting out the negatives of your opponents, without any fingerprints." According to a tranche of Kazakh government emails that were leaked online, Robertson's proposed plan of action in the Ablyazov's case included covert operations, cyber assaults and sabotage against the "Little Man" combined with "media manipulation globally" and outreach to every friend associate and family member in order to get into "every aspect of his existence, further undermining his confidence." The £3.25m contract between BTA Bank and World PR included funding a documentary on the case that was intended to portray Ablyazov in unfavourable ways. As the case progressed, Mukhtar Ablyazov, his family, lawyers and other close associates did report becoming aware of some of these covert tactics being used against them, as well as more overt approaches from Patrick Robertson at World PR to lawyer Peter Sahlas, which varied from foul-mouthed confrontations to more conciliatory offers to change sides and abandon his client.

In France, FTI, a consulting firm employing 4,700 people in 75 offices around the world, with a sizeable practice in "strategic communications" (FTI, 2019) was hired to work for the Kazakhs against Ablyazov. Analysis in the firm's proposal (Burgis, 2017) concluded that Mukhtar Ablayzov's objective would be to "win public opinion" and recommended a counter attack to deal with this based on a political communications and lobbying effort with French MPs. A core part of FTI's plan was search engine optimisation (SEO) work intended to ensure that search results related to Ablyazov and his case in Google would return and be associated with the term "fraudster" rather than "dissident" being pursued by a rogue President with support from President Putin of Russia, which is how he and his legal team were portraying him to the authorities in France and elsewhere in order to gain support for his case, which he was successful in mobilising from internationally recognised groups, including Amnesty International, Human Rights Watch and several members of the European Parliament.

Case Study 4.1

Interviews with practitioners in reputation management

The chapter concludes with extracts from interviews conducted by the author between 2015 and 2017 with individual executives who have worked for ten years or more on high-profile cases involving reputation management and privacy issues. The three summaries that appear here are from interviews with the founder of a London-based PR and reputation management firm, one executive at an international risk management investigations company and one director at a private security business in London.

> I worked as an investigative journalist for some years – mainly in documentary film-making – and the way I work and the work I do now is mainly a continuation of that. I look at publicly available information and then try and get more data beyond that as needed. The demand from clients varies but an important part is acting for funders and investors, in order to prove that people are who they say they are and that the assets they want to invest in actually exist. So we may be asked by a bank or private equity firm to check on someone seeking investment and to confirm it is a bona fide business.
>
> The reputation area comes into that sometimes because as well as not wanting to take on avoidable financial risk, banks and joint venture partners do not want to take on the unnecessary reputational risk of being associated with someone with problems in that area, or who is likely to cause reputational problems down the line. So the

first step in reputational countermeasures is to check the potential partner out and go from there.

      –Senior Investigator at US Corporate Intelligence Firm

The work we do in the PR and reputation space is mainly commissioned by law firms but sometimes PR firms as well who want what I call an investigative view. My background was as a detective in the Metropolitan Police, so I understand that world pretty well and can offer that investigative perspective. It can be corporate work but we are more often brought in by high net worth individuals who want something that could be damaging to their reputation – especially if it goes to court – to go away.

    As I say, typically that means we are brought in by someone on the reputation management side. That can be a PR firm or a law firm, or both. One thing that has happened over the past ten years or so is a crossover between the two in this kind of work, especially for high net worth individuals and celebrities. Lawyers are getting people in with some experience of PR and media, while the PR firms and teaming up with litigators. Typical instructions are for us to work with the lawyers to investigate the facts of a case and maybe talk to counterparties making a claim or thinking of making a claim. If the facts to support the case look weak, we can be explicit about that to the clamant and suggest another route to resolution via the law firm. So yes, that may mean someone being paid off rather than going to court with a claim, but that may be a decent outcome that avoids embarrassment all round.

    –Director, Private Security and Risk Management Firm, London

People hear that I work in the PR and reputation field and sometimes ask, "Who would you not take on as a client?" I have taken on arms dealers and some pretty unattractive politicians in the old Soviet Union with mixed records. I do draw the line at certain characters — proven predators, for example. But overall, as a former barrister, I take the view that there is a court of public opinion and that until proven guilty, everyone should have a fair chance and has the right to be represented well.

    For the most part, the clients I work for in this field are highly successful hard-nosed people who are used to winning. They hire us for the PR and reputation side because they want results and that is what we have our own reputation for delivering. Clients just don't

> hire us if they think we are just going to be pussy-footing around on their behalf. That is why we will always look to go the extra mile – beyond what the average big PR firm can offer – and team up with the right lawyer, investigator or whatever, in order to get an edge and get the right result for clients.
>
> –Partner in Mayfair-based reputation management firm

References

Banks, A. (2017) *The Bad Boys of Brexit*. London: Biteback Publishing.

Barber, L. (2017) Fake news in the post factual age: lecture to Oxford Alumni Festival; Oxford University. *Financial Times*, 16 September. Available at: https://www.ft.com/content/c8c749e0-996d-11e7-b83c-9588e51488a0

Benkler, Y., Faris, R. and Roberts, H. (2018) *Network Propaganda: Manipulation, Disinformation, and Radicalization in American Politics*. Oxford: Oxford University Press.

Bennett, M. (2017) Putin's holy war. *Politico*, 21 February. Available at: https://www.politico.eu/article/putins-holy-war/

Brenner, M. (2017) Deal with the devil. *Vanity Fair*, August, pp. 68–70.

Buncombe, A. and Garcia, F. (2017) Donald Trump Russia dossier: US intelligence confirms truth of some details. *The Independent*, 10 February. Available at: https://www.independent.co.uk/news/world/americas/donald-trump-russia-dossier-a7574536.html

Burgis, T. (2017) The information wars. *Financial Times Magazine*, 30 September, pp. 14–23.

Caesar, E. (2018) The reputation-laundering firm that ruined its own reputation. *The New Yorker*, 18 June. Available at: https://www.newyorker.com/magazine/2018/06/25/the-reputation-laundering-firm-that-ruined-its-own-reputation

Cadwalladr, C. (2019) So fed up with this disinformation. The IEA is not a "think tank". It's a dark money lobbyist. Twitter, 7 June. Available at: https://twitter.com/carolecadwalla/status/1137040543052156930?lang=en

Carter, G. (2017) A pillar of ignorance and certitude. *Vanity Fair*, March, p. 53.

Chaffin, J. (2019) Furriers find ally in fight to save their hide. *Financial Times*, 29/30 June, p. 4.

The Economist (2019) Press ownership: Sultan of the Standard. July 6, p. 25.

Entous, A. and Farrow, R. (2019) Deception Inc. *The New Yorker*, 18–25 February, pp. 44–55.

Financial Times (2018) Web influencers should be open about incentives. 18 August 2018, p. 6.

Fletcher, M. (2016) The man who bought Brexit. *New Statesman*, 14–20 October, pp. 24–33.

FTI (2019) Services: Strategic Communications. *FTI Consulting EMEA*. Available at: https://www.fticonsulting-emea.com/services/strategic-communications

Galloway, C. (2016) Media jihad: what PR can learn in Islamic State's public relations masterclass. *Public Relations Review* 42 (4), 582–590.

Gray, F. (2016) Trump's triumph. *The Spectator*, 12 November 2016, pp. 12–13.

Gray, J. (2018) Age of the Strongman. *New Statesman*, pp. 22–29.

Green, J. (2019) Exclusive update: open letter to speaker Cory Johnson from Harlem's Rev. Dr. Johnnie Green. *Harlem World*, 16 May. Available at: https://www.harlemworldmagazine.com/open-letter-to-speaker-cory-johnson-from-harlems-rev-dr-johnnie-green/

Griffiths, K. (2017) Schillings: from defamation defender to reputation bodyguard. *The Lawyer*, 23 August. Available at: https://www.thelawyer.com/schillings-abs-transformation/

Grunig, J. and Hunt, T. (1984) *Managing Public Relations*. New York: Holt, Rinehart and Winston.

Hardeman, M. (2018) Revealed: the Spear's Reputation Management Index 2018. *Spears*, 8 January. Available at: https://www.spearswms.com/revealed-britains-top-50-reputation-managers-2018/

Heath, R. (2006) Onward into more fog: thoughts on public relations research directions. *Journal of Public Relations Research*, 18(2), 93–114.

Kazmin, A. (2019) Activists accuse Modi TV channel of flouting poll rules. *Financial Times*, 6/7 April, p. 6.

Kerr, S. (2018) Top Saudi broadcaster caught up in Riyadh's corruption shakedown. *Financial Times*, 26 January. Available at: https://www.ft.com/content/a50075d2-0069-11e8-9650-9c0ad2d7c5b5

Klein, N. (1999) *No Logo*. Toronto: Knopf Canada.

Klein, N. (2017) *No is Not Enough: Defeating the New Shock Politics*. London: Allen Lane.

Leave.EU (2015) The science behind our strategy, Leave.EU, 20 November. Available at: http://web.archive.org/web/20160512002859/http://leave.eu/en/news/2015-11-20/the-science-behind-our-strategy

Lloyd, J. (2018) The new illiberal international. *New Statesman*, 20–26 July, pp. 30–35.

Mayer, J. (2019) The Fox News White House. *The New Yorker*, 11 March, pp. 40–53.

Mercury (2019) Capabilities, Mercury LLC. Available at: http://www.mercuryllc.com/capabilities/

Roberts, H. (2018) The dark side of five star. *The New European*, 26 April–2 May, pp. 24–25.

Schillings. (2019) What we do. *Schillings*. Available at: https://www.schillingspartners.com/

Topham, G. (2019) Ryanair ranked 'worst airline' for sixth year in a row. *The Guardian*, 5 January. Available at: https://www.theguardian.com/business/2019/jan/05/strike-hit-ryanair-ranked-worst-airline-for-sixth-year-in-a-row

Trump, D. (1987) *The Art of the Deal*. New York: Ballantine Books.

Walton, A. (2016) Is the Russian orthodox church a propaganda channel for Putin? *Christian Today*, 25 November. Available at: https://www.christiantoday.com/article/is-the-russian-orthodox-church-a-propaganda-channel-for-putin/102046.htm

Waterson. J. (2017) How to turn a campaign into a journalistic outlet approved by parliament. *Buzzfeed*, 1 August. Available at: https://www.buzzfeed.com/jimwaterson/vote-leave-campaigners-have-secured-a-place-at-downing

White, J. (2018) Politics, incivility and public relations. *Influence Online*, 31 October. Available at: https://influenceonline.co.uk/2018/10/31/politics-incivility-and-public-relations/

Winfield, N (2019). Italy's Catholic establishment faults Salvini for rosary. *Associated Press*, 20 May. Available at: https://www.apnews.com/5cb13f019ce64824b88150a1fec0e6bb

Wright, S. and Drake, M. (2015) Max Clifford and Rolf Harris hire private eyes to investigate alleged victims. *Daily Mirror*, 24 May. Available at: https://www.mirror.co.uk/news/uk-news/max-clifford-rolf-harris-hire-5750882

5   The rhetoric of certainty and division

Introduction

Instead of promoting dialogue in order to contribute to a fully functioning society as envisioned by Robert Heath (2006, p. 96), in post-classical public relations (PR), rhetoric is more usually deployed to dominate, to convey certainty about the cause at hand and to divide society in favour of that cause. The rhetoric of the Islamic State (IS) terror group, for example, seeks to divide the Middle East from the West, Shia Muslims from Sunni Muslims, Muslims living in the West from non-Muslims, in a way that undermines what it calls the "grey zone" of multiculturalism. President Trump's policy propositions on immigration during the 2016 election campaign were promoted using divisive rhetoric on halting all Muslims coming into the United States and building a wall on the US–Mexico border. In the United Kingdom, editor of the Politics.co.uk news web site Ian Dunt (2019) reported a new level of divisive commentary from Brexit-supporting Conservative politicians after the arrival of Boris Johnson as UK Prime Minister in July 2019, noting that it was "quite striking how many Tory Brexiters now revel in the use of aggressive political language. A useful indicator of when a tribe is no longer in contact with its better nature." Beyond politics, the digital public sphere of the social media platforms seems to have enabled and sometimes encouraged well-established lines of decency in public speech to be crossed and the destruction of some long-held norms of democratic debate. Crossing these lines can drive more restrained forms of argument as Ben Labe, has pointed out: "The effectiveness of the single insult is that it costs far less to assert than to disprove. Many of the best techniques of sophistry rely on apparently confusing one's interlocutor by showering him with nonsense. The key is to keep your opponent so busy trying to refute what you are saying that he never has time to assert anything himself" (Lee, 2016). This chapter explores the role of rhetoric in post-classical PR and how divisive and absolutist campaign messages have been used to influence audiences in an increasingly aggressive form of information warfare.

Divisive public communication in the age of anger

Steve Bannon, a founding member of the board of the right-wing news web site, *Breitbart News*, was named chief executive of Donald Trump's election campaign in August 2016 and went on to craft much of Trump's communications strategy and messaging in the US Presidential election. The Bannon playbook for political PR drew instinctively upon years of involvement in right-wing media production and a core element of his offering was the regular dissemination of divisive and provocative public statements that led to an outcry in the mainstream media and liberal society in general. These provocations and the media outrage they caused may have appeared like clumsy accidents but the style of communication was quite deliberate and intended to position the candidate as an outsider on the side of the people, who was willing to talk honestly in terms they can readily understand. Putting aside style and considering content, while some of these messages may be offensive to some voters, they can also energise the existing supporter base and extend it by waving the flag publicly for views that have previously been marginalised in mainstream debate. Besides Trump, the UK politician Boris Johnson appears to have deployed some of these techniques in the build up to his 2019 bid for leadership of the Conservative Party. Johnson's weekly opinion articles in the Conservative-supporting newspaper, *The Daily Telegraph*, were seen by many mainstream commentators and voters as unnecessarily offensive, divisive and provocative. In August 2018, Johnson's criticism of some Muslim women's dress as "absolutely ridiculous that people should choose to go around looking like letter boxes" gained widespread coverage – especially when he refused to apologise for the article. As well as being divisive in its content, it also positioned Johnson as someone willing to say what was on the minds of many Conservative Party members, but remained unspoken. Dividing out this audience and offering them the robust certainty of messages they wanted to hear proved a useful tactic in appealing to a niche audience that within 12 months would vote in the party leadership election that Johnson went on to win in July 2019, leading to him achieving his goal of becoming UK Prime Minister.

The tone and content of the public statements of the leaders of the two prominent Anglosphere nations, Boris Johnson and Donald Trump, plus those of their advisers and allies, is a long way from how Robert Heath envisaged PR operating in the public sphere. For Heath, PR should enable balanced debate in a market place of ideas in the public policy arena (Heath, 2000, p. 69) into which rhetorical contributions are made on behalf of different views or interests in order that all voices are heard in a fully functioning society. The ideal was that the balanced symmetric dialogue in these rhetorical exchanges would lead to optimal solutions that answered societal questions and resolved issues in ways that reflect widespread representation of varied views. The idealised presentation of PR as a rhetorical intervention emerged near the peak of the period of classical PR. Yet rather than reflecting the prestige of the involvement of PR in society, public experience and perception of the artificial and one-sided inputs of spin of the era had by this time led to rather dim view being taken of the field in terms of its status and benefit to society. As Coombs and Holladay (2007, p. 1) reflected on this period:

> People tend to regard anything labelled as "public relations" with great suspicion. [...] The negative impression given may lead people to wonder if society would be better off entirely without public relations.

One explanation for the growth of confrontational language in public life has been offered by Pankaj Mishra (2017), who has made links between the demagogues of the past and the way a more modern cocktail of mass politics, technological change and individualism has come together to produce what he has called an *Age of Anger* to use the title of his book on the topic. This angry and confrontation style of debate has manifested itself in varied modes of nationalism beyond the dominant Western examples of Trump and Brexit. For example, the main campaign message of the current Indian Prime Minister Narendra Modi (who has been in office since 2014) has been a form of Hindu nationalism that sought to promote that religion in a country that has the second largest Muslim population in the world. In 2008, Modi launched a web site in memory of the 1940s Hindu activist (and rival of Gandhi) Veer Savarkar in order to promote the work of a "legend" who has remained largely unknown because of misunderstanding and "vicious propaganda against him" (Veer Savarkar, 2017) Gandhi's assassin Nathuram Godse was a follower of Savarkar's ideology and in court, Godse spoke at length of how Gandhi's appeasement of Muslims had harmed India. Once in government, Modi's ruling BJP was accused of "fanning the flames" of religious division through routine dissemination of "fake news, targeting and demonising Indian Muslims" (Ayubb, 2018). As attacks by mobs on Muslims increased throughout 2018, Modi himself was accused by the same author of "creating a dangerous precedent before the next general election, setting the tone for an India whose syncretic values and democratic principles are under threat."

In Hungary, the rhetoric of division has had a distinctly cultural edge, with the site of confrontation ranging from the curricula of universities to musical theatre. In August 2018, chief of staff for the combative Prime Minister Viktor Orban announced there would be no more public funding for gender studies (even though it was only offered at one public university at the time) while in the same year, some performances of the Billy Elliot musical play were cancelled after the pro-government newspaper *Magyar Idok* criticised it as gay propaganda. For supporters of Orban's politics, the government was right to make changes:

> "Since 1989 the left has dominated the discourse about what constitutes Hungarian culture," said Gyorgy Schopflin, who represents Fidesz in the European Parliament. "Mr Orban's position is to nudge [the discourse] along so that the centre-right view of the world...has a much greater say."
>
> –Hopkins (2018)

This style of divisive rhetoric is no longer limited to a small number of countries and there is convincing evidence that it is growing. In 2019, *The Guardian* published the results of a study it commissioned from the *Team Populism* network of political scientists, which used textual analysis to scrutinise public speeches and statements by almost 140 world leaders in 40 countries over 20 years. The project concluded that a "two-decade surge in populist rhetoric has upended the global political landscape" and that rather than seeing any signs of a slowdown in their tracking of populist discourse in the world, "divisive populist rhetoric is on the rise" (Lewis *et al.*, 2019).

Partisan media and absolutist opinions

On 27 March 2019, three days before the United Kingdom was set to leave the European Union, The Rt Hon. The Lord Judge, ex-Lord Chief Justice of England and Wales, preached the sermon at the Temple Church, which serves as the church for the barristers and judges who populate London's Inns of Court at Middle and Inner Temple. Lord Judge, who had worked on several important media cases during his career, prioritised media matters and modes of public argumentation over law in this timely speech:

> With 24-hour news, and the perceived obligation to fill every minute of each 24 hours with excitement and stimulation and controversy, and plenty of individuals happy to join in, usually assertively, the news coverage has become intense and confrontational. We are becoming enured to intolerance. We have forgotten the societal need for moderation [...]
>
> During the last few months of debate and discussion too many on both sides have embraced what I describe as absolutist opinions. [...] There has been too much absolutism, and insufficient moderation. The constant use of intolerant language undermines our commitment to free speech. That is bad enough, but worse, the language here has damaged the body politic.
>
> –Lord Judge (2019)

As elements of the news media have become more partisan over the past ten years or so, with the emergence of networks such as *Fox News* in the United States on the right and online news sites in support of the left in the United Kingdom such as *The Canary*, it is not surprising that some of the more shadowy corners of social media have also become less balanced. Lord Judge's words quoted above are interesting for the clarity of his assertion that divisive and confrontational rhetoric have permeated mainstream news coverage as well as social media. In his evidence to a report by the UK Parliament's Committee on Standards in Public Life (2017) on the subject of Intimidation in Public Life, Lionel Barber, editor of *The Financial Times*, reflected upon the intersection of social media and comments on online news stories hosted by news outlets such as his own, pointing out that the economics of attention means that when social media posts adopt "extreme positions whether political or moral or abusive, you will get a rise in followers. There is an incentive to go to the extreme." This media logic helps to explain why deplorable appeals and shamelessness in public debate have become rhetorical calling cards of post-classical PR appeals and public performances.

In this divided atmosphere, there is growing hostility among those holding opposite views that all political parties have the right of access to the public airwaves. In a 2019 interview, the Labour MP David Lammy was critical of broadcasters including the BBC for allowing "extreme hard-right fascism to flourish" on the airwaves, citing the frequent appearances of Conservative politicians Boris Johnson and Jacob Rees-Mogg (Elgot, 2019). BBC journalist Paul Mason linked the divisive nature of political discourse with changes in media infrastructures, including the "new breed of overtly partisan talk radio stations" which have allowed totalitarian ideas to become "normalised" (Mason, 2019). Former head of BBC Television News Roger Mosey has suggested that national broadcasters in the United Kingdom have made "editorial lapses" in their portrayal, for example, of the Conservative Party politician Boris Johnson as "an engaging comedy act" and the overindulgence of United Kingdom Independence Party (UKIP) politician Nigel Farage as a "media personality" rather than a controversial politician whose views and policies should be scrutinised (Mosey, 2019).

Mediatisation and speech acts

While public perception of PR and its processes may be negative, it remains pervasive in a public arena characterised by the increased mediation of discourse by mass media. One result of this process of mediatisation in which media influences the shape of discourse and society itself (Runciman, 2006, p. 109) is the increased emphasis on words in the form of speeches, statements, opinion articles and even tweets when promoting and projecting ideas and information. Donald Trump's campaign slogan, "Make America Great Again" (MAGA) is an example of language as a call to action, as well as a Trump's habit of appropriating pieces of campaign rhetoric to suit his own purposes. The phrase was used by Ronald Reagan in the 1980 election and Trump registered a trademark application for the slogan in November 2012, days after President Obama defeated Mitt Romney in the Presidential election of that year. The slogan itself is on one hand a unifying call to action on behalf of the nation, but the stronger appeal is the way it is imbued with the fatigue that Trump and many of his supporters see as political correctness and promotion of diversity over nationalism, as captured in Hilary Clinton's "Stronger Together" slogan. Viewed in this contrasting light, the MAGA slogan is another skilfully deployed piece of campaign rhetoric that establishes dividing lines between Trump and Clinton supporters, while encouraging those in the middle to respond to Trump's call for voters to get involved in improving the future of America.

Reflecting on this trend, *The Economist* (2016) concluded that: "It is fair to say that pretty much the entire job of a politician unlike that of a woodworker or surgeon, is to talk, not to perform what might traditionally be called 'action'." Yet at the same time, rhetoric undertaken as part of PR work can have an action component when it forms what Austin (1975) described in his book, *How to Do Things with Words* as "speech acts" or "performative utterances." In the realm of linguistics and philosophy of language, speech acts are a category of pronouncements that involve performing an act as well as presenting information. Examples include "Can you come here?" which appears as a question about ability to walk across a room but is in fact a request for action. Austin made an important distinction between action in the real world ("illocution") and the speech act or "locution" that initiated it. The distinction is important and captures some of the risk in making public statements, set-piece speeches and other PR work because it addresses how the rhetoric of PR can take on commercial and geopolitical consequences when made by those in power. The public pronouncements of Prime Ministers and Presidents, for example, are received as commitments to specific policies or courses of action.

Such rhetorical pronouncements by public figures in a mediatised world form part of their day-to-day PR work within their organisation, whether they are the President of the United States, President of Oxfam or CEO of BP. Over time, these statements can also contribute to establishing a personal promotional presence for politicians, business leaders and others in power. Whether gained through print, broadcast, face-to-face or online engagement with audiences, this promotional presence or public image becomes a platform from which to undertake further public pronouncements, often with remarkably little action taking place to back up the communicative content. The personal dimension of this promotional presence is clearly important but also intersects with the corporate image and reputation. In August 2018, for example, the decision by Elon Musk, the CEO of Tesla, to tweet about his claim to have "funding secured" for the electric car maker from the Saudi Arabian sovereign wealth fund in order to take the company private led to the US Securities and Exchange Commission (SEC) taking legal action against him for causing market chaos and harming investors. Under pressure from short sellers who were betting on the fall of the Tesla share price, Musk's attempt at some personal financial PR via his Twitter feed led to the SEC fining him for recklessly making statements that were "false and/or misleading because he did not have an adequate basis in fact for his assertions" (O'Kane and Lapatto, 2018). The tweet from Elon Musk on taking Tesla private was received by shareholders and financial markets as a firm commitment that led to the share price rising. After Musk and the company were both ordered to pay $20m each in fines in October 2018, the Tesla CEO tweeted that he felt the fine was "worth it," possibly because it was followed by an 11% rise in the share price on the day of the tweet, temporally easing pressure placed upon the company by short sellers.

Confrontational and uncivil language as a positioning tool

In nationalist politics, the confrontational style of populism represents not only a new approach to politics, it is also an innovative PR strategy that can include bad manners, shock tactics and a focus on self. In media relations, the approach can include aggressive attacks on news outlets that publish criticism. A *Financial Times* editorial of September 2018 reflected on President Donald Trump's attacks on news media and placed it in the historical context of President Theodore Roosevelt's observation that the presidency itself was a "bully pulpit" for influencing public opinion:

> Donald Trump is also a devotee of public relations, but uses his bully pulpit in the modern sense: to intimidate those he disagrees with or regards as enemies. News media are a frequent target and this week President Trump added to the targets of his anger Google – in particular the search giant's news service. Its sin was to give prominence to stories that were critical of the President, including the CNN cable news network "They have it RIGGED, for me and others so that almost all stories and news is BAD" he tweeted.
>
> *—Financial Times* (2018)

Non-conformance extended to a lack of civility to customers combined with shock tactics such as regular attacks on regulators, governments and passengers by the discount airline, RyanAir. Despite conformance with many aspects of classical PR in his conduct both as a PR executive and politician, UK Prime Minister David Cameron began to display some of the incivility associated with post-classical PR with offensive comments describing members of the UKIP in 2006 as "a bunch of fruitcakes and loonies and closet racists," despite many being ex-Conservative voters that he would logically be seeking to win back to his more conventional politics. Beyond Cameron's outburst against UKIP, an offensive approach to political PR and public communication that combined rudeness with a macho public image had become the signature of several politicians around this time. One of the most prominent and enduring examples was Italy's Silvio Berlusconi who presented himself as the classic authoritarian strongman in his nine years as Prime Minister spread over several elections between 1994 and 2011, while in Canada, Rob Ford, Toronto mayor from 2010 to 2014 plumbed new depths of rudeness while also failing to resign after admitting substance abuse in 2013.

The online spaces of hyper-confrontation

On February 2019, the UK Member of Parliament (MP) Luciana Berger left the Labour Party after a sustained campaign of anti-semitism against her on what the Labour Party Deputy Leader Tom Watson described as the worst day of shame for the Labour Party in its 120-year history. Luciana Berger had been subject to a sustained campaign of online racist abuse in the United Kingdom, allegedly from Labour Party members as well as from right-wing activists in the United Kingdom and abroad. In the vanguard of the activity was the US-based *Daily Stormer* web site that derives its name from the *Der Sturmer* (The Stormer) newspaper of the Nazi era and which is run by the neo-Nazi, Andrew Anglin, who claims on the web site that it is "the most censored publication in history." In October 2014, Garron Helm, a young right-wing extremist in the United Kingdom, was jailed for four weeks for sending Luciana Berger an obscene message. The incident prompted Andrew Anglin to use the *Daily Stormer* as a channel to co-ordinate what he called "a new operation against the filthy communist Jewess, which will be known as Operation Filthy Jew Bitch." This call to action and its results were notable for the sheer volume of abuse dispersed through Twitter feeds and other social networks in ways that masked the original source as it made its way from one niche far right source for onward transmission via multiple accounts (some of which are anonymous or pseudo-anonymous). This tactic of online distribution via discreet infiltration into wider online networks has been a tactic of the alt-right as well as states such as Russia, which has used the twitter feeds of its RT news network and even interviews to introduce alternative storylines into the wider public sphere. The Luciana Berger case is notable for the repulsive racist call to action and also for the international nature of the operation. It is a tactic also suited to the divisive and racist messages associated with the "thirst for racial confrontation" that appears to exist on the extreme right and in some elements of extreme left, with the efficacy of the *Daily Stormer's* efforts in this field providing the alt-right in particular with "a blueprint for trolling projects that would go beyond anti-Semitic hate campaigns" (Wendling, 2018, p. 138). The aim of the individuals behind these sites seems to be producing an online promotional space of hyper-confrontation, which in turn attempts to force division and choice onto one side or the other of a debate, often leaving moderate mainstream opinion – whether from the public, business or politicians – in a powerless situation.

In evidence to a hearing on the topic of intimidation by the UK Committee on Standards in Public Life (2017, p. 17), the MP Ian Lavery described the pervasiveness of intimidation of politicians undertaken on social media: "It is torrid; this abuse is 24/7. It is not something that you can walk away from. When you go home, it is there with you and your kids. This abuse is constant." In her contribution, another MP, Rachel Maclean (2017, p. 26) stressed the detrimental effect on her mental health of "anonymous people" constantly directing "hatred and bile" via her publicly available Twitter feed and other social media channels. The BBC political journalist, Laura Kuenssberg, reported a noticeable worsening of the problem of divisive and intimidating verbal attacks in public life in the past 15 years: "I've been in and around lobbies since 2003 and have been in Westminster full time since 2014/15. There's been a sea change during that time in what's been experienced by MPs and candidates, especially women." (2017, p. 28). The report concluded that "Leaders of political parties should always call out intimidatory behaviour, even when it is perpetrated by those in the party's fringes" (2017, p. 15) but the more extreme examples of intimidation come from political actors who see such behaviour as justified by their political objectives.

Creating division: the alt-right digital PR ecosystem

The alt-right digital PR ecosystem exploits the characteristics of digital media in order to distribute its ideas and recruit supporters. It exploits digital media platforms in order to amplify what is often a quite insubstantial political proposition, that in turn can lead to it being reported on in mainstream media. In using tactics of shock, outrage and offence in their communications outreach, they are legally canny in ensuring that their claims avoid criminal proposition for inciting violence while making offensive and sometimes dangerous claims. Part of the shrewd avoidance of legal sanctions can extend to the use of alternative online platforms such as 4Chan, 8Chan, Reddit, Voat, Gab, Minds, Bitchute, as well as encrypted messaging applications such as Discord and Telegram.

A common feature of public statements and postings on social media by figures on the populist right of politics is the way oppositional arguments are used to position individuals as the upstart that draws audience attention through partisan breaches of democratic norms. The success of this alt-right style of political PR in Donald Trump's 2016 Presidential Campaign has been described as a form of "political punk rock" that is "loud, abrasive hostile, white, back to basics and fun" (Sailer, 2016). The rebel positioning of campaigners who pose as proud rather than ashamed of their brash appeal has pervaded both sides of the Atlantic. The book-length account of the unofficial Brexit campaign Leave.EU by Aaron Banks (2016) is proudly titled *The Bad Boys of Brexit: Tales of Mischief, Mayhem and Guerrilla Warfare in the EU Referendum Campaign*. The "bad boys" moniker was self-styled here but there are many examples of what were intended as terms of insult being eagerly mischievously adopted by those for whom they were intended. In the United States, soon after Hilary Clinton spoke of half of Trump supporters as a "racist, sexist, homophobic, xenophobic and Islamophobic 'basket of deplorables,'" the term was adopted by his supporters who used it as a badge of honour, proudly wearing it on t-shirts. In an interview after the campaign, Hilary Clinton said she regretted the way the term handed her opponent "a political gift" while apparently unsettled by the confrontation, bullying and rude campaigning style of the novice candidate Trump that breached the norms she was used to after years of political experience:

> I thought Trump was behaving in a deplorable manner. I thought a lot of his appeals to voters were deplorable [...] I thought his behavior as we saw on the Access Hollywood tape was deplorable.
>
> –Fang (2017)

Rather than balanced dialogue that respects another point of view, the aim of online alt-right rhetoric is to create division and offence, which can be seen as a PR success rather than failure, especially so if it gains mainstream media coverage because of the outrage caused. At the 2016 conference of the National Policy Institute, Nazi salutes were given hailing Trump's victory, with director Richard Spencer not apologising but describing the event as a PR success on which he would seek to capitalise (Schreckinger, 2017). Spencer spent time in US academia before founding Alternative Right web site in 2010 and from there developing "a raw online communications strategy" (Wendling, 2018, p. 20) that was framed in confrontation and ethnic and racial terms. As this academically minded group sought to define and project the alt-right's ideology to a wider audience, it did so through creating and distributing messages and narratives of hero worship of figures who had broken the norms and often the laws of anti-racism in civic society. In doing so, these online campaigns hollowed out the centre ground and extended the range of what was permitted public discourse on race and immigration issues – a theme that Donald Trump would develop as Presidential candidate with his campaign rhetoric on the specifics of Mexican and Muslim immigration.

One early example – and another case of transatlantic nature of the alt-right online discourse – was the case of a woman who was arrested on public transport in London for racially abusing fellow passengers. Richard Spencer praised her behaviour online and described her in heroic terms as the "Epic Tram Lady" whose feelings about "her native London being destroyed" were real and that her arrest showed up the "the true totalitarian nature of Cool Britannia" (Wendling, 2018, p. 21). In the terms of the new rules of public communication, such divisive, norm-busting and often illegal behaviour was no longer something to apologise for using PR techniques, it was something to celebrate. Stirring up the mainstream liberal media and generating controversy was no longer something to diffuse, it was the new communications strategy for some campaigning organisations for whom triggering and trolling became a core part of the online media relations toolkit.

The role of the platforms

In 2018, after the Cambridge Analytica scandal of data manipulation and intrusion had been uncovered by the media, the inventor of the World Wide Web, Sir Tim Berners-Lee issued an open letter in which he expressed his concerns with the levels of dysfunction in society. He wrote that these "unintended consequences" of aggressive and polarised debate had been enabled by the web, while it also distributed misinformation. In an interview with the BBC on the issues he had raised, Berners-Lee described the first decade of expansion of the web as mostly positive, but the effects were now turning negative and he was concerned with the spread of division, "nastiness" and destructive effects it was having on communication and society (Cellan-Jones, 2018).

While changes in politics are at the core of change in political atmosphere, the socio-technical characteristics of online media seem to offer an ideal incubator for divisive campaign rhetoric of unarguable certainty. The deterministic features include the way Facebook's content management system works to get and keep users' attention, by serving up targeted material that initially gets individual users engaged and then has the right characteristics of "stickiness" to keep them logged on. The most sticky content is likely to be the material that best matches the interests of the individual, is in accord with their interests and so on, thus creating the echo chamber effect in which users do not see a balanced diet of news and views, for example, but only material that accords with their interests, based on content already viewed, profile information and the multiple data points gathered by Facebook and fed into their algorithmic content management and server system (including age, sex, location, likely occupation and so on).

In response to this line of criticism, social media platforms have for many years maintained that they operate as utilities or "mere conduits" to use the legal term, rather than as publishers. In doing so, they avoided the need to pass judgement on the views and content expressed in posts – as well as avoiding responsibility for the effects of widespread trolling campaigns – on Twitter, Facebook and other platforms. However, breaches of terms of service and/or legal issues can lead to account suspensions although for some campaigners and communications specialists, these are viewed as one of the costs of campaigning. Rather than choosing to stay silent and minimise the embarrassment of having been caught out using the platform illegally or in breach of its service terms, some treat suspension as a further opportunity for publicity that helps their cause. When online campaigners are banned, the social media platforms that had provided such a free and easy operating environment for online campaigning are immediately presented as an enemy that stifles free speech. The platforms and any laws that have been applied are attacked as oppressive and as part of a minority conspiracy against the right of ordinary citizens to express themselves. In February 2019, the far right UK activist and founder of the English Defence League, Tommy Robinson, complained of his ban by Facebook and Instagram (where he had a combined following of one million other users) stating he had broken no "laws of Facebook" going on to ask "Where is free speech?" (Bridge and Donnellan, 2019). Robinson had been banned after complaints on Facebook about a series of abusive posts urging violence against Muslims in the United Kingdom.

Earlier, in July 2016, Milo Yiannopoulos, a right-wing British journalist known for bleached blonde hair, opposition to Islam and support for President Trump, went beyond the oft-used anti-free speech argument after he was banned from Twitter after a racialised trolling campaign against a remake of the *Ghostbusters* film. After the ban, he used the *Breitbart News* site to complain about the "cowardly suspension of my account" which he claimed meant that "Twitter has confirmed itself as a safe space for Muslim terrorists and Black Lives Matter extremists, but a no-go zone for conservatives" (Kew, 2016). He went on to place the ban as a totalitarian act against free speech: "Like all acts of the totalitarian regressive left, this will blow up in their faces, netting me more adoring fans. We're winning the culture war, and Twitter just shot themselves in the foot. This is the end for Twitter. Anyone who cares about free speech has been sent a clear message: you're not welcome on Twitter." Despite these selective bans, many well-known promoters of extreme views are still active online. Yiannopoulos himself remains active on Facebook (with two million followers) while the UK-based columnist Katie Hopkins remains live on Twitter (where she claims to be "telling the truths not being told"). In the view of *Wired* journalist, Will Bedingfield (2019), Facebook's decision to ban Robinson was "all about saving face, not stopping extremism" and left the company open to the charge that "it acts opportunistically rather than ethically, and that the primary motive guiding these bans is the defence of its reputation." In the same report, Dr Bharath Ganesh, a researcher at the Oxford Internet Institute went further:

> It seems the company is concerned by claims from the right that conservative voices, in both the US and the UK, [believe] their free speech is under attack. It's possible that Facebook's desire to be unbiased has some effect on [its] decision-making in taking down accounts.
>
> –Bedingfield (2009)

Conclusion: the contested effects of divisive rhetoric

Since Donald Trump's win in the 2016 election, journalists, academics and commentators have speculated about the role that trolling, 4chan, and the alt-right's skill in creating and distributing memes played in his success. Similarly, in discussions on the Brexit referendum, claims are made that brilliant digital campaigning by the leave side swayed the result. Certainly, the leave campaigns did not shy from using a divisive and certain rhetorical style, in the words and images they deployed. A typical Leave.EU post on Facebook warned voters that "immigration without assimilation equals invasion." A post about the dangers of "free movement" within the EU was accompanied by a photograph of ticking explosives. These sorts of posts on social media and their success in terms of audience reach and penetration, confirms claims made elsewhere in this text that the character and style of populist political PR and the nature of audiences aligns with the affordances of social media, particularly the divisive ping-pong of short Twitter posts on separate sides of an argument.

The confrontational rhetoric and non-conformist campaign style of Aaron Banks, head of Leave.EU, and his PR chief, Andy Wigmore, reflected their personalities, but also formed the core of their campaign's PR strategy. He told one interviewer, "We played the media like a Stradivarius," noting that "if we spent eight million in the referendum, we got thirty-five, forty million in free publicity" by outraging liberal commentators. This tactic had an obvious model across the Atlantic. "We are going to be blunt, edgy, and controversial, Donald Trump-style," Banks wrote in his book *The Bad Boys of Brexit*, adding, "If BBC Producers aren't spluttering organic muesli over their breakfast tables every morning, we won't be doing our job." Nigel Farage told an interviewer recently that Leave.EU, as a nonofficial platform, had some strategic advantages over the mainstream Vote Leave campaign.

> Banks created content that was very different in nature to what the establishment Conservative politicians were doing," he said. "It had more humor. It had more edge. Not everything they did was everyone's cup of tea, but hey, that's life. It was a much more populist campaign.
>
> —Caesar (2019)

The divisive populism of the Brexit campaign and the admissions by its protagonists that it was modelled at least partly on the Trump style of confrontational PR campaigning is interesting in itself for those concerned with PR efficacy, but what effects did it have on the result of the vote? Ben Page, who runs the polling company Ipsos Mori, has pointed out that the existence of an official and unofficial Leave campaign enabled the leave side to offer "a respectable (sovereignty) and less respectable (migrant scum) argument simultaneously" (Caesar, 2019). In considering the effect on the result, when a campaign runs as close as Brexit did, "anything can make a difference. Targeted Facebook advertising, the extra publicity, Farage, and the migrant poster – any or all of that could have swung it over the line." Such commentary offers a compelling media narrative but work by political scientists to analyse the result has suggested a more nuanced relationship between communicative cause and effect. While the rhetoric of division was present, sometimes compelling to observe, and certainly helped to amplify campaign messages, the results in the Brexit vote and the US Presidential election reflected a deeper set of changes in society and politics. As Clarke *et al.* (2017) detected in their analysis of the why Britain voted for Brexit, through longitudinal surveys and other empirical work, a complex mix of short-term and long-term factors underpinned the decision, rather than the rhetoric of digital media campaign alone.

While enthusiasm for and certainty about a point of view is understandable in some areas of public life, aspects of modern political PR have displayed excessive intellectual certitude on issues in the public sphere. Certitude has proved an effective approach to political communication in which audiences increasingly favour the "politics of absolutes" (Ganesh, 2018) in order to cope with the raised temperature of public life, which has been too high since the 1990s. Immoderate and divisive political rhetoric has come not just from new online channels such as those of the alt-right, but also the more longstanding sources such as talk radio stations and cable news channels, where its very divisiveness becomes a strength that enables micro targeting of niche audiences with specific political leanings. None of these niche or micro channels would be important if they did not gain audiences. Yet divisive and certain communication styles seem to meet the needs of increasingly "affective publics" (Papacharissi, 2014) who want an emotional connection with the products they buy, the places they go and the political goals they support.

Case Study 5.1

Islamic State and the divisive promotion of terror

During the most active years of its digital outreach work from around 2012 onwards, the IS integrated its PR and propaganda with digital marketing, data-analytics and search engine optimisation. Together, these tools delivered a computational form of PR that used algorithms and the optimisation of digital content to search online audiences, identify their interests, and then deliver messages to them directly. The name IS signifies division through the way it simultaneously combines inclusion and exclusion. The intention of this nomenclature is to intensify the value of belonging for recruits (who belong to a new state in effect) while annexing those who do not want to be involved or cannot because they are not Sunni Muslims. The rhetoric of IS propaganda on religious separation also promotes sectarian themes in the way it excludes Shia Muslims. Once the caliphate was established, IS rhetoric reflected its strategic intent of expansion, as well as divisive attacks on non-believers (*kufirs*) who are excluded from the IS and referred to as the far enemy.

This multiplicity of approaches reflected the multi-dimensional nature of IS – as terror group, state and Islamic welfare operation – and the multiple propositions it offered to recruits. The use of transnational digital communications technology has been a key enabler of IS and skilful deployment of limited resources has enabled IS to generate what Maher (2015) has called a "carefully curated asymmetry of fear." The online PR value chain that generated this asymmetric advantage starts with the creation of digital artefacts of terror that are designed to cause division through outrage, such as the notorious early videos of Western fighters beheading Western hostages such as James Foley in August 2014 and the burning alive of captured Jordanian airline pilot, Moaz al-Kasasbeh in February 2015. The choreography of these incidents, with Orange jumpsuits used as reminder of the humiliation of Muslims in Guantanemo Bay, along with the soundtracks of Islamic chants and rhetorical declarations or war on the West, is evidence of a media-aware performative dimension to IS's visual communications. In the terms of performance studies theory, the decisions about what to include and what to leave out renders these artefacts as performance (Phelan, 1992, p. 31) and rather than live and natural recordings, the films are deliberately "mediatized" (Auslander, 2008, p. 56) as part of the group's communications management. IS has recognised that beyond the terror of the act of murder itself, widespread attention and impact can be generated through exaggerated dramatisation in which terrorists are performers in specially designed media spectacles. That is to say, it is not enough just to be a terrorist and deliver acts of terrorism. In post-classical PR, these realities are choreographed and performed in order to render them compelling enough to be shared for maximum communicative effect as digital performative artefacts.

In considering its approach to managed communications, IS has combined message control with a digital liberalism in encouraging freedom in the use of social media that goes beyond two-way communication and embraces advocacy by its supporters. This mix of control of the core message (based on the strong ideological message structure) is balanced with freedom for a fragmented network of supporters to distribute existing material (through re-tweeting, for example). For fighters in the IS itself, there was the opportunity to create their own digital content that communicates their personal experience of IS in their own national register and language, creating a truly global outreach. In classical PR, such uncontrolled advocacy might be considered a problem but for IS, it has been an asset enabling a vocal minority to achieve asymmetric effects. So while web tools such as Google Analytics go some way to enabling micro-targeting of recruits, this approach becomes realistic to execute through the efforts of supporter advocates who are willing to spend time both seeking out potential recruits and building an online relationship, leading to the decision to commit to action in some form, whether that be travelling to Syria or other involvement.

References

Auslander, P. (2008) *Liveness: Performance in Meditatized Culture*. New York: Routledge.
Austin, J. (1975) *How to Do Things with Words*. Oxford: Clarendon Press.
Ayubb, R. (2018) Mobs are killing Muslims in India. Why is no one stopping them? *The Guardian*, 20 July. Available at: https://www.theguardian.com/commentisfree/2018/jul/20/mobs-killing-muslims-india-narendra-modi-bjp
Banks, A. (2016) *The Bad Boys of Brexit: Tales of Mischief, Mayhem and Guerrilla Warfare in the EU Referendum Campaign*. London: Biteback Publishing.

Bedingfield, W. (2019) Facebook's Tommy Robinson ban is all about saving face, not stopping extremism. *Wired*, 28 February. Available at: https://www.wired.co.uk/article/tommy-robinson-facebook-instagram-ban

Bridge, M and Donnellan, K. (2019) Facebook bans far right's Robinson for hate speech. *The Times*, 27 February, p. 23.

Caesar, E. (2019) The chaotic triumph of Arron Banks, the "bad boy" of Brexit. *The New Yorker*, 18 March. Available at: https://www.newyorker.com/magazine/2019/03/25/the-chaotic-triumph-of-arron-banks-the-bad-boy-of-brexit

Cellan-Jones, R. (2018) Tim Berners-Lee: 'Stop web's downward plunge to dysfunctional future'. *BBC News*, 11 March. Available at: https://www.bbc.co.uk/news/technology-47524474

Clarke, H., Goodwin, M. and Whitely, P. (2017) *Brexit: Why Britain Voted to Leave the European Union*. Cambridge: Cambridge University Press.

Committee on Standards in Public Life, (2017), The Committee's seventeenth report, intimidation in public life: a review by the Committee on Standards in Public Life, London: UK Government. Available at: https://www.gov.uk/government/publications/intimidation-in-public-life-a-review-by-the-committee-on-standards-in-public-life

Coombs, T. and Holladay, S. (2007) *It's Not Just PR: Public Relations and Society*. London: Wiley/Blackwell.

Dunt, I. (2019) Quite striking, @IanDunt, Twitter, 16 August. Available at: https://twitter.com/IanDunt/status/1162383690468605952

The Economist (2016) Doing by talking. 12 November, p. 81.

Elgot, J. (2019) David Lammy says comparing ERG to Nazis 'not strong enough'. *The Guardian*, 14 April. Available at: https://www.theguardian.com/politics/2019/apr/14/comparing-erg-to-nazis-not-strong-enough-says-david-lammy

Fang, M. (2017) Hillary Clinton: calling Trump supporters 'deplorables' handed him 'a political gift. *Huffington Post*, 10 September. Available at: https://www.huffingtonpost.co.uk/entry/clinton-trump-deplorables-2016-election_us

Financial Times (2018) Trump's dangerous claim to the internet that he wants. 31 August. Available at: https://www.ft.com/content/2c5b16e0-ad21-11e8-89a1-e5de165fa619

Ganesh, J. (2018) Politics of absolutes fuels ideological violence. *Financial Times*, 31 October. Available at: https://www.ft.com/content/becd97a4-dc39-11e8-8f50-cbae5495d92b

Heath, R. (2000) A rhetorical perspective on the values of public relations: crossroads and pathways toward concurrence. *Journal of Public Relations Research*, 12 (1), 69–91.

Heath, R. (2006) Onward into more fog: thoughts on public relations' research directions. *Journal of Public Relations Research*, 18 (2), 93–114.

Hopkins, V. (2018) Combative premier Orban sends chill through Hungarian culture. *Financial Times*, 22 September. Available at: https://www.ft.com/content/9c657408-b514-11e8-bbc3-ccd7de085ffe

Judge, I. (2019) *Sermon at Choral Evensong to Acknowledge Brexit*. Temple Church, London, 27 March. Available at: http://www.templechurch.com/wp-content/uploads/2019/03/032719-LordJudgeBrexit.pdf

Kew, B. (2016) Milo suspended permanently by Twitter minutes before 'Gays For Trump' party At RNC. *Breitbart News*, 19 July. Available at: https://www.breitbart.com/social-justice/2016/07/19/breaking-milo-suspended-twitter-20-minutes-party/

Lee, I. (2016) Understanding Trump's troll army, *Vice*. 13 March. Available at: https://motherboard.vice.com/en_us/article/bmvnq4/understanding-trumps-troll-army

Lewis, P., Caelainn Barr, C. Clarke, S. Voce, A., Levett, C. and Gutiérrez, P. (2019) Revealed: the rise and rise of populist rhetoric. *The Guardian*, 6 March. Available at: https://www

.theguardian.com/world/ng-interactive/2019/mar/06/revealed-the-rise-and-rise-of-populist-rhetoric

Maher, S. (2015) Jordan pilot murder: Islamic State deploys asymmetry of fear. *BBC News*, 4 February. Available at: http://www.bbc.co.uk/news/world-middle-east-31129416

Mason, P. (2019) David Lammy is right to encourage the left to unite against the far right. *New Statesman*, 15 April. Available at: https://www.newstatesman.com/politics/uk/2019/04/david-lammy-right-encourage-left-unite-against-far-right

Mishra, P. (2017) *Age of Anger: A History of the Present*. London: Allen Lane.

Mosey, R. (2019) Here's a question for the whole media: do we shut out or expose those with unpleasant views? *New Statesman*, 1–9 May, p. 25.

O'Kane S. and Lopatto, E. (2018) Elon Musk sued by SEC over 'funding secured' tweet. *The Verge*, 27 September. Available at: https://www.theverge.com/2018/9/27/17911428/sec-lawsuit-elon-musk-tesla-funding-tweet

Papacharissi, Z. (2014) *Affective Publics: Sentiment, Technology, and Politics*. Oxford: Oxford University Press.

Phelan, P. (1992) *Unmarked: The Politics of Performance*. New York: Routledge.

Runciman, D. (2006) *The Politics of Good Intentions*. Princeton: Princeton University Press.

Sailer, S. (2016) Political punk rock. *Takis's Magazine*, 7 September. Available at: https://www.takimag.com/article/political_punk_rock_steve_sailer/

Schreckinger, B. (2017) The alt-right comes to Washington. *Politico Magazine*, January/February 2017. Available at: https://www.politico.com/magazine/story/2017/01/alt-right-trump-washington-dc-power-milo-214629

"Veer Savarkar: A Legend" (2017). Available at: http://savarkar.org.

Wendling, M. (2018) *Alt Right: From 4chan to the White House*. London: Pluto Press.

6 Facts don't matter

Truthiness and fake news

Introduction

In a consideration of "PR, lies and post-truth politics," that drew upon Hannah Arendt's (1972) essay, Lying in Politics, Anne Cronin (2018, p. 113) proposed that "PR's capacities to both manage truths and broker new forms of promise place PR in a privileged position in today's new socio-political context." Public relations (PR) people pursue persuasive goals and seek to influence different institutions within the public sphere in the modern context of post-truth or what US comedian Stephen Colbert has called "truthiness." Colbert coined the phrase in 2005 and used it to denote the trend of statements being made and accepted on the basis of how truthful they felt rather than any basis in evidence, logic, intellectual examination or fact. My own understanding of post-truth is that is a social condition that arises from two communication behaviours: (1) The willingness of senders of messages to use falsehoods in public communication in order to win debates and influence opinion; (2) The willingness of audiences to accept the "truthy" messages and informational propositions of senders whose messages suit their opinions. In undertaking persuasive work in this context, PR people have the means, opportunity and incentive to exercise their informational intermediary role in a form of epistemological authoritarianism. That is to say, PR workers have the capacity to exploit their position of informational strength to influence debate, whether in the form of introduction of new facts or by controlling access to key players such as politicians and celebrities who make contributions to debate. Such informational power can be derived from the proximity PR people enjoy to the dominant coalitions in client organisations, whether they are political parties, corporations or charities. But there is a tension constraining the exercise of this power; PR people's role as providers of information to the public domain only endures over time if it is built upon high levels of trust and reliability with the media that use that material. In the case of mass media such as broadcast TV news, attempts to introduce falsehoods are normally swiftly identified and the source discredited. The knowledge produced by PR people in their role as informational intermediaries is intended to inform or to persuade, and is almost always part of broader plan to generate and distribute a message that will engage an audience and achieve a desired effect. The balance between the informational and persuasion priorities of PR is important to ethical and sustainable practice of PR, as well as justifying a social value as part of a process that introduces information to debates in the public sphere. The appearance of fake news in PR and campaigning is a result of a focus on persuasion only with little regard to the veracity of its information component, in a win at all costs style of aggressive campaigning. Yet the contribution of PR to the making of truth and introducing new facts to debate through press releases, research reports and other content, places the work of PR workers in the philosophical realm of "veritism," which denotes the way truth is attached to the people who produce and distribute knowledge (Fuller, 1988). This chapter attempts to explore matters of veritism in PR in the times of post-truth, and consider a style of public communication that views facts as irrelevant, holds expertise in disdain and replaces rationality with emotionality and distraction.

Post-truth and the media

In a sign of its ubiquity and importance, post-truth was nominated as word of the year by the Oxford English Dictionaries in 2016 (BBC, 2016). The varied backgrounds of writers on the topic (who have included those from the fields of media, politics and philosophy, for example) have produced an equally varied set of definitions. However, there is a notable coalescence around some core themes, scope and assumptions relating to the idea of post-truth and how it is linked to other communicative changes and phenomena such as fake news. For the political journalist, Matthew D'Ancona, the coming of the post-truth era has presented us with "a new phase of political and intellectual combat, in which democratic orthodoxies and institutions are being shaken to their foundations by a wave of ugly populism" (2017, p. 7). D'Ancona places post-truth as at the centre of political changes in the form of populism in general and he refers to the Brexit vote in the United Kingdom to leave the European Union in 2016 and the election of President Trump as examples of political campaigns that deployed post-truth tactics and in particular "slogans that were demonstrably untrue or misleading – but also demonstrably resonant" (2017, p. 8). The linkage of post-truth ideas and practices to political developments and its efficacy in the Brexit and Trump voting decisions is also made by James Ball (2017) in the set of analyses he offered in the stridently titled book, *Post-truth: How Bullshit Conquered the World*. These and other convincing accounts of the arrival of post-truth seem to reach back to a pre-truth or truthful era, or at least a general conception of a time of truth, that existed before the Brexit and Trump votes. But the reality is that lying by politicians, PR people and others has been present in public life and public communication for some time. The head of the UK's Ministry of Information in World War II, Brendan Bracken, who also worked on PR matters for Prime Minister Winston Churchill, was an almost compulsive liar, who simply laughed when caught out. Humour, laughter and a cheerful outlook have been the smokescreen used by political liars in more recent years, including Silvio Berlusconi in Italy and Boris Johnson in the United Kingdom. Just as Stephen Colbert's truthiness (word of the year for the American Dialect Society in 2005) heralded the arrival of post-truth as word of the year over 10 years later, the publication of Peter Oborne's (2005) book *The Rise of Political Lying* in the same year with its cataloguing of how being economical with the truth had become a jokey euphemism for the use of falsehoods in civic life, laid the way for the more recent wave of books on misinformation and post-truth in public communication almost 15 years ago.

Beyond the political sphere, changes in the production, distribution and consumption of media – and in particular the special characteristics of digital communication infrastructures and platforms – have enabled the swift propagation of fake news and the devaluation of what were previously viewed as reliable and truthful sources. In expanding the scope of post-truth studies to include media topics, it is clear that there are many types of media in play, with one type often working against the other in a confrontational style of public communication. Critics of the so-called mainstream media (MSM) claim that outlets such as the BBC and CNN in television news and *The Guardian* and *The New York Times* in the news sector are publishers of false narratives (or fake news) that favour and support an elite political orthodoxy that combines globalist politics with economic and social liberalism. These attacks and their propagation are enabled by the new digital media platforms and distribution systems, which include sites hosted by activist groups, alternative online news channels and conspiracy web sites often operated by one or two enthusiasts.

The promise of the internet and the World Wide Web was that more information than ever before would be easily searchable, giving more citizens of the world access to more facts than ever before. Yet in some fields – such as medicine with the anti-vax movement – it has given rise to folk narratives and irrational views based on superstition and hearsay that are more suited to the days before mass literacy. In an interview with Barack Obama on his leaving office in 2016, the US Presidential historian Doris Kearns Goodwin reflected on how different occupants of the White House had worked with the varied media that prevailed when they governed:

> In Lincoln's time, when your written word would be pamphletized, when everybody would be reading the entire speech and they'd be talking to each other about it. And Teddy Roosevelt was right for the era when punchy language worked. F.D.R. was perfect for conversational style on radio, J.F.K. and Reagan for the big TV networks. And you're governing in the age of the Internet, with its divergent voices and sound bites.
>
> –Goodwin (2016)

In addressing how he had chosen to communicate in the era of digital media and 24-hour TV news, President Obama focussed on questions of truth:

> There is a big part of me that has a writer's sensibility. And so that's how I think. That's how I pursue truth. That's how I hope to communicate truth to people. And I know that's not how it is always received. Because it gets chopped up. Or if it's too long, then it's dismissed as being professorial, or abstract, or long-winded.

Historical roots of post-truth: the Sophists and the inauthentic rhetoric of persuasion

The proposition of PR people enabling truthful rhetorical interaction and public discussion on issues, in ways that lead to mutual trust and resolution of differences, is central to Heath's (2006) theory of PR as rhetoric. Taylor (2009, p. 77) went further in proposing that civil society itself can be viewed as a "rhetorical public relations process" of organisations contributing to the mix of voices in the public sphere. Yet despite the positive claims by Robert Heath for the benefits of such an approach in the form of a fully functioning society, while PR people and processes undoubtedly contribute to the distribution of policy ideas into public debate, their status as agents acting on behalf of principals or clients means they are not always doing so with authenticity.

The work of the earliest relationship intermediaries or communicative "middle-men," the Sophists of fifth Century BC Athens, was criticised for its inauthenticity and tendency to twist facts when contributing to public debate. The Sophists provided rhetorical services that deployed their self-professed mastery in order to help paying clients win arguments. As such they were concerned less with the underlying issues, policies and goals of their clientele or with truth, than with the way they could combine their skills with circumstance in order to prevail in public debate. The Sophists offered a valuable service to their clients, in the form of communicative labour that combined innate expertise in the verbal arts with sensitivity to social context. Their awareness of the situations in which they operated, anticipation of trends in society and changing cultural conditions over time gave them flexibility to operate in response to varied briefs. Sophists also possessed an acute sense of timeliness that allowed them to adapt and take advantage of their circumstances in order to win clients and then exercise similar opportunism in order to win arguments. Such was the importance of this sense of timing (in the sense of an opportune time or moment rather than time itself) that the Ancient Greeks had the word *kairos* to describe this phenomenon against the standard *chronos* which referred to sequential time. A similar timely opportunism and enactment of the same rhetorical techniques by Donald Trump, in an unusual stylistic cocktail of American nationalism with new age positivity and business success literature, has produced a contemporary variant in the form of a "digital sophistry" for the twenty-first century (Lutz, 2018, p. 190).

The service proposition offered by the Sophists was a communicative advantage in the form of more efficacious persuasion resulting in a competitive advantage having won the argument. Like London taxis, barristers at law and many modern PR consultancy firms, the Sophists were ambivalent as to the nature and interests of their clientele. Their business development approach was simply to take on the next client who came along. The Sophists offered their rhetorical know-how to a range of messages and arguments, quite indifferent to issues such as the status, purpose or moral character of the end client. Although Socrates was critical of elements of the Sophist's approach – in particular the tendency to oversell their services to a sometimes gullible and often needy clientele – he recognised that in order to make a living, they offered something that was both needed and valued.

In this process of public debate, the use of spin and inauthentic expression in order to persuade and win an argument at all costs was prevalent from the outset of persuasive communications services being offered. Indeed, it was the stock in trade of the Sophists, who Steve Fuller has described as "the local post-truth merchants in fourth century BC Athens" (2018, p. 29). Fuller's historical perspective on post-truth and the contribution of communicative intermediaries to the post-truth condition contends that its origins can be traced to Ancient Athens circa 400 B.C., where "Plato believed that a well-ordered society had to restrict the post-truth condition to its ruling class, who then decides the terms of a common reality that apply to everyone else." In the modern jargon of post-truth political communication, Plato's view was that the well-educated elite should engage in political debate or contestation of any issue, after which – with the best result for society decided – the outcome is presented as the new truth that all should support.

Technology as an enabler of fake news

If we accept Steve Fuller's proposition that the Sophists were the first post-truth merchants, that means fakery and untruth in organised public communication have been around for two and half thousand years. The topic of post-truth has gained currency and urgency in the past decade, as a result of the general understanding that the technology of communication has acted an enabler of its growth. In an essay on modern media entitled "distraction stations" John Gray (2017) concluded that despite the emergence of some high-quality media outlets, the impact of new technologies on old media and the overall quality of the media landscape has been "mostly destructive," resulting in a miserable mix of fact and fabrication. Moreover, the characteristics of the digital media environment make it harder for audiences to discern fact-based news and analysis from fabricated stories.

> Manipulative language has been around as long as public debate. But today's lies linger because the internet has scuttled credibility, placing heaps of alluring junk beside small piles of dry honesty.
>
> –Rachman (2018)

The technical affordances of online news shape output through a "promiscuous mixture of fact, conjecture, partisan spin and fake news" which has been "deliberately constructed to gain attention and income" in the digital media economy (Lloyd, 2017). The audience stimulus that results from these economic drivers can be harmful to sustaining truth in online media, according to the BBC's Media Editor, Amol Rajan (2018), who has claimed that "the impulse to quick, strong emotion incentivised by social media, is often an enemy of the truth." This emotionalised media environment has proved comfortable for the media relations tactics of populists such as the blog of Italy's Five Star Movement leader Beppe Grillo which has garnered nationwide attention, while in the United States, in his Presidential election campaign, Donald Trump appeared "to command the US political scene through Twitter" (Lloyd, 2017). Both figures followed a media relations playbook of attacking the truthfulness of the media, with Grillo calling for citizens' juries to adjudicate on journalistic accuracy and Trump's repeated claims that the MSM was fake news. Yet despite his claims that anything critical of President Trump or his policy agenda was fake news, media audiences continued to find him fascinating and media outlets found it impossible to resist covering him. An analysis of three million articles of 2.5bn words that appeared in 8,000 news publishers in 50 countries throughout 2017 by Chartbeat for *The Economist* (2017) confirmed Trump's ability to attract readers, with his inauguration attracting 4.4m hours of readership. Although the women's march in Washington that followed attracted more people and more reader hours (six million), both were eclipsed by coverage of the attempt by the Trump administration to control inbound travel to the United States from Muslim countries which consumed 40m hours over the year. As *The Economist* report pointed out, "scandal sells," putting Trump on its cover nine times in 2017, which was a record for any individual in a year. The market value of scandal over time is a reminder that the forces at work in the online battle for attention are not only technical. "People have always told extravagant stories about their lives" as author Lawrence Scott (2019) has pointed out, wondering whether we are "all scammers now?" as a result of the limitless possibilities for self-invention in the digital world.

In May 2017, the former controller of BBC Radio 4, Mark Damazer (2017), wrote that we were living in an "age of lies" in which we have lost touch with the truth as a result of the dubious use of statistics and fake news. He is critical of the politicians who are coached by their PR teams to use sound bites repeatedly in sterile interviews, but also of the advisers themselves – "the Lynton Crosbys and Seamus Milnes of this world" (advisers on media and messaging to the Conservative Party and its leader Boris Johnson and the Labour Leader Jeremy Corbyn, respectively). Damazer's central point is that as well as untruthful campaign promises, there are numerous instances of politicians misleading the public with statistics, combining "cliches and almost idiotic numbers" without embarrassment. In their own deliberations on the emergence of fake news in recent years, coverage by some sections of the media has taken on the tone of epidemiology, discussing its growth as though it is a disease against which audiences need to take precautions and inoculate themselves. But rather than understanding fake news as a natural phenomenon that is spreading through society, it can also be more accurately viewed as the deliberate output of certain types of PR that introduces disinformation into the public sphere. Steven Poole encouraged re-orientation of the problem of growth of fake news away from the comparator of a spreading disease to a deliberately caused outcome with the following question: "But what if the thing that really needs to change is the way the masters of disinformation think?" (Poole, 2019).

Anti-vaxxers: fighting the facts

The metaphor of disease and disinformation is an apt one as 2018 and 2019 saw hundreds of outbreaks of infectious diseases in developed countries, with the United States alone experiencing its worst outbreaks of measles since 1994. The

World Health Organisation (WHO) has identified what it calls vaccine hesitancy among parents of small children in developed countries as one of the top ten threats to global health in 2019. Opposition to vaccines has resulted from years of campaigning by the so called anti-vaxxers, who have positioned themselves as victimised tellers of truth, struggling heroically against an alleged conspiracy of governments, the medical profession and big pharmaceutical companies (or big pharma). The campaign gained fresh momentum in the last five years or so, through association with various populist political campaigns, but had been festering since the 1998 publication of a paper in *The Lancet* medical journal by an English doctor working in London, Dr Andrew Wakefield, in which he claimed to have established a link between autism and administration of the combination measles, mumps and rubella (MMR) vaccine. The campaign has used the full mix of PR tools, including a documentary film – the 2016 *Vaxxed: From Cover-Up to Catastrophe* – as well as multiple conferences, rallies and celebrity endorsement from the model Elle Macpherson and Donald Trump. The anti-vax movement has been labelled as "perhaps the emblematic conspiracy theory of our times" and is generating "a giant threat to global health" (Lynskey, 2019). The survival and prominence of the anti-vax movement is also emblematic for the way its epistemological foundations rest upon a fraudulent report that was denounced by 10 co-authors and by the editor of *The Lancet* as "utterly false" (Buncombe, 2019). This long-running campaign of no facts or plain disinformation was quite simply based on the untruths of fraudulent research by Dr Wakefield, who was struck off as a doctor in the United Kingdom after being found guilty at a professional hearing of 30 different charges, including dishonesty.

Despite the core proposition of the anti-vax campaign having no basis in scientific fact and being a complex issue that requires expert knowledge to be considered seriously, Wakefield was able to gain momentum for the campaign having "remade himself in Donald Trump's America, travelling the country to promote views experts say have had deadly consequences and seemingly finding an ally in the president" (Buncombe, 2019). Agnotology, or the study of culturally induced ignorance, the strategic use of ignorance and a disregard for established facts, has been a topic of interest in science, medicine and linguistics for over 20 years. Verčič and Verčič (2016) have discussed agnotology in a PR context in a study of vaccination uptake in Slovenia, at a time that has seen otherwise well-informed parents throughout developed countries set themselves against medical science and campaign – with little if any specialist medical or scientific knowledge – against the vaccination of their children against communicable diseases The result has been the reappearance of some previously eradicated diseases such as measles in several developed countries, with the United Kingdom losing its measles-free status from the WHO in August 2019.

The continued prominence of the anti-vax movement is an example of a cultural trend of promoting ignorance in a strategic way as a virtue that empowers "ordinary people." This trend arguably gathered momentum in 2016 in both the US Presidential election and the UK's referendum on EU membership with Trump's celebration of his ignorance and the explicit disdain for experts by UK politicians in the Vote

Leave campaign. In the case of vaccination of minors, instead of interested parents cultivating knowledge on this complex matter, there is what verges on delight at ignorance among some of the campaigners, who position themselves – sometimes with a degree of grandiosity – as fighters against the mainstream. In addition to the Italian populist politician Matteo Silvani, who considers vaccines to be useless, the UK political commentator, Katie Hopkins, is another example of this grandiose but fact-less messaging against the mainstream that gives power and entitlement to the audience but demands no knowledge of or thinking on the subject from them, just an emotional response:

> Katie Hopkins, a reliable barometer of market opportunities for far-right grifters, recently jumped aboard the anti-vaccine bandwagon by combining scientific illiteracy with ****-you libertarianism: "You know what is best for your child. Your child is not an animal. The herd is not your concern."
> –Lynskey (2018)

The emotional appeal of the anti-vax movement to parents is that their children deserve better, in a way that gives status and a sense of privilege to the audience. That sense of privileged discovery by the audience and the sense that they are getting inside information was embodied in the tagline that accompanied Wakefield's *Vaxxed* documentary – "the film they don't want you to see." While persuasion is preferable to coercion, the uncontrollable and unpredictable nature of this misinformation contagion has led to calls for censorship of social media materials and posts on vaccination, with Pinterest having already decided to block searches on vaccine topics. Dr Phil Whitaker has argued that the way to combat the anti-vaxxers is through provision of "rational, evidence-based information that respects parents as responsible people capable of weighing competing perspectives, not by curtailing some groups' freedom of expression" (Whitaker, 2019). Dr Whitaker was writing after the UK Health secretary, Matt Hancock, had advocated a policy of partial censorship that in effect forced social media companies to take down false anti-vax material. Whitaker's classical approach to the issue of supporting a rational debate based on evidence is straight out of the playbook on the role of rhetoric in the fully functioning society. It contrasts sharply with Hancock's less-tolerant approach, which was perhaps informed by more familiarity with the realities of promoting and defending policy in the digital sphere and specifically a more canny understanding of the realities of coping with the onslaught of anti-vax campaigners posting post-truth propaganda that supports their case gained from his years as the UK's Minister of State for Digital and Culture. The anti-vaxxer example, which dates back 20 years, is an enduring example of the contagious nature of misinformation. The campaign tactics were to spread untruthful messages about vaccination that sounded viable, and the issue gained momentum in society long before talk of digital echo chambers and post-truth information wars. The seriousness of its impact on child health in the form of increased occurrences of preventable diseases makes it perhaps the saddest example of misinformation in practice, while also offering the challenge of generating a template of solutions for dealing with other instances of post-truth misinformation tactics:

> The tenacity of the anti-vaxx delusion, despite the considerable efforts of governments, journalists and health-care professionals, shows how hard it is to get the genie of fear and mistrust back into the bottle. Whoever can find an effective antidote to the anti-vaxxer virus will not just solve a medical crisis but a political one too.
>
> –Lynskey (2019)

False equivalence and belief in "people like me"

The anti-vax campaigners – along with the promoters of Brexit, of Donald Trump and climate change deniers – have benefitted from a media environment in the United Kingdom and elsewhere where obligations of impartiality have muddled with the need for fairness and for all voices to be heard. This has led to the false equivalence effect in public debate on these and other topics, in which the prevailing scientific evidence, expert opinion and other epistemologically sound material is heard alongside contrary views. Yet these contrary views sometimes lack any grounding in fact and are offered by media columnists, think tank spokespeople and others with links to vested interests. In the energy sector, these contrary positions are promoted alongside what one PR manager described to this author as "narcissistic self-publicists" speaking on behalf of often tiny or one-person campaign groups who appear do little else apart from offer such biased commentary at the request of 24-hour news channels and have little credibility outside that sphere on the subjects on which they pontificate. As the broadcaster James O'Brien has pointed out, the result of these broadcast set-piece clashes is often highly engaging television and radio partly because the climate change sceptics, anti-vaxxers and promoters of Trump are more entertaining: "They were bound to be. They were brass necks selling snake oil and self-interest while their more cerebral donnish counterparts were unwittingly cast as defenders of positions they'd never previously considered to be in need of defending" (O'Brien, 2018). Tom Nichols' (2017, p. 14) book, *The Death of Expertise: The Campaign against Established Knowledge and Why it Matters*, provided an in-depth exposition of this trend, claiming that over the past 20 years, the public space has become "increasingly dominated by a loose assortment of poorly informed people, many of them autodidacts who are disdainful of formal education and dismissive of experience [...] we now live in an age where misinformation pushed knowledge aside." A year earlier, during the Brexit referendum campaign, the UK cabinet minister and joint leader/convenor of the official Vote Leave campaign, Michael Gove, responded to a request to name any economist who was backing the leave campaign in a question and answer session on Sky News with the claim that "people in this country have had enough of experts" (Mance, 2016). In making this line of argumentation against expertise and fact-based position, Gove was giving status and grandiosity to the view of the ordinary voter against the prevailing political and economic wisdom from experts in those fields that remaining in the European Union was in the country's best interests. The appeal was primarily a status-building proposition for voters, who were encouraged to think that their view and feelings on a subject were equivalent or better than those of academics, politicians or experts who had studied these matters for years and/or had experience in areas such as international trade. This stance meant the rejection of expert views, which harmonised with the technological sense of empowerment of peer-to-peer social networks, which were used to share content and information that supported their position. In fields as varied as eating out, hotel accommodation and politics, people are increasingly relying on and influenced by crowd-sourced advice and opinion – as offered by Trip Advisor reviews in the case of restaurants and AirBnB's rating system in the case of accommodation – rather than the wisdom of restaurant or hotel guides compiled by experts. The erosion of the vertically oriented deference to expert sources such as restaurant guides and political scientists is due to consumers and voters embracing a technologically enabled horizontally oriented system of influence, that has been enabled by peer-to-peer networking and the social media applications built on top of this technology, such as TripAdvisor, which in turn enables the wisdom of the digital crowd to replace that of the individual analogue expert. As PR agency Edelman's annual Trust Barometer showed in 2016 when asking people in 20 countries who they trust, the effect of this aggrandisement of audiences through the expansion of horizontal channels of influence was a rising confidence not in experts but in "a person like me" alongside a high level of trust in digital technology. A persuasive conclusion on this finding offered by Gillian Tett (2016) of the *Financial Times* was that "we live in a world where we increasingly trust our Facebook friends and the Twitter crowd more than we do the IMF or the Prime Minster." Despite the promise of empowerment, this system of horizontal influence can lead to people falling prey to social fads and a divisive tribalism as Nick Barron at Edelman pointed out:

> The rise of "a person like me" has given birth to a post-truth era where comforting narratives and familiar messengers beat fact and argument. Social echo chambers prevent effective scrutiny of individuals, organisations and campaigns that we think we are on the right side of an argument. "My truth," "our truth" and "the truth" beat "objective truth."
>
> –Tett (2016)

Emotion, superstition and collective narcissism

While there has always been a balance between emotion and rationality in politics, communications and other spheres, there is now widespread discussion on the influence of emotion in public decision-making on topics such as Brexit, mass vaccination and the election of Donald Trump. The focus on emotion in public life in general is the theme of Will Davies' (2018) book *Nervous States: How Feeling Took Over the World*, which considers the way viral marketing has been applied to political campaigning, with the intent of generating an "emotional contagion" (p. 13) that will persuade pivotal voters and so sway the overall outcome. – in the chapter Democracy of Feeing – that Edward Bernays from the 1920s onwards understood that "what the public want in a democracy is a sense of intimacy with their rulers – not to be listened to or represented, but to gain a feeling of proximity to power" and that Bernays "government by education" was the way to achieve this. In his commentary on the way mainstream politics continues to prioritise words over the visual, he also cites Bernays' observation in the 1928 book, *Propaganda*, that politics had already been left behind by business "when it came to analysing the emotional dimensions of communication." At the same time, technology's effect on the information feeding in to democratic discourse as examined in Sunstein's (2017) *# Republic: Divided Democracy in the Age of Social Media*, in which he asserts that these social media platforms allow entrepreneurs of political polarisation to exploit confirmation bias resulting in diminished quality to the conversations needed to support healthy democracy. A broader examination of the nature of individual knowledge by the cognitive scientists, Steven Sloman and Philip Fernbach (2017), asserted that individuals think they know more than they do – and in fact have low levels of understanding on most matters – and that human success tends to come from the collective knowledge of experts.

Michal Chmiel (2018) has considered how the issue of individual and collective knowledge links to the problem of fake news in an innovative psychological study into collective narcissism in the post-truth era of PR. Collective narcissism is the tendency of having an exaggerated belief in the superiority of a group to which they belong – which can be a nation or religion, for example – while also harbouring underlying doubts about the true prestige and so seeking special recognition. Theodore Adorno used the concept to explain the ethnocentrism of the Nazis in the 1930s Germany and more recently, collective narcissism has been defined by Golec de Zavala and Federico (2009) as "an emotional investment in an unrealistic belief about the in-group's greatness." After the US Presidential election of 2016, Dr Agnieszka Golec de Zavala led a team of colleagues from Goldsmiths College and University of Minnesota's Centre for the Study of Political Psychology on a project that investigated voters' propensity to believe conspiracy theories, reporting that:

> Collective narcissism is not the same as just thinking your country is great, it's about thinking it is unique and, more than any other country, deserving of special treatment. [...] We have found evidence that collective narcissism predicts a general tendency to believe in conspiracies. This kind of thinking assumes a certain "them" plots to undermine "us": the them and us can be filled in by any particular content.
>
> –Wilton (2018)

Chmiel's (2018) experimental study of 240 participants, manipulated perceived similarity to the source of a fake message, while controlling for the collective narcissism trait and support for political ideologies. Results showed that people, who were led to believe that the originator of fake news (a passage about links between vaccines and autism in this experiment) is a person similar to them were more likely to share the message on social media, even though they assessed the credibility of the message as low. Another interesting result pointed to the moderating role of collective narcissism in sharing false information. Consistently with data obtained by other researchers, supporters of right-wing ideologies were more likely to share fake stories on social media. However, this effect was moderated by collective narcissism, i.e., only people high on this dimension and expressing a preference for right-wing politics were inclined to spread fabricated, untruthful information.

Alongside the views of crowds and the power of emotion in getting the trust of modern audiences, superstition is becoming a force that gets attention. Millennials are embracing the mystical and the occult, according to *The New Statesman's* "Digital Native" columnist, Amelia Tait. After attending a tarot evening, she concluded that a combination of hopelessness, helplessness and uncertainty has led to millennials turning to occult practices such as tarot, which has been re-branded through the internet (Tait, 2018). Her investigation uncovered over 500 tarot apps on Apple's App Store, over 3m #tarot hashtags on Instagram and a single video on how to learn tarot that had been viewed 800,000 times, suggesting a surprising scale of superstition – and corresponding lack of rationality and disconnection from facts – for a modern audiences with historically high levels of education.

In considering the BBC's attempt at even-handed political coverage and balance, during the Brexit referendum and its aftermath, an ex-employee Patrick Howse concluded that it had failed its greatest test since the World War II. One of his central points was that balance in discussion – a state to which PR seeks to contribute – breaks down when applied to areas such as Brexit, climate change and Holocaust denial. "The result is not balanced reporting, but a confused 'he said this but she said that' narrative that gives false equivalence to the truth and a pack of lies" (Howse, 2018, p. 8). Such discussion of the treatment given to truth and lies in news reflects the mixing of fiction and non-fiction in broadcast entertainment, such as in the work of Sacha Baron Cohen and his comic characters including Ali G. Borat and Bruno. The blurring of truth and fiction in Baron Cohen's 2018 series *Who is America*, which features a 2012 video blog from Donald Trump, was a prompt for the film academic Leshu Torchin to remind audiences of need for a new level of "non-fiction media literacy we all need in the era of Trump" (Torchin, 2018).

Epistemic volatility and post-truth

Steve Fuller (2018, p. 11) has argued that modern times have seen an intensification of "collective epistemic volatility" as the internet has become society's principal means of knowledge acquisition, as well as a principal channel of distribution for PR messages. Fuller makes parallels between the effect of the internet and the way Protestant Reformers took advantage of the arrival of the printing press by encouraging churchgoers to read the Bible for themselves, in order to undermine the legitimacy of the established Catholic Church. In the same way, anti-establishment campaigners in varied fields, including areas of politics and science, have used the direct communication enabled by the internet in order to distribute information and propaganda, and then encourage readers to make their own decisions on the evidence provided and override the view of experts. The approach of the UK Conservative politician Boris Johnson to truth and the way information is introduced to public debate has been described as "epistemic insouciance" by Quassim Cassam (2019), who defines the term as "indifference or lack of concern with respect to whether claims are grounded in reality or evidence." As Cassam, explains, epistemic insouciance is an attitude "that makes one a bull shitter and thereby causes one to spout bullshit" and includes moreover a "contempt for the truth, contempt for experts and, in the case of politicians, contempt for the public." The purpose of this cocktail of lies, nonsense and light entertainment, as the philosopher Harry Frankfurter explained in his essay and then book *On Bullshit* (2005), is to persuade without caring whether the arguments and information put forward to support a case are truthful or not. Insouciance to facts coupled with an often lively expression of contempt for inconvenient truths has generated the bitter tasting but dangerously potent cocktail that has variously been called post-truth or fake news. The practitioners of the art of fake news are almost always seeking to manipulate knowledge or information in ways that gives a persuasive advantage. They simply seek to deceive an audience through the misuse of facts.

When PR people used pseudo-events to create news, such as the torches of freedom event staged by Bernays in the 1920s New York, laying on the event was part of the PR performance, which was then faithfully reported by the media. The pervasiveness of digital media in more recent years means that the work of laying on a physical event in order to generate news has been left out. Instead, fake news can be generated simply through generating fabricated stories, which have often been created to exploit the digital advertising networks in ways that generate income for the author from online adverts if the story gained big audience viewings or went viral. This type of content came to mainstream attention around 2016, when it moved from the field of celebrity gossip and the entertainment and fashion industries – where hoax news stories of fake deaths and so on would go viral before being debunked – to politics where stories relating to Donald Trump and his Presidential campaign attracted millions of hits. Some of the more celebrated examples include the headline "Pope Francis Shocks World, Endorses Donald Trump for President" which was invented by one of the many fake news sites which were seeking to make money from online advertising networks through displaying advertisements alongside the widely viewed news content. While the dimensions of contemporary fake news operations vary, with most being small, it can extend to industrial-scale operations such as the fake news factories in Macedonia that exploited the workings of Facebook and Google to monetise the content they posted on specially created web sites. In 2016, the small town of Veles was found to be hosting over 100 sites in support of Donald Trump's US Presidential Campaign, leading to *Wired* magazine calling the place variously "fake news factory to the world" and "the Macedonian fake news complex" (Subramanian, 2017). This style of disinformation operations has been integrated into Russia's state-level propaganda apparatus for some years now. The Saint Petersburg based Internet Research Agency is one example of an organisation operating on behalf of Russia to undertake online influence operations, predominantly through setting up fake accounts on social media to post deceptive material, as well as trolling opponents. The Internet Research Agency employs around 1,000 people and was the institution indicted by a US grand jury in February 2018 for its attempts to interfere in the 2016 Presidential election.

Fake news and pseudo-events

Early PR as practised by Edward Bernays involved smaller scale deceptions, in the form of publicity stunts, such as his staging of a fabricated protest by women who lit and smoked cigarettes in the name of female emancipation during New York's 1920 Easter Parade already referred to here. The "torches of liberty" protest was in fact orchestrated by Bernays as a fake news story on behalf of the American Tobacco Company as part of a campaign to broaden the market for smoking by removing the taboo of women smoking in public. Fabricated news stories of this type were part of PR practice from the beginning and the years of high growth in the PR sector saw the industrial-scale manufacture of pseudo-events in order to gain media coverage (Boorstin, 1962).

Fake news is best viewed as a media artefact that results from conditions of post-truth in society rather than a component of post-truth. The term and its usage is a miserably compelling illustration of the relativism of post-truth, for the way it has been used – along with fake news – by both sides in contestation of truth matters. Rather than an absolutist judgement based on matters of fact, whether a report is fake news or not is a matter of perspective in which the party seen to be in error by the other is merely imposing a conceptual framework that the other party does not recognise. For example, while liberally inclined Democratic voters in the United States with an internationalist outlook media consumption may include reading *The New York Times, Washington Post* and *The Economist*, while watching ABC, CNN and other mainstream TV news channels, a nationalist supporter of President Trump will typically abhor such media channels as fake news and avoid exposure to them. Instead, the Trump supporter may typically consume partisan media channels such as the online *Breitbart News* site and other more extreme or niche news sites, while relying on the Murdoch-owned Fox News for rolling TV coverage and commentary. The point is that fake news is in the eye of the beholder – or in this case the media consumer – with the trusted channel of one community viewed with disdain and distrust by the other. This sense of distrust as a result of the post-truth condition has extended to outrage at the way fake news has been deployed as a campaign tool and also at the political losses (in the case of Brexit and Trump vs Clinton Presidential election, for example) that resulted. Beyond the discomfort of being on the losing side in polarised public policy arguments, there is an element of outrage from economic and social liberals that the techniques of deception and selective facts are used against them and their interests, rather than being deployed to maintain the status quo.

For some of the new political entrepreneurs such as Donald Trump, fake news is not a sideshow but a core tool of political PR. One study of 1,000 tweets from the @realDonald Trump twitter account in the first six months of the Presidency suggested that the term "fake news" was used tactically as a rhetorical device to discredit critical press coverage and more strategically as a "reputation management device" to undermine multiple media outlets who were pursuing critical lines of coverage, such as alleged Russian collusion (Davis and Sinnreich, 2018). Their study concluded that Trump used the term fake news as a rhetorical tool to attack those media outlets – such as CNN and others – that focus on facts in order to hold Trump to account and also that the new President tweeted most of his fake news claims while suffering the indignity of seeing supporters, staffers and even National Security Adviser Mike Flynn, being placed under investigation as part of the Mueller probe into alleged collusion with Russia during the 2016 election campaign. In her analysis of what she has named the "shock politics" of Donald Trump, Naomi Klein (2017, p. 55) offered the following summary of how fake news, alternative facts and the principle of the big lie are merged in his White House PR operation, in which the communications staff lie "for sport" rather than for any more strategic intent and compete amongst themselves on who can get "the biggest whoppers into print":

> If we know anything for certain, it's that hard facts don't matter in Donald Trump's world. With Trump, it's not so much the Big Lie as the Constant Lies. Yes he tells big ones, like the time he implied Ted Cruz's dad had a role in assassinating JFK, and his years of lies about Obama's place of birth. But it is the continuous stream of lies – notoriously offered to us as alternative facts – that is most dizzying.

The interplay of media and public relations in the post-truth era

Fake news is produced to suit both sides of a debate, and often replaces the hollowed out middle ground of MSM that offered society a shared view of the truth. So, there are often two or more separate – and in some cases extreme – variants either side of what was previously an agreed set of facts and priorities as formulated and distributed by MSM. The old consensus of the middle ground has given way to what the right populists see as a liberal, leftish elite of fake news as propagated by *CNN*, *The Guardian*, *New York Times* and others, while the liberals look on with disdain at the post-truth discourse of populists such as Donald Trump and the partisan media supporters such as *Breitbart* and Fox News that continue to report favourably on his Presidency.

Rather than building a productive relationship and working with the media as would have been the case in classical PR approach, Trump and other political entrepreneurs have undermined and attacked the MSM as a force that does not operate in the interests of the country nor of the majority of society. The MSM's patriotism has been questioned by Trump and he has also accused it of being in an alliance with left-wing politicians in order to support the interests of a global liberal elite. Individual journalists are also attacked as lazy lackeys of vested interests and as biased in their coverage. These public attacks signalled a new level of antagonism between some sections of the media and politicians, along with abandonment of the norms of political and media culture, to which both parties previously complied. As new political actors such as Trump have entered the field of politics – sometimes coming with experience of the entertainment industry, they have refused to conform to the norms associated with democratic media culture. Instead, they have sought out a communicative advantage through adopting the PR strategy of the upstart that ignores the norms of classical PR and gains attention by attacking MSM as out of touch.

Despite the low regard that populists have for the media, discussions with mainstream journalists and their public speeches confirm their enduring and earnest focus on pursuing and reporting the truth. In a 2017 lecture entitled "Fake news in the post-factual age," *Financial Times* editor Lionel Barber, whose father was also a journalist, spoke of how for him and his family, journalism was not only a profession, it was a vocation which conferred " a special obligation to attend to the facts and to pursue the truth" (Barber, 2017). This quest is a very similar aspiration to that of Carl Bernstein, the Washington reporter cited by Barber, who exposed the Watergate case, for presenting "the best obtainable version of the truth" for citizens to use as the basis for debate. Barber's speech went on to show concern with the negative effect of fake news on public trust in media and its exacerbation of the economic pressures facing news businesses. Beyond the news industry – although he acknowledged the claim of his *Financial Times* colleague and Reuters Institute of Journalism founder John Lloyd that "alternative facts and fake news have been part of the feedstock of politics and journalism for centuries" – Barber claimed that fake news was undermining "public confidence in our democratic discourse" and its spread and harmful effects highlighted the need for responsibility and possibly new types of regulation for a "fast-evolving media ecosystem." The same point has been made by Michiko Kakutani in her book, *The Death of Truth: Notes on Falsehood in the Age of Trump*, in which she records the most important effect of the "firehose of falsehood" comprised propaganda, disinformation and fake news on political life: "Without truth, democracy is hobbled."

Despite these high stakes, the interplay and interdependence of journalists with the political PR operators defending President Trump and sometimes telling lies on his behalf is often a relationship of servility, in which Washington journalists remain desperate to get close to power and show themselves as part of the political establishment. Journalist Mehdi Hasan reported on how journalists reacted badly to the performance of comedian Michelle Wolf at the 2018 White House Correspondents' Dinner. Her routine included a section referring to the White House press secretary Sarah Huckabee Sanders, who was at the dinner. "I think she's very resourceful. She burns facts, and then uses the ash to create a perfect smoky eye. Maybe she is born with it, maybe it's lies. It's probably lies" (Hasan, 2018). Wolf went on to capture the interdependence of the media and the Trump PR operation: "You guys are obsessed with Trump […] You helped create this monster, and now you're profiting off of him." Despite President Trump variously calling the assembled audience of journalists "scum," "slime" and sick people" in the preceding year, instead of congratulating Michelle Wolf on her performance, the journalists were highly critical and sided with President's spokeswoman, both at the dinner and in the public debate that followed. Hasan himself was surprised at the reaction, asking "Is there a more servile group of reporters anywhere in the West?", while also observing that "the obsequiousness pre-dates the arrival of Trump and his cronies." He cites the former press secretary to George W Bush, Scott McClellan, who wrote in his 2008 memoir of a "culture of deception" in the presentation of rationales for the Iraq war (which soon collapsed once the war was over), as well as a national press corps that was "probably too deferential to the White House and to the administration in regard to the most important decision facing the nation during my years in Washington." According to Mclellan, in order to justify the Iraq war, the White House media operation simply fed false propaganda to a complicit press in "a permanent campaign approach" (CBS News, 2008). The result some ten years on in the United States is "a democracy in which there are no shared facts and are only disputed opinions," according to the BBC News journalist, Nick Robinson (2018).

This evolving media ecosystem has involved a blurring of lines between independent, researched facts and what *The Guardian* journalist Carole Cadwalladr (2019) has called "PR guff" issued by policy think tanks such as the Institute of Economic Affairs (IEA), which she claims is not a think tank at all but rather a "dark money lobbyist" pushing out "disinformation" through a combination of research papers and media relations. In June 2019, Cadwalladr listed a set of appearances by IEA spokespeople on the BBC on different issues over a few days, including an appearance by its head, Mark Littlewood arguing against spending public money on climate change, without declaring that several parties interested in this issue including BP provide funding to the IEA, which as well as being misleading was also potentially in breach of the BBC's own guidelines on impartiality for the lack of transparency on the link between the interested funders of the IEA and the topic under discussion.

MisIndiainformation: fake news in the 2019 Indian election

In the run up to the largest democratic election in history in India in May 2019 – with 900 million eligible voters – the level of fake news being distributed led to the coining of a new word, "misindiainformation." The issuing of misleading messages spread on the messaging service WhatsApp about online voting led to the Election Commission in India warning voters to "Beware of fake news" as early as February 2019. As the campaign progressed, it became clear that the combination of rapid social media adoption in India and a strident, divisive politics based on religious identity was producing a media environment in which digital disinformation was deployed as a PR campaign tool. According to the India Digital Journalism Report (Reuters Institute for the Study of Journalism, 2019), one result of India's mobile first adoption of digital media is a media environment dominated by platforms such as Facebook and Google, with search engines, social media and messaging applications acting as agents of digital discovery of news. This discovery process through search was more trusted (45%) by users in the March 2019 Reuters study than news overall (36%) and even the news sources they use (39%).

BBC News online correspondent Soutik Biswas, who covered the 2019 Indian election commented that "India is in the grip of a fake news epidemic" in which politicians are using "fake news and propaganda to defame rivals," with chief of the ruling BJP, Amit Shah, encouraging social media campaign volunteers with the claim that "we are capable of delivering any message we want to the public, whether sweet or sour, true or fake" (Biswas, 2019). Biswas himself has observed that "the main conduit of fake news and viral hoaxes is WhatsApp" with the BJP creating more than 6,600 accounts on the platform ahead of the 2017 state elections in Uttar Pradesh "to spread the party's message" in a political PR campaign in which "the dividing line between legitimate messaging and fake news was blurred effortlessly" (2019, p. 40).

Conclusion

PR work produces meaning in society as a result of its attempts to regulate information flows on behalf of clients. In doing so, PR contributes to wider public discourse, which is the locus and process whereby knowledge and truth are discussed and circulated, which in turn may lead to outcomes in which power is either maintained or transformed. The pervasiveness of power in public discourse, in knowledge and in the circulatory apparatus of the media industry, which PR attempts to influence, came together to produce what Foucault called a distinct "regime of truth" or general politics of truth (1976/2000, p. 130). The past 30 years have witnessed significant changes in the media infrastructures and political apparatus that Foucault placed as controlling factors in the circulation and maintenance of regimes of truth. Yet as Jayson Harsin (2015, p. 327) has written, "this has not led to the demise of truth regimes but rather a more complex reorganization of functions, among which are efforts to mobilize a new digital 'participatory culture' to proliferate truth games – that is to generate an overall regime of post truth (ROPT)." So, contemporary public discourse is not only influenced by an emotionalised public sphere, it is also the site of a new round of power games using information, in which PR workers and processes participate in providing relevant content, in the form of statements, press releases and other material.

The increased scale of deception and a disregard for the truth in some modern public communication is also an indicator of a more aggressive type of PR, which is less concerned with persuasion and contributing information in order to build consensus in the public sphere and more focussed on winning at all costs. According to Charlie Beckett of the London School of Economics' Truth, Trust and Technology Commission, a cocktail of fake news, disinformation and lack of trust in some social media technologies has led to a "crisis in public information" for the United Kingdom (Beckett, 2018. While emphasis on the political origins of post-truth and the importance of modern media infrastructures in propagating the fake news artefacts (in the form of stories, image and video memes) are useful as a point of reference, post-truth is not an abstract that exists alone in digital media to be distributed by algorithms alone, it depends on living people for its delivery. Specifically, it is "a social order whose members are always and everywhere thinking both in terms of what game to play and what move to make" in an arena of public communications that "suspends the default assumption that its members have a common reality, and hence a common sense of truth conditions" (Fuller, 2018, p. 189). A major operational challenge for PR people in a regime of post-truth is how to engage and provide information to audiences who are showing decreasing trust in experts and specialist or academic knowledge.

Case Study 6.1

Kylie Jenner: from digital promotional presence to a woman of substance

In contrast to the classic intermediary PR infrastructure of message creators and media distributors working for a producer of physical goods, some fields of the modern fashion business have featured a more direct form of communication with audiences. In this post-classical mode of PR, the promotional presence itself comes before product development and its shape and scale affects the creation of the substantive underlying product line. The primacy of personal promotion in this process relates to the way in which PR is concerned with the creation of a public image, sometimes for a person and sometimes for a corporation, political party or other organisation. The link between the individual and the product is not one of endorsement based on celebrity but is based on the digital promotional presence that has been established by the individual. This logic explains why there is not always a direct correlation between the initial degree of celebrity derived from achievement in a field – such as in the case of the multiple endorsements of golfer Tiger Woods – and the extent and value of the promotional presence that is built up over time. The promotional presence of David and Victoria Beckham is an example of this effect. While David Beckham was a good footballer and Victoria a member of a successful girl band, their skills and achievements in those fields relative to others were not the driver of the promotional presence they share today as "brand Beckham" after careful cultivation of a European, American and now global promotional presence that transcends the origins of their initial achievements and resulting celebrity in football and music. So while sometimes linked to achievement in the fashion or entertainment business, the modern type of promotional presence has typically been acquired as a result of a sustained form of revelatory PR through posting of photographs or opinion-based text posts on social media sites and applications such as Instagram, Pinterest and Twitter.

Kylie Jenner was featured on the cover of Forbes magazine in August 2018 as America's youngest "self-made billionaire" as a result of the success of her online Kylie Cosmetics business which she started in

2015 and which has become a substantial enterprise despite practically no traditional marketing or advertising. The product line was created after Kylie Jenner had profited from paid endorsements for third-party cosmetics brands and was possible because her being celebrity as part of the Jenner family which had features on reality television shows and the resulting social media following she had achieved, with 131 million followers on the Instagram picture site and 26 million followers on the Twitter microblogging site by April 2019. The scale of the audience following her on social media gave Jenner a base that could be exploited for direct promotion of her own product line, using a form of PR and direct promotion that was perfectly in tune with Forbes described as "the era of extreme fame leverage" (Forbes, 2018). The point of value leveraged in this case was Jenner's promotional presence on social media, which included posting short, seemingly unorchestrated videos on Snapchat, which became so closely followed by users of the platform that a casual tweet about cutting back on her use of Snapchat led to that company's shares falling in value by $1.3bn due to the loss of user attention. While the use of a celebrity's face as endorsement for products is common-place, Jenner's case is important for the way she achieved a promotional presence on social media through a revelatory form of PR that offered an insider view of her daily life. In turn, this was leveraged to promote a cosmetics line, but "could have been cupcakes, sneakers or hair ties" according to Jeremy Paul of RLP Advisers (Nicolau, 2019, p. 11). Jenner's mastery of social media was achieved through a through a stream of self-revelatory text, images and video across multiple social media platforms that appealed to teenage girls, thus building up a complete digital PR and promotional system for her first line of cosmetics products.

For Kylie Jenner, promotional work is neither an intermediary function nor a support service to her cosmetics, it is the product locus without which there is no business. Rather than the more traditional route to market of a cosmetics company creating cosmetics on the basis of their research, expertise and knowledge of the sector and then promot-ing those products through PR and marketing communications (which may include forms of celebrity endorsement) the post-classical approach adopted by Kylie Jenner depends upon an ongoing digital promotional presence and coupled with direct communication using social media in order to build an audience which can then receive promotions in order to convert them into customers.

This instrumental exploitation of an online promotional presence to support – and sometimes to create – substantial real-world activity is not limited to the image-conscious fashion sector. In the realm of politics, the selection of candidates for the May 2019 European Parliament elections by the UK's new Change UK centrist party chose several candidates with significant promotional presence on social media, including the journalist Rachel Johnson and former BBC television presenter Gavin Esler, who is also Chancellor of the University of Kent, which describes itself as the UK's European University. According to the *Financial Times* (Payne, 2019, p. 3) the power of Facebook, Instagram and Twitter is that they "offer a swift, cost-effective alternative to membership databases or a regional structure" while at the individual level, "selecting candidates with ready-made support alleviates the pressure of establishing themselves as full-fledged parties ahead of the May 23 poll." As in the case of Kylie Jenner's relationship with her cosmetic product line, the recruitment of some Change UK candidates seems influenced by recognition that the new party can exploit the already established promotional presence of candidates in the media business in order to advance its core campaigning activity. Celebrity and number of followers alone is not the driver of whether this promotional presence has value. Change UK chose to turn down the application by the celebrated author and academic Richard Dawkins, for example, who has three million twitter followers. The reasoning was described by a member of the new party in the following terms: "Some people who have very high scores on social media can have the tendency to be Marmite and in some cases through the interview process, we concluded that would be distracting" (Payne, 2019).

References

Arendt, H. (1972). *Crises of the Republic; Lying in Politics, Civil Disobedience on Violence, Thoughts on Politics, and Revolution.* New York: Harcourt Brace Jovanovich.

Ball, J. (2017) *Post-Truth: How Bullshit Conquered the World.* London: Biteback Publishing.

Barber, L. (2017) Fake news in the post-factual age. Lecture to Oxford Alumni Festival; Oxford University. 16. September. Available at: https://www.ft.com/content/c8c749e0-996d-11e7-b83c-9588e51488a0

BBC. (2016) BBC News, 'Post-truth' declared word of the year by Oxford Dictionaries. *BBC News*, 16 November. Available at: https://www.bbc.co.uk/news/uk-37995600

Beckett, C. (2018). What do you mean by 'trust'? *Influence*, 16 October. Available at: https://influenceonline.co.uk/2018/10/16/what-do-you-mean-by-trust/.

Bernays, E. (1928) *Propaganda.* New York: Horace Liveright.

Biswas, S. (2019) Misindiaformation. *Influence*, Q2, pp. 38–41.

Boorstin, D. (1962) *The Image: A Guide to Pseudo-events in America.* New York: Vintage Books.

Buncombe, A. (2019) Andrew Wakefield: How a disgraced UK doctor has remade himself in anti-vaxxer Trump's America. *The Independent*, 4 May 2018. Available at: https://www

.independent.co.uk/news/world/americas/andrew-wakefield-anti-vaxxer-trump-us-mmr-autism-link-lancet-fake-a8331826.html

Cadwalladr, C. (2019) So fed up with this disinformation. The IEA is not a "think tank". It's a dark money lobbyist. Twitter, 7 June. Available at: https://twitter.com/carolecadwalla/status/1137040543052156930?lang=en

Cassam, Q. (2019) *Vices of the Mind: From the Intellectual to the Political.* Oxford: Oxford University Press.

Chmiel, M. (2018) Fake News, My News, Real News. Source credibility crisis and the rise of PR professionals as indirect gatekeepers. Paper presented at 25th BLEDCOM International Public Relations Research Symposium, 5–7 July. Lake Bled, Slovenia.

CBS News (2008) Exclusive: McClelland whacks Bush. CBS News, 27 May 2008. Available at: https://www.cbsnews.com/news/exclusive-mcclellan-whacks-bush-white-house/

Cronin, A. (2018) *Public Relations Capitalism.* Basingstoke: Palgrave.

Damazer, M. (2017). Gaming your future with numbers. *New Statesman,* 19–25 May, pp. 23–25.

D'Ancona, M. (2017) *Post Truth: The New War on Truth and How to Fight Back.* London: Ebury Press.

Davis, D. and Sinnreich, A. (2018) Tweet the Press: "Fake News" as a Reputation-Management Device in President Trump's Tweets. *Voices,* ICA 68th Conference, Prague, 24–28 May.

Davies, N. (2008) *Flat Earth News.* London: Vintage Books.

The Economist (2017) Charting the News. 23 December, p. 41.

Forbes Magazine (2018) How 20-year-old Kylie Jenner built a $900 million fortune in less than 3 years. 31 August. Available at: https://www.forbes.com/sites/forbesdigitalcovers/2018/07/11/how-20-year-old-kylie-jenner-built-a-900-million-fortune-in-less-than-3-years/#11f3a63faa62

Foucault, M. (1976/2000) Truth and power. In: Faubion, J.D. (Ed.) *Power: Essential works of Foucault 1954–1984.* New York: New Press, pp. 111–133.

Frankfurter, H. (2005) *On Bullshit.* Princeton: Princeton University Press.

Fuller, S. (1988) *Social Epistemology.* Bloomington: Indiana University Press.

Fuller, S. (2018) *Post-truth: Knowledge as a Power Game.* London: Anthem Press.

Golec de Zavala, A. and Federico, C. (2018) Collective Narcissism and the growth of conspiracy thinking over the course of the 2016 United States Presidential election: a longitudinal analysis. *European Journal of Social Psychology* 48 (7), 1011–1018.

Goodwin, D. (2016) Barack Obama and Doris Kearns Goodwin: the ultimate exit interview. *Vanity Fair,* November, pp. 170–173.

Gray, J. (2017) Distraction stations. *New Statesman,* 11–17 August, p. 36.

Harsin, J. (2015) Regimes of post-truth, post-politics, and attention economies. *Communication, Culture & Critique,* 8 (2), 327–333.

Hasan, M. (2018) Inside America: even in the age of President Trump, White House correspondents find it hard to stop bending the knee. *New Statesman,* 4–10 May, p. 33.

Heath, R., (2006) Onward into more fog: thoughts on public relations' research directions. *Journal of Public Relations Research,* 18 (2), 93–114.

Howse, P. (2018) The Beeb and an illusion of balance. *The New European,* 16–22 August, p. 8.

Kakutani, M. (2018) *The Death of Truth: Notes on Falsehood in the Age of Trump.* New York: Tim Duggan Books.

Klein, N. (2017) *No is Not Enough.* London: Allen Lane.

Lloyd, J. (2017) *The Power and the Story: The Global Battle for News and Information.* London: Atlantic Books.

Lutz, B. (2018) Digital sophistry: Trump, Twitter and teaching about fake news. In: Lockhard, M. (Ed.) *President Donald Trump and His Political Discourse: Ramifications of Rhetoric via Twitter*. New York: Routledge, pp. 190–205.

Lynskey, D. (2019) Vaccine hesitancy is a giant threat to global health and the conspiracy theory of our times. *New Statesman*, 31 May–6 June 2019, p. 37.

Mance, H. (2016) Britain has had enough of experts, says Gove. *Financial Times*, 3 June. Available at: https://www.ft.com/content/3be49734-29cb-11e6-83e4-abc22d5d108c

Nichols. T. (2017) *The Death of Expertise: The Campaign Against Established Knowledge and Why It Matters*. Oxford: Oxford University Press.

Nicolau, A. (2019) Kylie Jenner, social media's first billionaire youth star. *Financial Times*, 8 March. Available at: https://www.ft.com/content/7935b4da-40e6-11e9-9bee-efab61506f44

O'Brien, J. (2018) Media impartiality is a problem when furious ignorance is given the same weight as expertise. *New Statesman*, 23 March 5 April, p. 27.

Oborne, P. (2005) *The Rise of Political Lying*. London: Free Press.

Payne, S. (2019) Social media puts insurgent parties into the fast lane. *Financial Times*, 26 April.

Poole, S. (2019) Mastering misdirection. *New Statesman*, 5–11 April, pp. 44–45.

Rachman, T. (2018) Writers gonna write: maintaining standards in the digital age. *The Times Literary Supplement*, 19 January, pp. 8–9.

Rajan, A. (2018) The social media impulse is an enemy of truth. *New Statesman*, 27 April-3 May, p. 59.

Reuters Institute, (2019) *India News Report*. Oxford: Reuters Institute for the Study of Journalism. Available at: https://reutersinstitute.politics.ox.ac.uk/sites/default/files/2019-03/India_DNR_FINAL.pdf

Robinson, N. (2018) Remainers attacking the BBC should be careful – they could end up with a British Fox News instead. *New Statesman*, 6–17 April, p. 27.

Scott, L. (2019) The age of the hoax. *Financial Times* (*Life and Arts Section*), 16–17 February 2019, pp. 1–2.

Sloman, S. and Fernbach, P. (2017) *The Knowledge Illusion: The myth of individual thought and the power of collective wisdom*. London: Macmillan.

Subramanian, S. (2017) Inside the Macedonian fake news complex. *Wired*, 15 February. Available at: https://www.wired.com/2017/02/veles-macedonia-fake-news/

Sunstein, C. (2017) *#Republic: Divided Democracy in the Age of Social Media*. Princeton: Princeton University Press.

Tait, A. (2018) Digital Native. *New Statesman*, 10–16 August, p. 38.

Taylor, M. (2009) Civil society and rhetorical public relations process. In: Toth E., Heath, R., and Waymer, D. (Eds.) *Rhetorical and Critical Approaches to Public Relations II*. New York: Routledge, pp. 76–91.

Tett, G. (2016) Why we no longer trust the experts. *Financial Times*, 2/3 July 2016, p. 46.

Torchin, L. (2018) The perfect antidote to fake news. *The New European*, 19–25 July, p. 27.

Verčič, D. and Verčič, A. (2016) Agnotology and Democratization of Public Relations. Paper presented at the 18th Annual EUPRERA Congress, How strategic communication shapes value and innovation in society, Gronigen, Netherlands, 29–30 September. Available at: https://www.youtube.com/watch?v=BwTTua4y2ss&t=26s

Whitaker, P. (2019) To jab or not to jab? *New Statesman*, 17–23 May, p. 59.

Wilton. P. (2018) Why do some voters fail for conspiracy theories? *Goldsmiths College, London*. Available at: https://www.gold.ac.uk/news/conspiracy-thinking-us/

7 Performativity and public communication

Introduction

Previous chapters have proposed that public relations (PR) has contributed to the post-truth condition through its role in the confection of fake events, clandestine influence campaigns and other communicative artifices in the public realm. A question that arises in respect of this proposal is who are the actors in these communicative performances and how are they staged? In the field of populist politics, it is striking that several of the political entrepreneurs to emerge in recent years share experience of mass media, either as performers in reality television (Donald Trump), talk radio (Nigel Farage) or television comedy and satire (UK Prime Minister Boris Johnson, Beppe Grillo of the Five Star Movement in Italy and President Volodymyr Zelensky of Ukraine). This chapter discusses the aspects of dramatic performance by actors in the public sphere – whether corporate leaders such as Michael O'Leary of Ryanair or politicians – and how it has been used as a tool of influence and persuasion. This section concludes with a case study, based upon extracts from interviews with PR workers, journalists and other original research on the performative populist communication style of President Rodrigo Duterte, President of the Philippines since 2016.

The performative element of post-classical public relations

In considering the performative element of post-classical PR, well-established theories of dramatic performance can helpfully inform discussion. Writers in this area have already attended to the way in which decisions are made about what to include and what to leave out of public performances – such as interviews, speeches and public appearances, along with how such projections are deliberately "mediatized" by communicative actors (Auslander, 2008, p. 56). This dramatic perspective reflects aspects of Ranciere's philosophy on inclusion and exclusion in political discourse that he called the distribution of the sensible, which was mentioned in Chapter 1. While Auslander's thoughts on "liveness" in the art of theatrical performance are useful in that they fit with modern televisual and digital mediums of transmission, it is worth noting that they run counter to Peggy Phelan's (1993, p. 31) canonical theory of performance that draws a clear boundary between the "ephemeral nature" of performance art that means it "cannot be documented," with the implication that once it appears in any documentary form such as a photograph, a stage design sketch or a video tape, it "ceases to be performance art." In the same way that PR work needs an audience to influence, definitions of performance art depend upon the physical and temporal co-presence of performing actors and audience, in order that both parties share an experience simultaneously. In this definition, performances are deliberate, crafted acts carried out for a defined audience with deliberate communicative intent.

The populist rallies of Nigel Farage's Brexit Party and Donald Trump's continuous programme of arena events in the United States have become part of modern politics, and both are examples of the way in which dramatic performances are deployed as part of PR outreach. In business, the performance of publicity stunts is pervasive and used, for example, to promote airlines by Sir Richard Branson of Virgin, Michael O'Reilly of Ryanair and betting shops and pastries by Paddy Power and Greggs in the UK retail market. The political meetings staged by populist politicians include similar elements of performance and production values to those used by preachers in American mega churches. Donald Trump has been described as a "big fan" of Joel Osteen, "a maestro of high-tech religious marketing" who preaches a prosperity gospel at his Lakewood Church. As well as catching Trump's attention, Osteen has also been a subject of study for political scientist John Green of the University of Akron, Ohio, who noticed parallels of his approach with modern political communications and stagecraft:

> Preachers like Osteen know how to work the modern marketplace. They are like the mega mall of religion.[...] Politicians like to associate with fame. At the end of the day, they are all in the popularity business.
>
> –Luce (2019a)

Just like drama in the theatre, performative acts of PR – whether press conferences by chief executives, political rallies or visual stunts such as Sir Richard Branson picking up the model Dita von Teese to launch new routes of Virgin Atlantic from London to Las Vegas – depend upon the co-presence of an audience and are often designed specifically to appeal to the media. Through their participation in these performances as actors, leaders of businesses and populist political projects alike become the "articulators" of the relevant ideology, message or sales proposition, and offer a "performance of health, strength, sexuality and strong corporeal presence" (Moffitt, 2016, p. 52). In enacting their performance, leaders in the public eye confront the dilemma of wanting to be seen as of the people while simultaneously transcending the ordinary citizenry and presenting themselves as in possession of extraordinary talents that enable them to single-handedly solve political problems that have failed others. The performative style of PR is often linked to personal charisma and a vibrant rhetorical style, as exemplified by the flowery public speeches of UK politician, Boris Johnson, for example. But populist leaders also perform "ordinariness" in their PR outreach through the use of bad manners and lowering the tone of civic discourse through taunting opponents or making exaggerated political claims. Recent examples of the performative politics of bad manners being put into action include Beppe Grillo of Italy's Five Star Movement establishing and staging regular V-Day rallies, the purpose of which is to show the V-sign (the Italian expletive *Vaffancullo*) to more conventional Italian politicians.

Performativity and the media: "I love your show" and other stories

This new brand of political showmen and women have exploited a media landscape that places an increasing premium on public figures being entertaining. Ex-UK Prime Minister and PR executive David Cameron recalled his own experience of this inversion of politics and entertainment, when asked in a street in New York: "Are you David Cameron? The guy from Prime Minister's Questions? I love your show" (Nelson, 2016, p. 13). During the April 2019 Presidential election in Ukraine, celebrity combined with social media communication in the candidacy of comic actor, Volodymyr Zelensky, a man of with huge name recognition but no political experience. He was elected after a campaign against seasoned politicians during which the satirical entertainer primarily used social media to communicate with the electorate. Zelensky's celebrity and the specificity of being well known for playing a teacher who becomes President enabled him to break through to the public, gain TV coverage and establish momentum. There was little clarity on his policy proposals but the vacuum of substance in this political PR performance was deliberate. In order to avoid the Marmite effect of voters either loving or hating his policy proposals, Zelensky's social media campaigning was engaging, but said little about his plans in order to avoid dividing the vote. Instead, the telegenic Zelensky "ran an ingenious campaign that aimed not so much to transform him from celebrity to president but to blur the lines between entertainment and politics" (Hall and Olearchyk, 2019). Rather than the debates with rivals, in-depth interviews or policy proposals, the campaign that followed was little more than a mix of jokes and showmanship, ending in Zelensky's election as President.

The election result in Ukraine was not a one-off and comedy increasingly seems to be a component shared by several populist politicians in their communicative political performances. The writer who was paid to write jokes for President Barack Obama in what already seems like a distant and more serious era of political communications, David Litt has acknowledged that President Trump has combined a great feel for his audience with the skillset of a comedian to produce an all-encompassing comedic performance in which politics is treated as a "joke filled prank" (*The Economist*, 2019a). This approach accounts for the rambling and unscripted monologues from Trump at press conferences, rallies and other PR encounters that resemble stand-up comedy more than the more scripted format associated with set-piece political speeches.

The growth of celebrity culture offers one possible explanation for the success of a comic actor in Ukraine and other instances of the electoral success of performative politicians such as Beppe Grillo, Boris Johnson and Donald Trump, whose ability to deliver an enactment of amusing political performance seems to be at least as important as their political proposition. Yet the roots can also be traced to the arena of political PR, in which being on message consistently is so prized that it has led to a perceived superficiality in the way politicians, business leaders and other public figures communicate with the public via the media. Audiences have simply grown tired of this artifice over time, concluding that political actors offer no expertise, capability or insight that cannot be replicated by actors. This perception is often unwittingly encouraged by the logic of a media system on which seeks to portray politics in terms that combine telegenic sports and entertainment. Robert Shrimsley, editorial director at the *Financial Times*, has reflected on how the prominence of an entertainment component in political PR – including the arrival of comedic and performative public communication – is a logical response to contemporary media logic:

> Too many leading figures and the media that report them have created the impression that they see politics as a game, where winning is more important than governing well. [...] Unfortunately, in the desire to win an argument and build support, they have too easily succumbed to cynicism, political games and playing to the gallery.
>
> –Shrimsley (2019)

Channelling Trump and the public relations performances of distraction

In October 2016, as the momentum behind his campaign in the US Presidential election seemed to falter, *The Economist* magazine (2016a) reported that Donald Trump was exploring the possibility of an online TV channel to serve the substantial fan base he had built up as a result of his candidacy. Jeff Gaspin, the former chairman of NBC Universal, who produced *The Apprentice* reality TV show that featured Trump, concluded that the candidate's divisive comments on Muslims, Hispanics and women during the campaign had made his brand too toxic for mainstream media companies. For this reason, online streaming was being considered for delivery of a few hours of daily TV content funded through a subscription model. On Mr Gaspin's projections, the new Trump TV service could attract between 250,000 and 500,000 paying customers recruited from the committed political fan base that follows Trump on social media, where he boasted 24 million followers on Twitter and Facebook at the time. With Trump's canny eye for self-promotion and a circle of media supporters who share his willingness to exploit the outrage of conservatives, Mr Gaspin expected subscribers would pay up to $100 a year for this type of programming, giving a revenue stream of $25–50m a year for around $7–8m of production costs. The result would be a recurring revenue stream and an enduring media property from which Trump and his family could promote their varied commercial and political projects, underpinned by programming that consisted of little more than Donald Trump raging on his recurring themes of trade wars and immigration.

In the hollowed out politics of division, in which moderate, consensus, middle of the road views are marginalised by the louder online promotion from extremes of the right and left, a niche media channel offering divisive content as political entertainment is commercially viable. The viability of the subscription streaming model has been proven by the success of the ex-Fox News presenter Glenn Beck, who launched an online content service in 2011 which he claimed attracted 300,000 customers paying $9.95 a month. These types of media projects raise questions about the boundaries between entertainment and news, reality and performance. In a sign of this dilemma, for the first half of 2016, the US news web site *Huffington Post* covered Donald Trump's Presidential campaign in its entertainment section before including his pronouncements in the politics section once he had secured the Republican nomination. The new communicative entrepreneurs in politics have demonstrated similar media awareness and agility in using slick PR techniques to exploit existing media in order to promote commercial or political propositions. Moreover, once they have established a digital promotional platform with sufficient momentum and follower base, such as Trump has achieved with his Twitter following for example, the new political actors can enter the media sector themselves.

The triumph of showmanship over statecraft?

Trump's presidency, like the planning for his TV channel, proved an important marker of the potential for show business and performance to triumph over policy argument and statecraft in politics, although the 45th US President cannot claim to be the first interloper from show business to enter politics or the White House. Arnold Schwarzenegger observed of his election to Governor of California between 2003 and 2011: "I was kinda the first populist that was elected, when the people were discouraged and disenchanted" after campaigning that positioned him as "a Republican outsider who had appealed to Democrats" and "channelled public anger at the political class" (Mance, 2019). Trump's performative and sometimes outrageous style of political communication throughout the 2016 Presidential election race swept aside the slick but more conventional campaigns of established political operators such as Jeb Bush (who had raised $130m of funding), Ted Cruz and Marco Rubio, partly because of the free air time given to his rallies and statements:

> Every news show wanted Trump on air; he would call in, chew the fat, throw out a few incendiary remarks and suck all the oxygen out of the news cycle. He was a spectacle: like in a car crash, no one could help themselves from slowing down to look. It was too easy to treat him and his candidacy as a joke. [...] He was known for his vulgarity, his divorces and his improbable hair
>
> –Lewis (2016)

The unattractive aspects of Trump's character and his capacity to offend in public statements seemed to increase media appetite for the inflammatory spectacle he offered on the campaign trail. His on-screen political performances in interviews, talk shows, debates and press conferences as a bullying alpha male were a continuation of the character he displayed in *The Apprentice* reality TV show. In another transfer from reality television, the firings in the Trump White House became almost normalised for a US TV audience that was accustomed to hearing the phrase "you're fired" on *The Apprentice*. Among the record-breaking short tenures were Mike Flynn, as National Security Adviser, who lasted only 24 days before being forced to step down and White House Communications Director, Anthony Scaramucci (also known as The Mooch) who lasted just 10 days before being fired by Trump, apparently for making a series of obscene remarks about members of the White House staff to a journalist on *The New Yorker* magazine.

The success of the performative approach to political PR is not only an opportunistic PR coup over the media, it is deliberately cynical and debasing of serious debate. It also represents the triumph of showmanship over statecraft and a decline in serious political argument. Moreover, many journalists in mainstream media have been complicit in this process, unwittingly promoting division as they seek to bring entertainment motifs into political programming:

> Though people often talk about political polarisation in America, they rarely mention the incentive for exacerbating it. In politics and punditry, nuance, and consensus don't sell. Plumbing ever-lower depths most certainly does.
>
> For the networks and media, the increasing polarisation and void are desirable: a necessary part of business. The worse the better. These bosses have encouraged the transformation of politics into WWF wrestling: a fake sport in which participants and observers sometimes seem complicit – except some poor saps mistake it for real life.
>
> –Murray (2016)

Naomi Klein (2017, p. 51) made a similar observation that besides his performances *on The Apprentice*, Trump also had experience as a promoter and performer in professional wrestling, which she described as "another blockbuster entertainment genre that is also based on a cartoonishly fake performance of reality." The media format of reality television has become a recurring motif and exemplar of a distinct form of PR and political campaigning that requires a specific genre of performance from the communications actors, many of whom have had some experience of the television, entertainment or media sectors. While Trump could reach to his reality TV experience to inform his political PR performances, the format of politician as a communicative performer had been established in the 1990s by the chairman of the Italian media company, Mediaset and ex-Prime Minister of Italy, Silvio Berlusconi, whose template has been revived more recently by other outspoken politicians, including Roderigo Duterte in the Philippines, Recep Tayyip Erdogan in Turkey, Viktor Orban in Hungary and Vladimir Putin in Russia. In late 2016, Brendan Simms made some predictions on how the emergence of a new style of political promotion and a new approach to political discourse – which in the USA included a new empowering of white supremacist narratives – would develop and affect international global politics over time:

> Style will soon become substance. At best, a Trump presidency will lead to the "Berlusconification" of international politics, which will become extended reality-TV events, at least as far as they relate to the United States. More seriously, his antics will empower and encourage a coarsening of the discourse between states and about world problems.
>
> –Simms (2016)

In the United Kingdom, Ayesha Hazarika, a former adviser and speechwriter to Labour Party leader, Ed Miliband who has worked as press officer, stand-up comedian and journalist, made a similar observation on the way public conversations on Brexit are being managed compared with previous norms of political debate:

> I was taught that compromise was normal and good. There's no desire to compromise because there is little reward for it these days. The Lib Dems got punished for their time in coalition yet have fared better on a clear "B★★ocks to Brexit" line. Jeremy Corbyn is tanking with his halfway-house position on Brexit.
>
> –Hazarika (2019)

Another prominent example of the trend for performative PR in politics was the way UK politician Boris Johnson avoided a vote on a third runway extension at Heathrow Airport by absenting himself on a contrived and unnecessary trip abroad. One journalist wrote that the episode confirmed that "showmen have taken over our politics" and that while in contemporary political campaigning, "performance is all that matters," the consequences are serious as unrealistic political propositions that cannot be delivered:

> Politics based purely on performance is unsustainable in a democracy. At some point, campaign pledges are meant to become law. Candidates are meant to make the transition from actor mode to lawyer mode. But what if there is no lawyer mode? First, the actor dreads disappointing and so losing the audience, therefore the performance gets increasingly outrageous to sustain the ratings. [...] This is where the cult of individual celebrity leads: to the inflation of individual vanity until it squeezes out old-fashioned notions of due process and the rule of law. This is why British politics can do without so many charismatics, cartoon characters and comedians.
>
> –Behr (2018)

Reality TV and other low brow entertainment in the economy of attention

As a businessman, Donald Trump filed for bankruptcy on behalf of corporations he controlled or was involved with four times. He made more money in the entertainment business by performing as a tycoon on the TV show, *The Apprentice*, than he did in reality by actually being a businessman. His success in reality TV gave Trump insight into the dynamics of the celebrity economy in an age when social media was blurring lines between mainstream and self-generated media. Simultaneously, reality TV was blurring lines between performance and actuality, especially for its biggest stars. In his 2011 book, *Time to Get Tough*, Trump demonstrated his understanding of these new dynamics of performance, audience attention and communicative value, when he wrote: "You can be a horrible human being, you can be a truly terrible person, but if you get ratings, you are a king" (Roberts, 2015).

In Russia's March 2018 election, the official opposition candidate to President Putin was the ex-model, actress and journalist, Ksenia Sobchak. She had gained fame as host of the Russian reality television show, Dom-2, and acknowledged ahead of the election that it was not a realistic contest but rather a "high budget show." The show started with an announcement on YouTube and resembled previous attempts by the Kremlin to "absorb the protest vote" (*The Economist*, 2017a). In contrast to this high-budget effort in Russia, Donald Trump's campaign communications were low cost and appeared amateurish and unpolished from the start. Instead of carefully considered phrases and neat sound bites putting forward policy propositions, Trump's public performances were a cocktail of divisive chants ("lock her up" for Hilary Clinton, for example) gibes, mimicry and casual insults, including "Pochahontas" for Elizabeth Warren, in a gibe that mocks the Democratic candidate for alleged exaggeration of her native-American ancestry. Berkeley University Professor of Linguistics, George Lakoff, has argued that although the rambling rhetoric may seem chaotic, Trump is "very careful and very strategic in his use of language" and discourse mechanisms such as the way he repeatedly addresses the audience as "folks" in order to generate intimacy and the way he leaves some sentences unfinished in order to deepen the connection by bringing the crowd in to finish the fragment and so make it their own (Lakoff, 2016). The resulting performances of political communication are complete in themselves and rather than forming part of a distraction strategy, they are essentially all that Trump has to offer. As *Financial Times* journalist Simon Kuper (2017) concluded: "He is a lowbrow entertainer, so he produces lowbrow entertainment."

This lowbrow entertainment has proved a highly effective and engaging form of political promotion, with the conduct of the early days of the Trump White House resembling a reality TV show at its most compelling, with media coverage to match. Beforehand, during the 2015 Presidential election campaign, the UK political journalist Sarah Mackinlay (2016) concluded that she could not recall "any other political performance that has been anywhere near as entertaining or engaging" in over 10 years of writing on politics, recording that "this rambling style has created a powerful discourse that grips us – even though over here we can't vote for him."

The comedic public relations performances of political clowns

The example of Trump TV confirms the value of an entertaining and performative presence for political actors in post-classical communication. Some modern political campaigns, candidates and their communication approach can also seem like comedy or a series of ironic jokes rather than the lively presentation of policy proposals. Indeed, once elected, the Trump presidency was likened to a display of tragi-comic reality television at its most compelling, synchronising political PR with a media logic that was simultaneously able to satisfy his supporters and sustain audience attention. Trump's media performances also provided a seemingly never-ending series of distractions from the more troubling questions of US domestic politics and foreign policy, as Simon Kuper of the *Financial Times* explained at the time:

> The broader problem is that we the viewers – the smartphone generation raised in peacetime – have no concentration spans either. Trump is the fitting president for our era. No wonder that another merchant of distraction, Facebook's Mark Zuckerberg, thinks he can be president next.
>
> –Kuper (2017)

In 2009, the Italian comedian Beppe Grillo founded the Five Star Movement as a combination of activist group and ironic political joke. The party gained popularity on the back of Grillo's comedic blog and videos on his web site, going on to be the largest party in the Italian Parliament following the 2018 general election and forming a coalition government. Since leaving a full-time journalistic career (but continuing to write lucrative columns), the UK politician Boris Johnson has cultivated the image of a superlatively educated Latin-speaking man of the letters with that of a political clown. By July 2019, he was UK Prime Minister. The comedic component of his political offer had been in the ascendant since he began appearing on a satirical BBC TV show, entitled *Have I Got News for You* in 1999, going on to be a regular fixture on the highly rated programme. The prominence these appearances gave to Johnson in national life and the way he was able to present himself as uniquely amiable, charming and funny led to Sky News – in June 2019, as Johnson moved ahead in the contest for leadership of the ruling Conservative Party – accusing *Have I Got News for You* panellist Ian Hislop of being culpable for giving Johnson too much of a platform to promote himself (Jankowicz, 2019).

Nigel Farage, one-time leader of the United Kingdom Independence Party (UKIP) also appeared on *Have I Got News for You* in a series of performances that seemed to consciously blur the line between serious politics and knockabout comedy. As a PR exercise and despite the exaggerated nature of some of the politico-comedic performances, the longer term effect is quite subtle. By personally directing a controlled demolition of norms and personal dignity through self-mockery on live television, both Farage and Johnson shifted the rules of political PR by making jokes at their expense almost redundant, as they had already done worse to themselves than anything third-party media could offer. Professor Diane Roberts (2015) of Florida State University made a similar point in an article about Trump, entitled "The man who can't be parodied," in which she observed that the excesses and comedic performances of this "cornucopia of frenetic egotism" had made satire redundant. One effect of comedic performance making candidates joke-proof relative to their more serious counterparts is that the new breed of comedic politicians are able to avoid blame for past and current misdemeanours by using humour in a strategy of plausible public denial. Even serious allegations are either brushed aside or dealt with as yet another joke. For example, in 2019, when Nigel Farage was exposed by the UK's Channel 4 News as having secretly received £450,000 of funding from businessman Aaron Banks, his onscreen reply when confronted in the street by reporter Matt Frei was a jocular and mocking retort of "terrible, isn't it?" (Channel 4, 2019).

The surface lightness and comedic aspects of performative PR are rarely light in their long-term effects and often mask darker and sometimes sinister political projects or conceal attempts at state influence, censorship and propaganda. After watching Trump win the 2016 US election, the Hungarian prime minister Viktor Orban rejoiced that "we can return to real democracy – what a wonderful world." In Hungary, after winning the 2018 election, Orban claimed a new mandate for his own brand of "illiberal democracy" and announced plans to build a new era based on this message. Specifically, Orban intended to curb the freedom of the media, the arts and academia in order to "embed the political system in a cultural era," which was to include proactive promotion of "a national identity, Christian cultural values, patriotism, attachment to the homeland and family" (Hopkins, 2018). These postures are typical strongman political PR, with associated messaging that sets up the country in a nationalistic and cultural struggle against others, as Peter Kreko of the Political Capital think tank observed:

> The Orban regime is striving to liquidate all forms of independent institutional autonomy, and the leadership of the system want to put all issues in the frames of a war between different world views and civilisations.
>
> –Hopkins (2018)

Retrospective military messaging and performance

One recurring component in the messaging of performative politicians is a harking to the past. This is present in the claims of lost sovereignty put forward by the Brexiteers and the way the nation will able to return to a great global role if it leaves the European Union. The year after the Brexit referendum saw box office success for films released in 2017 that featured the country's fight against Nazi Germany in World War II, including *Darkest Hour* on Churchill's wartime leadership and *Dunkirk* on the evacuation of British troops from France in 1940. Trump has described his own anti-establishment revolt as "Brexit plus-plus-plus" in nativist rhetoric that echoes Charles Lindbergh and the America First isolationists ahead of World War II. In his book *The Shipwrecked Mind* (2016) Mark Lilla has described how Trump's Make America Great Again slogan carries the same retrospective imaginary of a lost greatness that can be reclaimed through his politics, with supporters encouraged to step back in history to recover what they imagine was lost. Similarly, in France, Marine Le Pen's language "caters to nostalgia, anxiety and antipathy to the liberal international order" with slogans that vow to make France great again too, such as "No to Brussels, yes to France" (*The Economist*, 2016b).

For over 240 years, the 4th July holiday in the United States has been a national celebration of the "distinctly civilian declaration of independence when Thomas Jefferson announced the right of all Americans to 'life, liberty and the pursuit of happiness'. It is about the birth of an idea, not a military battle" (Luce, 2019b). Yet in 2019, in Washington, President Trump turned the event into a celebration that glorified America's military and also focussed on Trump himself, who tweeted that the day would feature an address by "your favourite President, me!" Trump's

4th July *Salute to the Military* pageant was apparently inspired by his experience of France's Bastille Day Parade which he had witnessed as a guest of President Macron. However, rather than unifying the nation in celebration, Trump's version of the "Fourth of July – with tanks" managed to outrage his critics, an outcome that would prove "equally delightful for the President" according to *The Economist* (2019b). The bombastic pageant that resulted was a divisive example of populist and performative political communications. The day was a physical embodiment and performance of the way Trump had already appropriated the military in his digital media presence by using images of himself with serving members of the armed forces and veterans featuring as the home page on his Twitter feed for long periods (it was changed to the image of a campaign event in the run up to the 2020 Presidential election).

The thoroughness of planning for this performance included issuing all military personnel with PR talking points to help handle interviews with the media and discussions with the public, with the guidance notes stating "these messages and tips apply to all communications, not just interviews:"

> The Department of Defense would like service members to be clear that they are "proud" on several levels. Under the overall messages, the guide suggests: "I am proud of my job and my vehicle/tank. I am glad to share my experience with American People." It also proposes that they say: "I am proud to honor the Nation and the Armed Forces during this Independence Day Celebration."
> –Cohen (2019)

Trump's inclusion of the military in his promotional outreach was an example of the increased visibility of military motifs, symbols and rituals in the civic and political sphere from around 2007 onwards. The presence of serving military along with the emergence of more vocal veteran campaign groups in the United States and United Kingdom reflected the role of both countries as the largest and second largest contributors, respectively, of troops to the US-led invasion of Afghanistan in 2001 and the 2003 coalition invasion of Iraq. In the years following these two operations, aspects of military life become more visible in civic society, through physical incursions such as tributes to the armed forces at sporting events and the presence of military personnel in uniform as guests in sports stadia (Fischer, 2014). Public support for both operations eroded as casualties rose and the financial cost increased. In a 2009 opinion poll, 47% of the UK population opposed the war in Afghanistan with a similar split over timing of the withdrawal of British troops. In the same period, the popularity of Prime Minister Tony Blair fell to below 30% from over 60% for much of the time before the wars. The fall in public support moved in an inverse proportion to the rise in casualties to a level not seen by the UK military since the Korean War, with troops returning home having survived terrible injuries on the battlefield.

In the nationalistic politics of UKIP in the United Kingdom and the Tea Party movement and Trump supporters in the Republican Party in the United States, an unquestioning approach to supporting the military prevailed. Specific examples include the policy statements of the UKIP which branded itself "the party of defence" and promised the services "more funds, more respect and more support" (UKIP, 2015). Ahead of the UK's 2016 European Union membership referendum, the Veterans for Britain group campaigned for Brexit with shrewdly organised media relations outreach, such as photo opportunities of Battle of Britain veterans who urged readers not to give away "what we fought for" (Cole, 2016). This level of veteran visibility in mainstream politics was novel for Britain, but was eclipsed by the Veterans for Trump coalition in the 2016 US Presidential election. Veterans appeared at many Trump campaign events and Donald Trump committed "to make the VA (Department of Veteran Affairs) great again by firing the corrupt and incompetent VA executives who let our veterans down" (Trump, 2016).

The business of showmanship

In business and financial journalism, the performative, entertaining and high-profile CEO has become more common in recent years. This typology of business leader differs from the celebrity CEOs who became prominent in the 1980s and 1990s as global economic expansion joined with the increased individualism of the Reagan era in the United States and the premiership of Margaret Thatcher in the United Kingdom and wider coverage of business topics in the media, through new publications and more human interest stories on business in the mainstream media in separate special sections such as the Business section of the *New York Times* and *The Sunday Times* in London, for example. Celebrity CEOs of this period were commemorated as heroes on the cover of *Business Week, Forbes, Fortune* and other publications throughout this era. The face of Jack Welch of GE was prominent in the US media, while Alan Sugar of Amstrad featured in the United Kingdom, in profile stories orchestrated by PR teams and in which they pledged conformance to following the rules of business, society and politics that prevailed at the time.

Over the past 40 years or so, some new entrants to the highly competitive airline industry have integrated elements of showmanship into their PR tactics, as small and sometimes disruptive operators attempted to break in to a crowded marketplace of much larger incumbents. In the 1980s and 1990s, Sir Richard Branson went further than his hero Sir Freddie Laker had in the 1970s in promoting Laker Airways' Sky train transatlantic flights, undertaking a series of publicity stunts. These included serious record-breaking feats, such as attempting twice (in 1995 and 1998) to circumnavigate the globe in a hot air balloon, alongside more frivolous gestures such as dressing as a female flight attendant and even wearing a wedding dress to promote his Virgin Brides retail wedding store in 1996. Numerous web sites now record these projects by what one calls the "undisputed king of the publicity stunt" who was himself open about using the PR tactic of extreme stunts in the early years of Virgin Atlantic as a way to gain publicity for the airline when competing against the might of British Airways and its marketing budget that dwarfed that of Virgin.

Having launched its web site in 2000, Ryanair's PR strategy in the even more competitive short-haul market of the late 1990s onwards was that "Short of committing murder, bad publicity sells more seats," according to chief executive Michael O'Leary (Eleftheriou-Smith, 2013). O'Reilly's approach to PR was deliberately aggressive, confrontational and non-conformist. Moreover, unlike Sir Freddie Laker and Sir Richard Branson, whose PR campaigns positioned them as outsiders fighting on behalf of customers whom they respected. O'Reilly seemed to revel in any conflict with customers, especially so if it was on the subject of costs. There seemed to be a deliberate effort to use bad publicity to convey a consistent PR message that the Ryanair proposition was all about low cost. After a summer of cancelled flights in 2018 due to a dispute with its pilots, Ryanair attracted further negative publicity and passenger outrage when it sent unsigned compensation cheques that bounced when attempts were made to cash them. As one journalist covering this story reflected: "He does not embarrass easily. Any attendant bad publicity – and there has been plenty – has been regarded instead as an opportunity to emphasise that Ryanair would do whatever was required to keep its costs lower than those of its rivals, which it would then pass on to customers in lower fares" (Cooper, 2018). O'Reilly also showed a shrewd understanding of the logic and crowd dynamics of social media, cheerfully embracing the consequences of poor customer service that would be seen as negative by other airlines, as well as an understanding of the role of performing publicity stunts. When asked by one interviewer if the Ryanair could survive on publicity stunts and press coverage alone, O'Reilly replied:

> Well I have 29 years of evidence suggesting that it can. [Richard] Branson has been doing it for years. As long you run around generating noise, which is now easier because you've got all these halfwits on social media ranting and raving, inventing stories, it drives people on to our website. And we don't spend €50m or €100m on marketing companies to do it. […] Negative publicity generates so much more free publicity that it sells more tickets.
>
> –Eleftheriou-Smith (2013)

Case Study 7.1

The performative political communication of President Rodrigo Duterte

Introduction

In the Philippines, the performative political communications of President Duterte began with his positioning of himself at the start of his election campaign as an outsider with a strategy of stirring up grievance politics in a long-established democratic country with reasonable economic growth, despite being a member of one of the country's oldest political families.

Duterte combined political nous with canny use of social media throughout the campaign, including special channels to reach expatriates, with the entire effort supplemented by online trolls. In an edited volume, Curato (2017) has offered an overview of the Duterte's campaigning to win the election and the ongoing vitriol, hyper-masculinity and "spectacle driven politics" that has characterised his rule and political communication. Once in power, his PR approach was to "dominate the news cycle on a daily basis and gain free airtime by making outrageous off-the-cuff remarks" (Reed, 2018). One message of the PR effort was to create a "manufactured crisis" which portrayed the country as at risk of becoming a "narco-state beset by drugs and crime and in desperate need of strong leadership" (Heydarian, 2018, p. 13), using rhetoric and style that was anti-elite and populist, despite his own origins in Philippine politics. The PR messaging in the early years of the Presidency placed the appropriation of melodrama at the centre of politics alongside antagonism against the establishment, with Duterte positioned as a saviour, who posed in PR photographs with a rifle about to take the fight to the streets himself on behalf of the people. Duterte named his armed action against the illegal drugs market "Oplan Tokhang," or, "Operation Knock and Plead" and started raids in June 2016. A statement from the National Police Commission dated 1 July 1 2016 described the aim as the "neutralization of illegal drug personalities nationwide." The policy saw 5,000 people killed by police or others in the first two years of the Duterte Presidency, according to official figures, although human rights groups including Amnesty International have claimed the death toll could be two or three times that figure. In October 2018, the President issued a statement to the press saying that he had only been "playful" when admitting that his "only sin was extrajudicial killings" rather than the corruption which he associated with most politicians (Reed, 2018). According to his media spokesperson, Harry Roque, the admission was also a sign of authenticity: "That's the President just being himself, being playful, highlighting the point that he is not corrupt." The high-profile militarised political PR performances of Duterte attracted approval from President Trump, who commended Mr Duterte in a phone call in early 2017 for doing an "unbelievable job" fighting drugs (*The Economist*, 2017b), although the same report suggested that Duterte's campaign against drug dealers and users had led to 9,000 deaths. Having seen the persuasive power of social media in elections, Duterte then deployed it as a channel of harassment, intimidation, or threats on behalf of his interests. In particular, Duterte's campaign team masterfully appropriated the use of trolling as part of its political outreach and was so able to influence moods, framing of issues and the scope of public conversations, leading to his success in the 2016 election.

> This campaign method influenced public opinion by deploying messages that vilified elite-driven politics and a conniving media, thus allowing Duterte's camp to strategically frame and shape the election narrative on issues such as criminality and drugs, among others.
> —Aguirre (2018, p. 545)

Interview summaries

In investigating the case study that appears here on Rodrigo Duterte, Miguel Cortez conducted content analysis of 40 news releases and articles issued by the PR department of the Philippines Drug Enforcement Agency (PDEA) in 2017 and also undertook extended qualitative interviews with journalists and PR professionals in The Philippines. The results of the content analysis suggested that the government's PR operations were positioning the war on drugs within a frame of prevalent conflict on the streets, against which citizens were powerless to take action. This finding is consistent with government efforts to brand its anti-drug operations as much needed law and order measures. Interviews with PR people and journalists provided further evidence that a message of imminent danger and conflict was being used to consolidate power:

> The war on drugs is a fabrication. It aims to solve mere symptoms of a larger problem – poverty. Its policies ignore human rights and its enforcers carry out violations with the blessing of the president. The war on drugs will never be won because its champions need the war on drugs to legitimize their power.
> —Radio broadcaster and journalist

The interviews showed how media were swift to pick up on the contrast between normal political PR and the new aggressive and "raw" performative PR style of Duterte:

> He's tough talking, down to earth, couldn't care less if media was all around. Media was not ready for this kind of president. They were so accustomed to those who had some kind of media training, would spin stories or apply "PR terms" for tough media questions. This was as raw as you could get.
> —TV journalist and presenter

One interviewee pointed out that bloggers had created a media environment that allows errors and misreporting of Duterte and his campaign against drugs to be amplified:

> The traditional concept of government-media relations is naturally adversarial. However, if you would look at the present climate, it is not President Duterte who has a problem with the media. The hardcore supporters most specifically the bloggers are creating the environment where errors are amplified. The President has not changed his mannerisms since he was a mayor and he likes to hold impromptu press conferences and media discussions.
>
> –PR manager

Despite misgivings about Duterte and his style of governance, the impact of his unorthodox approach to Presidential media relations with its emphasis on action and canny use of social media is admired by one interviewee who had previously worked in government PR:

> From an outsider's point-of-view, I do have to admire the communication tactics of his team, though. They were able to present a persona of Duterte that feeds Filipinos' id – a macho action man who can get things done by posturing and blustering his way through things.
>
> His social media team is also insane. I don't know if they are paid trolls or if they are people who truly believe in the cause, but I can't help but be amazed at how they continue to convince people that what's happening in the country is okay. Even though I don't agree with what they are doing, I have to recognize just how smooth their comms work has been. As someone who previously worked for the government, I can attest to just how difficult it is to sell the government to the people.
>
> –Former government PR manager

The former government PR professional also admired the way Duterte's media performance and choice of words generates repeat coverage. This interviewee also offered some useful commentary on the scope of responsibility and effectiveness of Duterte's press spokespeople:

> Duterte is quotable, and not always in a good way. His words are preposterous enough that the media can't resist quoting him. This means that his lines can easily be taken out of context. I would say

he needs a PR person, but that's supposedly the job of Andanar and Abella*. Abella whitewashes what Duterte says, so much so that his "interpretation" is completely different from what the president said. Andanar is a joke. Furthermore, Duterte's bombastic ways have become his identity, so suddenly shifting into a prepared speech will seem even more unbelievable than him spouting his own words.

*Martin Andanar was appointed head of Duterte's Presidential Communications and Operations Office from 2017. Ernesto Abella was President Duterte's official spokesperson until replaced by Attorney Harry Roque in October 2017.

Several interviewees were critical of how Duterte's macho public performances and personality-driven approach to PR, which has included posing with machine guns on raids himself, has had negative effects in Philippine politics by normalising more personal attacks on opponents. While the high-impact performances helped Duterte to control the communications and media agenda, by distracting from policy questions and resulting in less detailed discussion of policy matters, there have been other negative systemic effects. One interviewee went as far as to suggest that Duterte's approach to presidential communications was putting independent and impartial reporting in the country at risk:

The government is strengthening its propaganda machinery in traditional as well as social media in order to sway public opinion and control information. The tenets of journalism are under assault.

–Broadcaster

References

Aguirre, A. (2018) The Duterte Reader: Critical Essays on Rodrigo Duterte's Early Presidency. *Philippine Studies: Historical and Ethnographic Viewpoints.* 66 (4), 542–545 Available at: https://www.researchgate.net/publication/330355436_The_Duterte_Reader_Critical_Essays_on_Rodrigo_Duterte's_Early_Presidency_ed_by_Nicole_Curato

Auslander, P. (2008) *Liveness: Performance in Meditatized Culture.* New York: Routledge.

Behr, R. (2018) From Heathrow to Brexit, showmen have taken over our politics. *The Guardian*, 26 June. Available at: https://www.theguardian.com/commentisfree/2018/jun/26/heathrow-brexit-politics-boris-johnson-commons-vote

Channel 4 News (2019) Nigel Farage's funding secrets revealed. 16 May. Available at: https://www.channel4.com/news/nigel-farages-funding-secrets-revealed

Cohen, M. (2019) Pentagon guidance to troops in Trump's July 4th event: say I love my tank. *Mother Jones*, 3 July. Available at: https://www.motherjones.com/politics/2019/07/pentagon-guidance-to-troops-in-trumps-july-4th-event-say-i-love-my-tank/

Cole H. (2016) Battle of Britain: WWII vets plead with Brits 'don't give away what we fought for' urging voters to back Brexit. *The Sun*, 20 June. Available at: https://www.thesun.co.uk/news/politics/1313861/wwii-vets-plead-with-brits-dont-give-away-what-we-fought-for-urging-voters-to-back-brexit/

Cooper, M. (2018) Bounced cheques, cancelled flights – why do we still fly Ryanair? *The Guardian*, 23 August. Available at: https://www.theguardian.com/commentisfree/2018/aug/23/ryanair-michael-oleary-airline-pilots-strike

Curato, N. (2017) *A Duterte Reader: Critical Essays on Rodrigo Duterte's Early Presidency*. Quezon City, Philippines: Ateneo de Manila University Press.

The Economist (2016a) Channelling Trump. 22 October, pp. 60–61.

The Economist (2016b) League of nationalists. 19 November, p. 63.

The Economist (2017a) Centre ring. 28 October, p. 32.

The Economist (2017b) Meet and retreat: Donald Trump has friends, but few ambitions, in South-East Asia. 4 November, p. 60.

The Economist (2019a) Funny business. 18 May, p. 55.

The Economist (2019b) Lexington: the calm before the storm. 6 July, p. 38.

Eleftheriou-Smith, L. (2013) Ryanair's Michael O'Leary: short of committing murder, bad publicity sells more seats. *Campaign*, 1 August. Available at: https://www.campaignlive.co.uk/article/ryanairs-michael-oleary-short-committing-murder-bad-publicity-sells-seats/1193681

Fischer, M. (2014) Commemorating 9/11 NFL-style: insights into America's culture of militarism. *Journal of Sport and Social Issues*, 38 (3), 199–221.

Hall, B. and Olearchyk, R. (2019) Ukraine comic's poll challenge is no joke. *Financial Times*, 30/31 March, p. 4.

Hazarika, A. (2019) Polarised Britain has lost the art of compromise and it is putting the country and future in danger. *Evening Standard*, 3 July, p. 13.

Heydarian, R. (2018) *The Rise of Duterte: A Populist Revolt Against Elite Democracy*. Basingstoke: Palgrave Macmillan.

Hopkins, V. (2018) Orban's chill wind blows through Hungarian culture. *Financial Times*, 22/23 September, p. 6.

Jankowicz, M. (2019) Ian Hislop would never vote for Boris Johnson but defends giving him a platform. *The European*, 19 June, Available at: https://www.theneweuropean.co.uk/top-stories/have-i-got-news-for-you-and-boris-johnson-1-6114486

Klein, N. (2017) *No is Not Enough: Defeating the New Shock Politics*. London: Allen Lane.

Kuper, S. (2017) The Trump Show – reality TV at its most compelling. *Financial Times Magazine*, 12/13 August, p. 5.

Lakoff, G. (2016) Following Trump's use of language. *Berkeley Blog*. Available at: https://blogs.berkeley.edu/2016/08/24/following-trumps-use-of-language/

Lewis, H. (2016) The politics of whitelash: Donald Trump lied, scammed and won by appealing to America's bases instincts. *New Statesman*, 11–17 November, pp. 22–23.

Lilla, M. (2016) *The Shipwrecked Mind: On Political Reaction*. New York: New York Review Books.

Luce, E. (2019a) Blessed are the Wealthy. *FT Weekend Magazine*, 20–21 April, pp. 14–21.

Luce, E. (2019b) Donald Trump creates 'Red Square on the Potomac'. *Financial Times*, 5 July. Available at: https://www.ft.com/content/d8dabfa2-9efb-11e9-b8ce-8b459ed04726

Mackinlay, S. (2016) Star-spangled banter. *The Spectator*, 4 November 2016, p. 23.

Mance, H. (2019) Breakfast with the FT: Arnold Schwarzenegger. *Financial Times* (*Life and Arts Section*), 25/26 May, p. 3.

Moffitt, B, (2016) *The Global Rise of Populism*. Stanford: Stanford University Press.

Murray, D. (2016) Lights camera, politics. *The Spectator*, 15 October, pp. 12–13.

Nelson, F. (2016) Jolly good show. *The Spectator*, 15 October, p. 13.

Phelan, P. (1993) *Unmarked: The Politics of Performance*. New York: Routledge.

Reed, J. (2018) Rodrigo Duterte and the populist playbook. *Financial Times*, 26 July. Available at: https://www.ft.com/content/98589db0-8132-11e8-bc55-50daf11b720

Roberts, D. (2015) The man who can't be parodied. *Prospect*, November 2015, p. 16.

Shrimsley, R. (2019) Actors in politics? You could not make it up? *Financial Times Magazine*, 6/7 April 2019, p. 10.

Simms, B. (2016) What would a Trump presidency mean for the rest of the world? *New Statesman*, 7–13 October, pp. 26–31.

Trump, D. (2016) *Donald J. Trump's 10 Point Plan to Reform The Department of Veterans Affairs*. Available at: https://www.donaldjtrump.com/policies/veterans-affairs-reform

UKIP (2015) *UKIP is the party of defence*. UKIP, 7 April. Available at: http://www.ukip.org/ukip_is_the_party_of_defence

8 The digital mixology of online engagement

Introduction

Post-classical public relations (PR) has enthusiastically combined the conventional work of messaging, targeting and distribution with the tools and skills of digital marketing, including data-analytics and search engine optimisation. The product of this combination is a hybridised form of computationally based campaigning that blends PR messaging and content creation with online marketing. Corporations, individuals, political parties and others have used this model of online public engagement, persuasion and advocacy in campaigns that are sometimes enabled by the third-party service providers with political links such as Cambridge Analytica, a UK-based service provider that closed in 2018 after accusations of wrongdoing and malpractice in its use of the data of individual Facebook users The intensive targeting process used in this computational style of communication leads in turn to intense advocacy by followers who voice their support in debates on social media in a manner more usual among sports fans or lovers of a rock band than political engagement by citizens in civic society. This chapter seeks to unpack the components of this digital mixology and consider how the technical affordances of social media platforms and the digital advertising networks they host have been re-purposed as instruments of engagement in online influence campaigns. The chapter concludes with a case study on aspects of the Chinese government's use of online engagement in its state-level PR, digital diplomacy and internal communications. The case study is based upon interviews conducted in China in 2018 with members of the *Wumao* community of social media commenters paid to post material by the government as part of its online engagement work, as well as journalists, critical of this state-sponsored form of artificial digital advocacy.

Computation, data and online engagement

At the forefront of the post-classical PR repertoire is a digital mixology of tools, techniques and trickery that shrewdly takes advantage of the affordances of online media, just as classical media relations techniques took advantage of the characteristics and culture of print journalism. For modern PR workers, an ideal digital PR skillset now includes mastery of search engine optimisation (SEO) techniques, the workings of social media news feeds, distribution and display algorithms, alongside understanding how content management systems control what audiences see. The aim of this mixed repertoire is to optimise the synchronicity of client messages with the chosen digital format (a social media post or captioned photo on Instagram, for example) and the communications technology used for transmission in order to achieve maximum influence on an audience. This normally clandestine digital mixology of post-classical PR came into public view in 2018, when reports emerged of Cambridge Analytica's scope of online engagement work, which spanned producing political campaign films, setting corruption traps and social media profiling via Facebook. Lionel Barber (2018, p. 1) editor of the *Financial Times* and someone familiar with the receiving end of PR campaigns, tellingly classified Cambridge Analytica as "a political advertising PR operation." It is a perfect description of the firm – and also defines some important aspects of post-classical PR – yet is clearly at odds with the classical style as defined by Grunig and Hunt in the 1980s and successors and predecessors back to Bernays in the 1920s that has dominated PR scholarship for almost 100 years.

The increased specialisation and development of advanced industrial nations such as United States, Germany and the United Kingdom throughout the twentieth century led to services making up an increasing proportion of the economy, with business and professional services, including PR, also expanding throughout those years. As well as an increase in the number of PR people and activity, the recent modern era has been affected by the emergence of the so-called digital economy (Tapscott, 1995) in which audiences become communicators themselves using the directness of digital media platforms (Negroponte, 1995). For one populist communications strategist, the start point for understanding and engaging with audiences online was the field of video games. Like the social media that was to follow, online video game culture was a largely invisible channel that had highly engaged users, many of whom were young men enacting aggression in the games setting using the anonymous cover of the internet. Trump's election campaign strategist Steve Bannon was an investor in the online video games market from 2005 onwards, and here he learned how to engage and communicate with niche audiences, and harness the "troll army from 'World of Warcraft'" before moving his focus on online media to the right-wing news site, *Breitbart* (Snider, 2017).

From optimistic beginnings to a "cesspool" of misinformation

During the early years of mass-market internet adoption in the 1990s, there was widespread optimism about the potential benefits it could bring to civic society. Habermas was one of those initially interested in the potential of civic engagement through an online public sphere, and there was widespread expectation that the global internetworked technology infrastructure would enable dialogue across borders on global political challenges such as conflict, climate change and unequal distribution of property. More than 20 years after positive pronouncements by President Clinton and Vice President Gore of the United States on the potential for good of the internet at the start of mass-market internet adoption, in 2018 the

UK government published a Digital Charter that seemed to ignore much of the disruption and controversy of the intervening period. "The internet is a force for good" that "serves humanity, spreads ideas and enhances freedom and opportunity across the world" the report from the Department for Digital, Culture, Media and Sport (2018) intoned. This uncritical view of communications technology having deterministic power appeared somewhat dated, but reflected a ten-year-old ortho-doxy that had developed to complement mass-market internet adoption. While serving as US Secretary of State, Hilary Clinton remarked in 2010 that "inform-ation has never been so free" and that the internet offered an unrivalled power to people to share ideas. Beyond these observations by politicians, the revolution on communication technology seemed largely to pass by the way democratic govern-ments engaged with voters. In contrast, authoritarian governments viewed commu-nications technology not only as a medium to be controlled (as occurred in China with its blockages on some foreign content and Iran, which operates a national "halal internet") but also as a medium for controlling citizens by monitoring them online as well as distributing PR messages.

Yet rather than reflecting the open, global inter-connective nature of the inter-net's technical infrastructure, the layer of social media applications and platforms such as Facebook, Google and Twitter that sit on top of the core network have developed closed, proprietary digital empires that exploit user's private informa-tion through a system of surveillance capitalism (Zuboff, 2019). The affordances of social networks such as Facebook have generated a contrary trend that narrows tolerant discussion and taps into nationalistic tribal instincts. Social media's narrow-ing of information choices may well be an unintended effect of the way content management systems operate but the end result of exposure to what Steven Poole (2019) has called an "enormous cesspool" of misleading information can be dismal:

> People with an attention span of much longer than five minutes can easily get sucked by profit-maximising video-recommendation algorithms down the vortex of fake-news doom, ending up where an interest in conspiracy theories always ends up: anti-Semitism and Holocaust denial.

World Wide Web inventor, Tim Berners-Lee, had always envisioned that the medium could become a destructive force, but by 2018, he confessed that he was "devastated" by the negative effects that his creation was having, particularly through the effects of mass surveillance and fake news (Booker, 2018). Berners-Lee's state-ment of regret came after the media had exposed Cambridge Analytica's wrongful use of data gathered from Facebook accounts and other sources during the 2016 Brexit referendum on behalf of Leave.EU as well as on the Trump Presidential campaign. By 2018, in the view of the computer scientist and writer, Jaron Lan-ier, the dominant social media and search platforms such as Facebook and Google had become dangerous "behaviour manipulation empires" that should be resisted (Lanier, 2018). In an interview to promote his book, *Ten Arguments for Deleting Your Social Media Accounts Right Now*, Lanier made a compelling case that the pervasive surveillance and subtle manipulation of these platforms and the constant "weaponised advertising" they serve up are not only "unethical, cruel, dangerous and inhumane," but also "polarising society, destroying democratic debate, and turning us into assholes" (Thornhill, 2018). As social media has replaced, displaced or at least made less significant some traditional media such as newspapers, it has also had sinister effects on the way information on issues in society and politics are shared. In considering how social media can act as a distribution channel for extreme views, David Omand, the former head of the UK's signals intelligence service, Government Communications Head Quarters (GCHQ), has claimed that social media platforms are having harmful deterministic effects that go beyond any claim that they merely act as neutral conduits:

> Twitter and Facebook have a darker side. I have seen them encourage the growth of radical voices, most worryingly on the far right, where alt-right and other extremist tendencies have in recent years gained ground. These forces are now becoming so powerful they now threaten the foundations of Western democracy.
>
> –Omand (2018, p. 11)

Omand's point is that social media channels enhance the capability of hostile actors within or outside a nation to take advantage of the vulnerabilities of modern, relatively open democratic states in order to manipulate public opinion. They do so by taking advantage of the characteristics and technical affordances of the social media platforms directly affects the way policy positions and ideas are advocated in the public sphere. The short format of Twitter, with its limit of 140 characters in posts initially and later expanded to 280, seems to encourage snappy but increasingly extreme opinions, as the climate of discourse on a topic grows more divisive with each iterative round of posts by users. Such online anonymity is having harmful effects on democracies, according to David Omand (2018):

> Anonymity lends the online world an especially nasty flavour. It encourages a crudeness that would not be tolerated face to face. [...] These characteristics have left us vulnerable to demagogues and extremists: social media enhances the subversive agendas of states like Russia.

Russia has certainly been a prolific user of social media as a distribution channel for digital propaganda and PR material in support of its foreign policy goals. During and after the 2014 invasion of Ukraine by Russian and Russian-sponsored forces, a former aide to the Ukrainian President Petro Poroshenko claimed that it felt like the entire country was being hacked as Russian social media content was distributed across the country using Facebook and other channels. Actors were hired to make films alleging cruelty by Ukrainian soldiers, for example, in a sustained campaign of disinformation that was deliberately provocative. Facebook was weaponised by the Russians, according to Dmytro Shymkiv, who confronted the technology group about the "aggressive behaviour" of the Russians as they waged an "information propaganda war" on the platform. When Shymkiv explained the extent of fake news being generated and distributed on Facebook channels to senior Facebook executives, they were apparently more focussed on emphasising their commitment to democracy and to free speech than taking action to control the spread of disinformation: "Their response was: 'We are an open platform. We allow everybody the possibility to communicate.' That's all I got" (Kuchler and Olearchyk, 2017).

Facebook: social network or people-centric propaganda engine?

According to Martin Moore (2018, p. 256), Vote Leave was the first political campaign in the United Kingdom to put "almost all" of its spend into digital communication, which was then controlled not by political PR or campaign specialists but by people "whose normal work was subjects like quantum information." The resulting campaign exploited the blurred boundaries between advertising, news and features content on social media platforms. In the case of Facebook, the blurred lines were no accident but a deliberate decision by the company's leadership to be vague about the source and category of content in order to maximise advertising revenues and justify its high stock market valuation. Advertising is increasingly an online activity, with over 50% of advertisements now displayed online and 67.3% of those displayed on mobile devices (Enberg, 2019). So Facebook has an economic incentive to offer users advertisements for which they are paid alongside images, videos and stories that are relevant and have the capacity to grab attention, in order to fulfil its commercial goal of growing its audience and the amount of time they spend on the site. The result has been that under the guise of offering compelling content Facebook transformed itself from social network into "a people-centric propaganda engine," (Moore, 2018, p. 158).

Because of the level of personal data shared by Facebook members with the site (often while thinking they are sharing just with their online friends), the company was able to build personal profiles that could be segmented for use by advertisers. The profiles were the outcome of a micro-targeting exercise based on the information on an individual's affinities, attitudes, life stage, relationship status, purchasing record that Facebook made available to the third-party advertisers and data analysis firms that was normally harvested unknown to the user. Around the same time, Google responded to Facebook's entry into the personalised campaigning sector with a change to the terms and conditions of its privacy policy. The change to terms enabled the search engine company to extract personal data from the varied accounts that individual users may have for applications owned by Google – GoogleMail, YouTube and so on – and aggregate these into a single data picture of an individual from these sources. The result was a set of saleable data analysis tools and audience targeting services, including Google Customer Match. This service enables organisations to use "information customers have already shared with you" (possibly without their knowledge or active consent through cookies or other forms of online tracking) along with "online and offline data to reach and re-engage with your customers across Search, YouTube and Gmail" (Google, 2019) while at the same time targeting "customers like them," that is individuals whose online data profiles match the profile of existing customers, voters and so on. In the 2016 US Presidential election campaign, both Facebook and Google made these types of tools available to political campaigners in an approach that maintained a level of neutrality on messages and means of transmission that was more associated with utility operators than media operators. In this digital media propaganda system, campaign managers and PR planners were granted access to an audience along with the capability to control how campaign messages could be segmented and micro-targeted based on life stage, relationship status, likely political affinities and issues of concern. Kreiss and McGregor (2018, p. 160) reported how platform companies including Facebook, Google, Microsoft and Twitter were promoting campaign data services such as a virtual Oval Office where influencers could post Instagram images at the US Democratic Party Convention, while in the same election, experts were loaned to assist Trump's Presidential run for the Republican Party. As Trump's campaign progressed throughout 2016, one Facebook secondee was named "most valuable player (MVP)" in the campaign team according to a Buzzfeed report (Warzel, 2016).

Based on years of experience in the online advertising (or AdTech) business, Facebook, Google and other platform operators had enabled and witnessed the power of invented news or other forms of "compelling content" to generate digital footfall and enable advertising revenues as a result. The algorithms that drove the content management served up by these platforms and the way humans engaged with the material that was served up meant that the most incendiary, divisive and hyper-partisan types of material proved the most effective in gaining attention as well as the cheapest to post because of the way the financial model of online advertising worked. Indeed, the automated digital payment system supporting this media logic led to widespread fraud in online advertising, as the platforms offered economic incentives to generate click-throughs and page impressions of advertisements and articles by users as an end in itself. This had already led to sites inventing news and posting news-type stories in order to create income from the advertising networks running on Facebook and Google. This unique micro-targeting capability was the basis for a suite of services offered by social media platform companies including Facebook and Goole who touted their offerings as "the best way for political propagandists to reach just the right people with just the right message at just the right time" or "micomoment" (Moore, 2018, p. 163).

This exploitation of so-called "big data" at the individual level pre-dated the emergence of social media platforms, or indeed mass-market internet adoption. John Mashey, chief scientist at Silicon Graphics and previously a systems designer at MIPS Computer Systems, coined the phrase big data and promoted the term in the early 1990s from a computer science perspective. Around the same time, the marketing business was becoming more alert to the prospects of what Don Peppers and Martha Rogers described in the title of their 1993 book as *The One to One Future* of "building relationships one customer at a time." The opportunities of personalised marketing and communication based on databases of customer information were also advocated by the advertising and direct marketing agency heads, Stan Rapp and Tom Collins, in a series of books published around this time including *Maximarketing* (1987) and *The Great Marketing Turnaround* (1990). The high costs of computer processing and storage meant that acquiring, storing and manipulating consumer data only made sense for high-value repeat purchases. So some of the early programmes based on consumer data were airline loyalty schemes targeting high-value business travellers, including the American Airlines AAdvantage scheme based on the Sabre reservations system launched in 1981.

Throughout the 1990s, engineering advances led to cheap computer power, particularly the advances in data storage enabled by specialist companies such as Boston-based EMC, which saw widespread adoption of its Symmetrix storage systems making it one of the fastest growing companies in US business history. Combined with cheaper and faster processing power, low data storage and manipulation costs enabled the emergence of specialist consumer information companies such as Caci, CMT, ICD, NDL and others, that collected data from door to door surveys, return of paper guarantees for electrical goods and discount coupons in order to create what they called lifestyle data, that could then be used in marketing campaigns. A Caci employee, Clive Humby, left the firm to set up Dunn Humby with his wife and together, they created the Tesco Clubcard. The project went live in 1974 and had ten million active memberships by 2000, attracted by its proposition of discount vouchers in return for brand loyalty. The success of the scheme's trial in three stores led Tesco Chairman Lord MacLaurin to comment: "What scares me about this, is that you know more about my customers in three months than I know in 30 years" (Mesure, 2003). His observation reflected the depth of consumer data gathered from transaction which could then be mapped onto lifestyle, life stage and residential data in order to predict demand and customise offers in order to increase spend at Tesco. For example, if the data from ClubCard showed that a City worker was buying expensive ready meals in the City store, lived in an affluent suburb but was never buying wine, Tesco was able to target that individual with special high end wine offers with home delivery.

Likes, content and the flywheel of social media engagement

One of the most powerful innovations in the field of optimisation was the innocuous-looking thumbs-up "like" button that Facebook implemented in 2009. As users adopted the new function and "liked" different pages, people and companies, they created a network of connected data points that could be tracked over time and analysed by Facebook in order to serve relevant advertisements and messages, that would in turn enhance engagement. The like button became a driver of what one Facebook employee called a flywheel of engagement that enabled the platform to guess what type of content and messages users would like to see most and then served it up. As Facebook looked towards its 2012 Initial Public Offering (IPO), it needed to demonstrate the future potential of a sustained revenue stream from the distribution of paid content such as advertising. In turn, the capability to deliver a targeted audience depended on the levels of engagement, which became a key metric at Facebook. This goal was pursued by serving up content that the engagement algorithms had computed users would most want to see and find enjoyable. Ahead of the 2012 IPO, while CEO Mark Zuckerberg and other executives were still spreading the mantra that Facebook was focussed on creating a "more open and connected world," the social network company started to establish commercial relationships with lifestyle information companies and consumer data brokers who could offer a view on Facebook users' life stage, spending habits, political orientation and multiple other behavioural and lifestyle details. This new profile data was overlaid on the existing Facebook dataset of each user, taking exploitation of Facebook's most valuable asset of user data to new levels of sophistication in targeting, creating a powerful system for personalised message creation and delivery. As the Austrian digital privacy activist Max Schrems has pointed out, the reality for users is that Facebook is "always looking" and knows what you are doing at what place and at what time (PBS America, 2019), in the manner of the TV-like apparatus in George Orwell's novel, 1984, that was always watching the activity in the room occupied by the book's central character, Winston Smith, and able to communicate individually at any time, while at the same time pushing out continuous propaganda.

The most powerful marketing tool an extremist could hope for

This prioritisation of engagement through the distribution of affinity material that Facebook judged users will like may appear harmless if the content is fashion stories or celebrity gossip, but during times of political upheaval, the effects can be more serious. Before the 2014 example of the use of social media by Russia in its invasion of Ukraine already referred to earlier in this chapter, governments throughout the Middle East expressed concerns to Facebook about the speed at which rumours and disinformation were spreading on social networks throughout the so-called Arab Spring of 2010 and 2011 in ways that undermined political stability. Bob Igler, the Walt Disney CEO has been similarly critical of the corrosive effects on the social fabric of social media platforms in the United States, claiming that they are consuming public discourse and shaping the country in ways that are contrary to the principles of civility, human rights and basic decency:

> It's the most powerful marketing tool an extremist could ever hope for because by design social media reflects a narrow world view filtering out anything that challenges our beliefs while constantly validating our convictions and amplifying our deepest fears. Hate and anger are dragging us toward the abyss once again [...] Hitler would have loved social media.
>
> –Sharma (2019)

In their study of the online political campaigning of the Israeli-based Psy-Group, Adam Entous and Ronan Farrow (2019) cited Uzi Shaya, a former senior Israeli intelligence officer, who summed up the attractions of social media platforms for influence campaigns:

> Social media allows you to reach virtually anyone and to play with their minds. You can do whatever you want. You can be whoever you want. It is a place where wars are fought, elections are won and terror is promoted. There are no regulations. It is a no man's land.

The same article gave details of the scope of a 2016 campaign that Psy-Group ran in order to keep a board member, Parmod Kumar, in post at the Tulare Regional Medical Centre in California for commercial reasons. The plan was for Psy-Goup staff to assume fake identities online in order to "uncover and deliver actionable intelligence" on opponents and then proactively use non-attributable web sites that appeared to be part of a grass roots movement to spread negative material about the opposition candidate.

According to Charlie Beckett of the London School of Economics' Truth, Trust and Technology Commission, social media technology has played a role in luring in audiences "with kittens and news of our friends' children" before going on to deliver creepy personalised advertising (2018). Concerns over the placement of advertising alongside extreme and inappropriate content led to some advertisers withdrawing from YouTube in 2017, only to return on the back of promises by the platform to take down extreme material more swiftly and deploy new algorithms to assist in monitoring content. However, by April 2019, Procter and Gamble chief brand officer, Marc Pritchard was voicing doubts, stating that there was still no "brand safety" for corporates on social media platforms. *PR Week's* (2019) report of his speech highlighted his call for "a digital ecosystem that prioritizes quality, civility, transparency, privacy and control" and that Procter and Gamble would only engage with platforms that "promote civility."

Computation, emotion and attention

In an article entitled "The age of the hoax," the author Laurence Scott (2019) argued that "people have always told extravagant stories about their lives – but in the digital world, the possibilities for self-invention have become almost limitless," going on to ask readers the question "So are we all scammers now?" The article describes in depth the way US novelist Dan Mallory created a promotional public image on social media, which seemed to be crafted to generate "intense emotional responses from his audience" through social media posts that included sharing of "macabre declarations about his ill-health and the invented deaths of family members" along-side more the mundane "self-puffery of false qualifications and professional achieve-ments." For social media influencers, who inhabit a promotional realm somewhere between reality and fantasy, Scott argued that a contemporary "obsession with grabbing others' attention is proving increasingly lethal" as competitive pressures in the "online economy of vloggers and influencers" get more intense, leading to a situation in which "the search for online acclaim has real world perils." Over 2017 and 2018, examples of these perils included three stars of a YouTube extreme travel show dying after a waterfall plunge and a US video blogger accidentally killing her boyfriend with a gun while making a video.

PR, advertising and marketing firms are often at the forefront of analysing and working within the fierce competition for attention in the online economy. Since it was launched on Facebook in 2017 – and subsequently rolled out on Instagram and Snapchat – the "Stories" function that allows a series of photos and/or videos to be uploaded on the platform by users has not only grown in popularity, it has also become seen by digital PR and marketing professionals as the ideal format of online promotion. According to author Laurence Scott (2019), the aim of much online campaigning is "to make storytelling a dominant aspect of our lives as consumer citizens" since stories not only build our social prestige and involvement, they also stay in the mind. Scott goes on to quote neuroscientist, Paul Zak, whose work has considered how neurology can be integrated into the digital economy, concluding from his work on the physiological effects of storytelling that "stories that are personal and emotionally compelling engage more of the brain and are thus better remembered than simply stating a set of facts." Scott concludes by asking whether the power and "commercial centrality" of the story in online promotion encourages all of us – but especially digital communications professionals, perhaps – to blur the lines between fact and fiction in order to offer a meaningful narrative to audiences.

Wikipedia and online public relations

The move to digital media has posed challenges to the traditional media relations practices of classical PR. In particular, while plurality of provision has emerged in online media as predicted by Negroponte (1995), there has been a concentration of consumption into relatively few titles, leaving many more with small readerships. This skewed or heavy-tailed audience distribution has made Wikipedia increasingly important as users spend more time on the site, which is one of their favoured and most-frequently visited resources for facts. By 2014, online metrics provider Alexa (2014) rated Wikipedia as the sixth most popular site on the World Wide Web and the highest ranking fact-based content site. This concentration effect has intensified because of the way Wikipedia's scale of content – along with levels of usage and links to and from the site – fits the algorithms of Google search criteria so well. This means that any Google search on a topic will often display Wikipedia at the top of the suggested pages. So rather than diversity and plurality in online media, the top-ranked search engine Google recommends the top-rated information site, Wikipedia. In effect, this turns the web into a feedback loop between the two and in this digital duopoly, "the amateur-written encyclopaedia has become the world's all-purpose information source. It's our new Delphic oracle" (Carr, 2007).

The new digital Delphic oracle of Wikipedia, with content generated and managed by a polycentric structure of multiple volunteer editors, has presented difficulties for some PR practitioners who have struggled to adapt to – or even adequately understand – such a fluid and dispersed institutional structure. Lord Bell, for example, described Wikipedia as "a ridiculous organisation ... created by a bunch of nerds" (Cave and Rowell, 2014, p. 95). The fact that Wikipedia is free to use, is not copyrighted and is produced by a loose group rather than named individuals marks it out from traditional media. O'Sullivan (2009, p. 1) has described Wikipedia as a community of practice which is "alien to our cultural traditions in several ways." The organisation's volunteering and community nature differs from the individualism of society in general and the commercialism of traditional media in particular. These points of difference (summarised in the following table) are

Table 8.1 Old media and Wikipedia: points of institutional difference

	Old Media	Wikipedia
Ownership	Clearly defined Either corporate (e.g., GE) or proprietorial (e.g., Rupert Murdoch, Richard Desmond, Barclay Brothers)	Less clear/Not for profit Web site is owned by the not-for-profit Wikipedia Foundation. Content is owned by the original authors but published under a Creative Commons licence
Management structure	Clearly defined Highly visible owner, hierarchical management structure with editor	Peer-based structure Loose affiliations of volunteers who remain anonymous. Governance by not-for-profit Wikipedia Foundation.
Content production system	Named professionals Named journalists generate content for sections of paper or programme with editors co-ordinating content creation	Anonymous groupings Anonymous, amateur and part-time volunteer Wikipedia editors write material with no (or minimal) co-ordination
Interaction with PR and corporate interests	Not transparent or visible Negotiations, interactions and information exchanges are not seen by readers	Transparent and visible Interactions are recorded in the Wikipedia editing system and can be tracked back to the previous version
Opportunity for revisions	Limited Corrections can be made but the article is set once published. Corrections are made reluctantly and given little prominence	Extensive The ongoing content creation system and additions is at the heart of Wikipedia which means revisions occur continually. Online corrections can be made easily
Economic model	Paid – protected content Either paid subscription or purchase for paper version or online pay per view – plus advertising revenue in both cases. Copyright protected.	Free Wikipedia is non-proprietary and free at point of use. The content is not copyright protected and can be shared freely under the Creative Commons Deed. Relies on donations.
Role of readers	Passive Limited opportunities for action or interaction in print and online. While comments are welcome, content creation opportunities are rare.	Active/opportunities for action Readers can create and amend articles in Wikipedia and are encouraged to do so as long as they comply with the Terms of Use.

having profound impact on the nature of PR interactions with Wikipedia and other common pool media.

After being caught out altering Wikipedia pages on behalf of clients using multiple fake identities in 2012, Lord Bell invited the Wikipedia founder Jimmy Wales to address fifty of his London staff. In an earlier response to the incident, Bell Pottinger insisted that it had "never done anything illegal," (Bradshaw and Pickard, 2011). According to one account of the 2012 meeting, Mr Wales alleged that Bell Pottinger had a "history of wrongdoing" on Wikipedia, including concealing changes to pages in the required descriptions of edits (Bradshaw, 2012), while in response, Lord Bell was unapologetic about the content changes that had been made, maintaining that "we have done absolutely nothing wrong whatsoever," which attracted particular criticism from Jimmy Wales, in which he emphasised the ethical and normative aspects that apply to Wikipedia, as well as the commercial downside to the agency as a result of its clandestine editing work:

> I am astonished at the ethical blindness of Bell Pottinger's reaction. That their strongest true response is that they didn't break the law tells a lot about their view of the world, I'm afraid. The company committed the cardinal sin of a PR and lobbying company of having their own bad behaviour bring bad headlines to their clients and did so in a fashion that brought no corresponding results.
>
> —Burrell (2014)

Despite these warnings from Wikipedia, it seems that as the number of entries has grown along with online viewers on the demand side, so has the importance of Wikipedia in reputation management firms such as Bell Pottinger. Bell Pottinger was one of a clique of PR firms that combined to make London what *The Guardian* in 2010 called the "world capital of reputation laundering" (Booth, 2010). The resulting commercial pressures have been described by James Thomlinson, head of digital at Bell Pottinger, as "the pressure put on us by clients to remove potentially defamatory or libellous statements very quickly, because Wikipedia is so authoritative" (Bradshaw, 2012). In reacting to the two episodes, chair of the UK's Public Relations and Communications Association (PRCA), Francis Ingham did not urge members to abide by the Wikipedia terms of use and engage with the good faith culture. Instead, he stated that "while we would not condone PR professionals anonymously amending Wikipedia entries, we understand why frustration sometimes drives them to do so" (Cartmell, 2012). Ingham also claimed that the site's internal process for amending inaccurate or inflammatory material was "opaque" when in fact every revision is displayed online and is fully transparent.

From press officers to content producers: the new digital work of engagement

In July 2019, David Beckham launched a content production and media company, Studio 99, in which the retired footballer took an executive role alongside his long-time adviser Dave Gardner and Nicola Howson as managing director. Nicola Howson is ex-CEO of the London-based PR agency Freuds – where she founded the corporate division – before moving to the corporate PR firm Portland. Howson began working for the Beckham organisation in May 2019, leading a team with an eclectic but revealing mix of skills for the modern PR repertoire. An ex-visual director from Stella McCartney was hired as creative director for photo and video shoots and product creation, while Lewis Hamilton's ex-head of social and digital media was hired to manage Beckham's own online media and digital partnerships (Delahunty, 2019).

The intention is that the new Studio 99 venture will produce and manage all content creation and social media distribution for Beckham's 57 million followers on Instagram and 52 million on Facebook. In addition, the newly formed Studio 99 "content studio" will develop documentaries, TV shows and other formats as a commercial agency for the third-party clients, executing campaigns across traditional, digital and social-media channels, according to an exclusive report in the entertainment newspaper *Variety*, which described the aim of the project as Beckham "making a run at Hollywood" and quoted his goals for the new media venture:

> I have always enjoyed creating content of all kinds and working on set with creative people. It's amazing to see what guys that I admire so much, like LeBron and Maverick, have achieved. It's inspired me to see what's possible in my world. It's just very cool to be working with friends and meeting so many new people who are doing great things and want create exciting new projects with us.
>
> –Spangler (2019)

The transmutation of David Beckham's media operation from an extravagantly configured press office for a retired footballer to a digital "content studio" is an interesting moment for celebrity PR. It is another staging post that sees celebrities who used to be the focus of media attention and who would contribute to media in the form of words and pictures from their PR teams, move on to become producers of their own media content and even proprietors of their own media studios in the case of Beckham's project, with that content being orchestrated by PR professionals. This extension of the scope of the PR and media generation operation reflects the success of David and Victoria Beckham in rising above their previous country-specific careers as UK footballer and singer – and the associated media presence in terms of local coverage – to a global "brand Beckham." Maverick Carter, CEO of LeBron James' media venture Uninterrupted, made this point when commenting in the *Variety* article on plans for working with Beckham's Studio 99: "David Beckham typifies the 'More Than an Athlete' mentality" — referring to an Uninterrupted series centred on James produced for ESPN Plus — "and we're excited to be partnering with him and Studio 99 on this new development deal and documentary." Today, the Beckhams' online promotional presence through social media – with a combined Instagram following of nearly 85 million – transcends their original achievements in sport and music, and most of their portfolios of commercial and promotional projects are detached from those fields. For example, Victoria Beckham's main venture is her own fashion brand which is quite unconnected to her original achievements in music with The Spice Girls.

In the case of David Beckham, Studio 99 marks a transformation from being the subject of media attention for achievement in one sector to media content producer for PR and promotional goals, for himself and for the third-party clients of the new agency. Kylie Jenner managed a similar change from a celebrity media subject to a self-contained and self-sustaining PR promotional presence but at a much faster rate accelerated rate, with the real acceleration to her becoming one of the most-followed people on Instagram (with around 130 million followers) and launching her cosmetics line occurring over less than five years from 2012 to 2017 (see case study in chapter 6 on Kylie Jenner for more detail).

Social media influencers

Audience preference for authenticity in communications means that messages with a less corporate feel that do not feel forced or contrived are favoured in social media channels. Marketing and PR people have taken advantage of this preference through the marketisation of digital influence and the third-party endorsement online. What used to be informal word of mouth commentary in the analogue world has been shaped into an industry in which PR people seek to capture value from social media influencers. This new category of digital influencers are third-party endorsers, who are able to combine sufficient following in terms of their presence and authority in a specific field with numbers of followers. A combination of authoritative presence plus followers means that individuals are judged as able to influence audience attitudes through their blogs, tweets or other types of posts on social media. A core attraction for marketing and PR people of such influencers is their perceived authenticity, with advocates of this channel arguing that social media influencers can present messages to audiences in a natural way, whether this is done overtly or covertly.

In 2018, the Competition and Markets Authority (CMA) announced it would be scrutinising the activity of social media influencers, following allegations that some had been blurring the boundary between spontaneous/unsolicited testimonials and commercially sponsored endorsements in their posts. The move by the CMA followed a 2017 demand by the US Federal Trade Commission for high-profile celebrities to confirm instances of when they had been paid to make online endorsements that had in fact appeared on their social media feeds – including Facebook, Instagram and twitter – as routine posts. The UK's CMA's solution was to introduce more transparency by insisting that paid endorsements be labelled as such using descriptive hashtags such as "#sponsored," alongside the posts. The regulator's moves were in response to the enormous growth in social media use and the power of existing celebrities and newly minted social media stars in the digital media ecosystem for their efficacy in harnessing audience attention. As a *Financial Times* report on the CMA move observed, while the third-party endorsement is a desirable and enduring benefit of PR work with organisations "eager to trade on the influencers' reach" and the temptation may for some not to declare a commercial relationship, marketing executives at some larger companies are sounding as concerned about the risks as the regulators:

> We need to take urgent action now and to rebuild trust before it is gone forever" said Keith Weed, Unilever's chief marketing officer, in June, announcing that the conglomerate would cease working with influencers who buy followers."
> *—Financial Times* (2018)

At the centre of the dilemma the regulators are seeking to resolve with influencer marketing is the lack of a clear boundary in digital media between the core media content and advertising that existed in the case of television and print media. Instead, in the case of social media, audiences are exposed to a growing sprawl of paid marketing messages – some of which are little more than advertisements – that attempt to offer intimacy with the celebrities or bloggers on social media while pushing products or a point of view. The sprawling pile of marketing messages is itself layered on the mass of social media content that is being produced by audiences and PR people, who are replacing journalists as generators of stories and other material online.

Case Study 8.1

Chinese government public relations on social media

Introduction

In October 2017, at the party's 19th congress President Xi Jinping urged delegates to "tell the China story well and build China's soft power," using social media. In speeches, President Xi repeatedly emphasised the communicative goal of "spreading positive energy" and so disseminate positive messages about Chinese society from the perspective of being a citizen. Beyond China and Chinese citizens, for the last ten years or more, the Communist party has increased its outreach using Western social media platforms to show upbeat videos about Chinese society, as well as funding private studios to post images, short films and memes in a public/private co-operative campaign of what Professor Wanning Sun, of University of Technology Sydney has termed "indoctritainment" (2002, p. 116). One of the most ambitious examples of this trend for promotion of Chinese political ideology and nationalism using cinema was the 2018 action film, *Operation Red Sea*, which portrayed a fictional protected evacuation of Chinese citizens from a Yemini port using a range of Navy assets of the of the People's Liberation Army (PLA) Navy, which co-operated with the director Dante Lam throughout its making. The film is notable as a piece of cinematic propaganda in China for the role it played in commemorating the 90th anniversary of the PLA and was also presented first to the 19th National Congress of the Communist Party of China in 2017. Besides its propaganda value, *Operation Red Sea* was also a commercial success, grossing $579 million (US), which made it the fourth highest earning film in China and top earning Chinese film in 2018.

From the early years of social media, China raised a volunteer troll army of real people, most of them young men, to go online and attack its enemies, paying patriotic supporters 50 cents for each positive social media posts, earning them the nickname of *Wumao* denoting the 0.50 Rembini, or 50 cents payment they received for each post (Yang, 2017). More recently, over the past two years, Beijing has set up initiatives to encourage the "good netizen" who spreads positive messages about China, such as the Communist Party youth league's "Volunteer Campaign to Civilise the Internet" initiative. The summary interviews that follow are intended to illustrate the effects of the Chinese firewall that blocks Western social media sites and also how local social media platforms, such as Weibo, are used by the government of China in its PR outreach. Four in-depth interviews were conducted in China in 2018 with social media promoter with the intention of better understanding the online activity of the Central Committee of the Communist Youth League and People's Daily on Weibo, that targets young people, with a particular investigative focus on the operating methods of the *Wumao* or paid social media posters. The extracts below are a summary from an interview conducted in China in 2018 with a 26-year-old male *Wumao*, or paid social media promoter, who undertakes promotional work writing posts in support of the government on the Sina Weibo social media platform.

The role of the Wumao

Wumao is a broad term that covers plenty of people. Some of them co-operate with the government and some others do not even know that the government controls some processes related to social media. Some people co-operate with each other and organise groups while others act on their own and use their own judgement, So *Wumao* are diverse. Yes, I am one of them but I won't tell you more. *Wumao* are good people who protect their state. However, I cannot share information about them. I hope you'll understand me.

The *Ziguangge* are a great representative of the party and the government. (*Ziguangge* is an online community linked to a magazine of the same name run by the Central Committee of the Communist Youth League, which is the most active media account of the Communist Party on Weibo) They are especially good with the youth due to their innovative approaches to generating content. I think that CYL is very smart in microblogging. They communicate propaganda messages, you know, indirectly. Most people cannot say they had a propaganda post since it is hidden.

—Wumao/social media promoter (aged 26)

The public relations messages promoted by the Chinese government on social media

I think that our government promotes simple ideas. Unity. Understanding. World peace. Sometimes it puts things in ultra-patriotic light, but this is just to promote the idea that our state is stable and effective. Well, look at the recent statistics about GDP and all. We will outrun the USA soon and the government tries to make sure that all Chinese see this success.

We have achieved impressive success in politics, economy and social life. Our GDP is skyrocketing and we are on a short track to become the largest economy in the world. Of course, Western countries don't like it and try to stop us. They cannot use military mechanisms, but they try to take advantage of information warfare. They've defeated the Soviet Union this way and they wouldn't mind to use the same mechanism to defeat us. At the same time, we are no longer on the defensive. Our internet will become the weapon in the future. Plenty of people in the world cooperate with our companies, and they use Weibo ad WeChat in this process. Eventually, we will make numerous people use our networks and it will be the instrument of our influence in the Western states.

—Wumao/social media promoter (aged 26)

Methods used by Chinese government in digital propaganda and network control

As you know, we have the firewall that blocks access to many Western websites. People here do not access Facebook, Twitter or Instagram. However, we have our own networks that are far better that those Western sites. The government has a set of network offices that monitors the activity of different users. The system is linked to some keywords. The minute a user writes some restricted keywords, the system detects him and sends his information to thee offices. Specialists there see the situation and make a decision either to ignore it in case there is nothing bad in their user's opinion or close his account. They also use background monitoring to make informed decisions.

Many people think the system exists to spread propaganda, but it actually helps citizens. Look at the Western websites. There is plenty of bad content there. Popular networks sometimes overlook porn videos, which makes the youth exposed to serious risks. You've probably heard about all these scandals on Facebook with the theft of personal data and information attacks. I don't want our people to be exposed to such content. That is why I think the government does the right thing in blocking access to Western websites.

The restrictions serve the national interests of the state. It is a matter of national security. We protect our sovereignty. To a certain extent, these restrictions isolate China from the rest of the world, but these measures are justified.

—*Wumao*/social media promoter (aged 26)

References

Alexa (2014) The top 500 sites on the web. *Alexa*, 2014. Available at: http://www.alexa.com/topsites

Barber, L. (2018) Bannon and the big question. *Financial Times* (*Life and Arts*), 31 March, p. 1.

Becket, C. (2018) What do you mean by trust? *Influence*, 16 October. CIPR, London. Available at: https://influenceonline.co.uk/2018/10/16/what-do-you-mean-by-trust/

Booker, K. (2018) 'I was devastated': The man who invested the World Wide Web has some regrets. *Vanity Fair*, August 2018, pp. 51–56.

Booth, R. (2010) PR firms make London world capital of reputation laundering. *The Guardian*, 3 August. Available at: https://www.theguardian.com/media/2010/aug/03/london-public-relations-reputation-laundering

Bradshaw, T. (2012) Wikipedia in clash over editing rights. *Financial Times*, 13 January. Available at: http://www.ft.com

Bradshaw, T. and Pickard, J. (2011) Wikipedia probes edits by Bell Pottinger. *Financial Times*, 7 December. Available at: http://www.ft.com

Burrell, I. (2014) International PR firms sign agreement to stop abusing Wikipedia. *The Independent*, 14 June. Available at: http://www.independent.co.uk

Carr, N. (2007) The net is being carved up into information plantations. *The Guardian*, 17 May. Available at: http://www.theguardian.com/technology/2007/may/17/media.newmedia

Cartmell, M. (2012) PR industry blames 'cumbersome' Wikipedia for Finsbury editing issue. *PR Week*, 12 November. Available at: http://www.prweek.com

Cave, T. and Rowell, A. (2014) *A Quiet Word: Lobbying, Crony Capitalism and Broken Politics in Britain*. London: Bodley Head.

Delahunty, S. (2019) Former Freuds CEO named in David Beckham's new brand, PR and commercial team. *PR Week*, 14 May. Available at: https://www.prweek.com/article/1584604/former-freuds-ceo-named-david-beckhams-new-brand-pr-commercial-team

Department for Digital, Culture, Media and Sport (2018) *Digital Charter: A response to the opportunities and challenges arising from new technologies*, 25 January. London: UK Government. Available at: https://www.gov.uk/government/publications/digital-charter

Enberg, J. (2019) Digital ad spending 2019. *Emarketer.com*, 28 March. Available at: https://www.emarketer.com/content/global-digital-ad-spending-2019

Entous, A. and Farrow, R. (2019) Deception Inc. *The New Yorker*, 18–25 February, pp. 44–55.

Financial Times (2018) Web influencers should be open about incentives, 18 August, p. 6.

Google (2019) About customer match. Available at: https://support.google.com/google-ads/answer/6379332?hl=en-GB

Kreiss, D. and McGregor, S. (2018) Technology firms shape political communication: the work of Microsoft, Facebook, Twitter and Google with campaigns during the 2016 presidential cycle. *Political Communication*, 35 (2), 155–177.

Kuchler, H. and Olearchyk, R. (2017) Ukraine says it warned Facebook of Russia fake news in 2015. *Financial Times*, 31 October. Available at: https://www.ft.com/content/c63d76d4-bd1e-11e7-b8a3-38a6e068f464

Lanier, J. (2018) *Ten Arguments for Deleting Your Social Media Accounts Right Now*. New York: Henry Holt and Co.

Mesure, S. (2003) Loyalty card costs Tesco £1bn of profits – but is worth every penny. *The Independent*, 10 October. Available at: https://www.independent.co.uk/news/business/analysis-and-features/loyalty-card-costs-tesco-1bn-of-profits-but-is-worth-every-penny-90728.html

Moore, M. (2018) *Democracy Hacked: Political Turmoil and Information Warfare in the Digital Age*. London: OneWorld

Negroponte, N. (1995) *Being Digital*. New York, New York: Alfred Knopf/Doubleday

Omand, D. (2018) Agents of our own destruction. *Prospect*, July 2018, p. 11.

O'Sullivan, D. (2009) *Wikipedia: A New Community of Practice?* Farnham: Ashgate Publishing.

PBS America, (2018) *The Facebook Dilemma*. 12 June. Available at: https://www.pbs.org/wgbh/frontline/film/facebook-dilemma/

Poole, S. (2019) Mastering misdirection. *New Statesman*, 5–11 April, pp. 44–45.

PR Week (2019) Read Marc Pritchard's landmark speech on creating a 'new media supply chain'. *PR Week*, 12 April. Available at: https://www.prweek.com/article/1582002/read-marc-pritchards-landmark-speech-creating-new-media-supply-chain

Rapp, S. and Collins, T.L. (1987). *MaxiMarketing: The New Direction in Advertising, Promotion, and Marketing Strategy*. New York: McGraw-Hill.

Rapp, S. and Collins, T.L. (1990) *The Great Marketing Turnaround: The Age of the Individual, and How to Profit from It*. Englewood Cliffs, New Jersey: Prentice Hall.

Scott, L. (2019) The age of the hoax. *Financial Times*, (*Life and Arts*), 16/17 February 2019, pp. 1–2.

Sharma, V. (2019) Disney CEO Iger takes a dig at social media, says Hitler would have loved it. *Variety Reuters*, 11 April. Available at: https://uk.reuters.com/article/us-disney-bob-iger/disney-ceo-iger-takes-a-dig-at-social-media-says-hitler-would-have-loved-it-variety-idUKKCN1RN2IQ

Snider, M. (2017) Steve Bannon learned to harness troll army from 'World of Warcraft'. *USA Today*, 18 July. Available at: https://eu.usatoday.com/story/tech/talkingtech/2017/07/18/steve-bannon-learned-harness-troll-army-world-warcraft/489713001/

Spangler, T. (2019) David Beckham launches media company Studio 99. *Variety*, 10 July. Available at: https://variety.com/2019/biz/news/david-beckham-studio-99-media-venture-1203263110/

Sun, W.S. (2002) Semiotic over-determination or 'indoctritainment': television, citizenship, and the Olympic Games. In: Donald, S.H., Hong, Y. and Keane, M. (Eds.) *Media in China: Consumption, Content and Crisis.* London: Routledge.

Tapscott, D. (1995) *The Digital Economy: Promise and Peril in the Age of Networked Intelligence.* New York: McGraw Hill.

Thornhill, J. (2018) Lunch with the FT: Jaron Lanier. *Financial Times (Life and Arts Section)*, 7/8 July 2018, p. 3.

Warzel, C. (2016) Trump fundraiser: Facebook employee was our "MVP". *Buzzfeed*, 12 November.

Yang, Y. (2017) China's Communist party raises army of nationalist trolls. *Financial Times*, 30 December. Available at: https://www.ft.com/content/9ef9f592-e2bd-11e7-97e2-916d4fbac0da

Zuboff, S. (2019) *The Age of Surveillance Capitalism: The Fight for a Human Future at the New Frontier of Power.* London: Profile Books.

Conclusion

At the outset of this book, I set out three questions I would seek to address: How do we make sense of the post-truth style of public relations (PR), what is its scope and how is it practised? The notes that follow are intended to draw a close by summarising some answers to these three questions, drawing upon the discussion and examples from the preceding chapters.

Making sense of post–classical public relations

The central proposition of this book is that a post-classical style of PR has emerged in the last ten years in response to the post-truth condition in society. It is a variant of the classical PR that we can now look back upon over the past 100 years or so and has taken advantage of the post-truth environment in order to optimise delivery of messages to audiences. As already explained here in Chapter 6, post-truth is a social condition caused by many factors, but as preceding pages have made clear, some aspects of PR undertaken on behalf of clients who demand a win at all costs approach have contributed to fragility of the idea of a common truth in an already divided and high temperature public sphere. So the post-classical style of PR is both an evolutionary response to the post-truth condition in society and also a contributor to that condition through almost 100 years of inserting unreliable or false information into the public sphere through the creation of stunts (dating back to Bernays fabrication of the torches of freedom protest on the 1929 Easter Parade in New York), inventing news stories and spinning the truth for commercial advantage. More recently, the effect of PR interventions in the digital sphere of public information has been to increase rather than dampen down epistemic volatility. The growth of social media platforms and demise of mass media channels over the past 20 years has resulted in any sense of shared truths based on universally agreed facts fading, leading to the loss of a common set of truths or facts as the basis for debate. The drive to win at all costs in a crowded and competitive PR marketplace, the opportunities for digital deception offered by online media and the decreasing costs of getting caught out lying in the public sphere mean that some post-classical PR work has created further uncertainty about the reliability of sources and facts, thus adding to the post-truth condition in society rather than resolving its challenges through enabling balanced debate and factual contributions.

In attempting to understand this post-classical style of PR, I have referred to the Sophists in Ancient Greece for historical perspective and also to inform the analysis of contemporary communicative work that practitioners working in the field do or say they do. A consideration of these two historical extremes, along with many examples of communicative labour in the years in between, suggests that most PR workers function as communicative intermediaries, who act as specialist agents on behalf of a principal client organisation or individual they represent in this agency role. From the days of the Sophists through to the PR firms of modern times, the very nature of this agency role means that all such intermediaries have practised at least some degree of communicative artifice. PR people create communications materials, and then operate as representatives of a third party on whose behalf they are deployed, and so some degree of inauthenticity has always been present in PR work. This intermediary process is not always transparent to audiences. Indeed, this lack of visibility has enabled clandestine practices being used at high volume by PR firms in their orchestration of astroturfing campaigns that have included the creation of multiple front groups by the firms themselves.

As audiences became more aware of PR processes and tired of the inauthentic style of communication that classical PR delivers, they also became resistant to what they perceived as manufactured modes of engagement and persuasion. While post-classical PR includes aspects of communicative artifice, some adopters such as President Trump in the United States and Beppe Grillo in Italy have been successful at delivering what appears on the surface at least to be a more authentic style of public communication. Trump's words are accompanied by the vulgar pomp of his public performances in interviews and at campaign rallies, using a style that was honed to high-impact perfection after years appearing on the ultimate artifice of modern media, reality television. Yet despite the digital confection behind the promotional presence of several public figures discussed, including Donald Trump, Beppe Grillo and Kylie Jenner, all the examples cited have generated a sizeable audience online and are seen by that audience as representing an authentic tone of voice. The paucity of individuals with a million or more followers suggests that PR voices perceived as authentic by audiences are rare and that they command a premium in the online economy of attention.

The scope of modern communicative labour

The work that prominent PR firms such as Burson Marsteller, Hill and Knowlton and others undertook to create front groups and run astroturfing campaigns, as described in Chapter 3, is an uncomfortable truth for the PR sector, especially so as at the same time PR practitioners were using the cover of the construct of Corporate Social Responsibility (CSR) to justify their own civic contribution and that of their clients. The deceptive interventions in Wikipedia by UK PR agencies described in Chapter 8 is another example of the potential inauthenticity of PR in both the messages intended for insertion into public discourse and the methods used for content creation and distribution. Rather than making a positive contribution to society or showing social responsibility, the attempts at clandestine editing of Wikipedia were arguably a form of pollution of the media commons, which arose because of the economic incentives involved when acting for clients who demanded results. Similarly, the sophisticated integration and co-option of seemingly independent think tanks into PR campaigns, also described in Chapter 3, represents a similar degrading of the world of new policy ideas. The type of communicative labour in these examples is not undertaken for social gain or as part of two-way dialogue but solely to achieve a communicative advantage. As one of the interviewees in the case study on reputation management in Chapter 4 confirmed, powerful clients who are used to winning in business and politics hire PR specialists to reduce their risk of losing and increase their chances of winning in matters of influence and public opinion. As this set of interviews established, post-classical PR has increased its communicative firepower by co-opting legal and investigative resources in order to try to make inconvenient facts go away for powerful clients, even if that means undermining the information introduced by claimants against them. The evidence of success and growth of this sector confirms that powerful clients are willing to meet the high costs of this variant of post-classical PR, in which lawyers and investigators are on the payroll alongside PR people in the mixed repertoire of modern reputation management.

In considering scope, the preceding chapters have made the case that modern post-classical PR combines performativity with a digital mixology of online engagement and persuasion, based upon the exploitation of user profile data from social media applications such as Facebook. The focus on the PR work of communicative intermediaries led to the inclusion here of two prominent firms in the field that failed in the two years before the date of writing, but whose mode of operating is still present in the industry. Although Bell Pottinger ceased trading in 2017 after its use of racialised online campaign messaging in its work for the Gupta family in South Africa was exposed, the firm had been one of the dominant PR operators in London for a decade or more, offering a global corporate and political clientele a form of geopolitical sophistry that helped in elections and on state-level reputation management. Similarly, the work of Cambridge Analytica up to its demise in 2018 was a form of transatlantic digital sophistry for political and corporate clients worldwide, with a particular focus on political and corporate PR work. The work of both firms seems to confirm that in the new digital game of disinformation, power and audiences that makes up this line of work, the first rule of ethical practice seems to be to "do what is needed to prevail but don't get caught." In modern China, the scope of communicative intermediary labour includes the work of the *Wumao*, who are a volunteer army paid by the government to post positive messages about the Communist Party and life in China on social media. The low fee of 50 cents per post is indicative of a global oversupply of PR labour, especially in developed economies. This means that it is getting rarer for PR people to be bold advisers who speak truth to power, rather clients are more likely to use power to overcome inconvenient truths and take only the advice they want to hear.

As a reviewer of this text pointed out, the period of classical PR proposed from around 1920 to 2010 coincides uncannily with the era of mass media and availability of news on limited spectrum broadcast media, supplemented by cinema newsreels until the arrival of mass market TV in the 1950s onwards and vibrant print journalism until after 2000. The comment was a useful reminder of the context of media technologies in which PR work takes place. BBC Radio started broadcasting news in 1920 and by 2010, smartphone market penetration rates and internet usage had changed the way news was consumed. The growth of social media simultaneously transformed the practice of PR away from the traditional media relations to content creation for the new digital media platforms. One result of these changes in media production and distribution is that large sections of the modern audience expect news to be an endlessly entertaining variant on show business. Simultaneously, partisanship in audiences is driving a political economy of divisive rhetoric that is designed specifically to suit a specific demographic or point of view, along with an accompanying bundle of fake news for each side of a debate. In the fake news supply chain, demand is driven by the confirmation bias of partisan publics who want to read, hear and watch material that is in harmony with what they believe, rather that yield to a centrist middle road of a truth as laid down by mainstream media. While emotionality, superstition and lack of rationality in audiences is a problem for traditional PR practice, it is also an opportunity to be exploited by a new generation of post-truth merchants in the media supply chain. As political consensus has been hollowed out by more extreme views on the right and left, the middle of the road audience has shrunk and the news and information flows they depend upon have also become more divided, leaving PR people working to influence increasingly partisan publics and media channels. So as the post-truth condition continues to produce unfolding effects in society – and as fake news has posed threats to mainstream journalism and also mainstream or classical PR – it has simultaneously created opportunity for providers of partisan content such as *Breitbart News* to grow their readership and revenues. The resulting environment of truthiness is one in which anything goes and which enables post-truth PR operators such as Russia's Internet Research Agency and RT's (Russia Today) broadcast and online news network to get their business done.

The practice of post-classical public relations

Post-classical PR represents an evolution of the practice to meet many conditions in society, including post-truth and the partisan publics with whom they engage. As the era of curated and edited media in the form of printed newspapers, magazines and newscasts gave way to a more fragmented pick and mix of online media, audiences have become accustomed to addictive content on demand offered by online content providers such as Netflix. This level of provision has exacerbated the challenges of engaging audiences who were already more comfortable with light entertainment and conspiracy theories than the delivery of dull news and facts about the world. Audiences are also more open to being persuaded based on emotional appeals rather than facts and sustained rational argument on important issues such as mass vaccination, as the continued anti-vaxxers campaign described in Chapter 6 shows. The net effect of these changes in audience attitudes and the volume and pace of modern media content is that audiences have higher expectations for the messages, narratives and content they consume beyond what routine facts can offer. One response of post-classical PR to this demand is a performative mode of practice which includes the production of engaging and sometimes comedic political PR presentations, such as those put on by Beppe Grillo in Italy, President Duterte of the Philippines, President Trump in the United States and Prime Minister Boris Johnson in the United Kingdom. Central to the success of this approach is the enactment of the role of strongman by the principal actors. As one interviewee in the Philippines case study in Chapter 7 commented in relation to President Duterte's PR style, his "raw" form of engagement through public performances as a gun-toting strongman going out on the streets on anti-drug raids cuts through to gain public and media attention. For the principal actors such as politicians and senior business people, one benefit of delivering successful comedic or authentic performances is that where there was once shame in being caught lying or cheating, it is now possible to ignore or laugh off such accusations.

There is a similar rawness, directness and eagerness to cause offence in the political PR and campaign rhetoric of President Trump, reflecting the current disruption of long-established boundaries, benchmarks for propriety and legality in public communication. There have been official complaints and even legal challenges over public statements by President Trump and Prime Minister Boris Johnson in national politics, and both continue to push at the edges of rudeness, truth and legality. On the right-wing fringe in the United Kingdom, activist Tommy Robinson has been banned from the major social media platforms and was jailed for contempt of court in 2019 for posting on a live trial, but others such as the *Another Angry Voice* blog in the United Kingdom and Andrew Anglin's *Daily Stormer* site in the United States continue to carefully tread the boundary of legality in the extreme and divisive stories they post. The combined effect has been to establish new norms for the type of messages, narratives and language that is acceptable in public debate, with standards set not by mainstream media but by the degrees of abuse and polarisation that have become the new normal in the wild west of social media platforms such as Twitter. Before digital media, new political groups would hold meetings, publish pamphlets and build a base of supporters over time before gaining press coverage and votes because of their momentum of support. Now, social media applications such as Facebook and Twitter provide a platform for immediate publication and distribution of uncensored and unregulated online content. Beyond the legalities relating to hate speech, defamation and so on, it has become clear over the last ten years or so that the affordances of social media platforms align neatly with the character and style of populist political communications. The mediated world that results leaves audiences vulnerable to manipulation by communicators who are able to exploit the vast data and processing power of the digital forces of Facebook, Google and other platforms. As the data of users of social media are segmented and digital surveillance layered on top in order to enable customised messaging by advertisers, PR firms and political campaigns, it is questionable whether this type of communications outreach is in the interests of audiences or of value only to the platforms themselves. Modern media is about scale and exploiting the value of a large audience, as the success of Facebook, Netflix and others has demonstrated. Yet despite the rhetoric of empowerment of social media users that the platforms sometimes use and their emphasis on the role of audiences as producers of content, they have given little consideration to the interests of the audience as a whole nor to minority interests, until forced to do so by regulators and lawmakers.

Social media has shifted the shape of communication in society, contributing to the erosion of professionally curated media in the form of newspapers and broadcast news and a redrawing of day-to-day PR practice. Alongside this demise of the reach and influence of mainstream media, the power and value of the gatekeeping function of editors has also eroded, removing a distribution node that PR people influenced for many years through media relations skills. In the resulting hybridised media environment, that blends old and new media channels, successful PR work matches its message and distribution plans with the social context, audience preferences and media logic in which it operates. The media logic of a system that combines 24-hour news with a continuous blend of global information and entertainment tends to favour constantly changing and controversial content that gains attention through the level of outrage generated, as the success of the ex-reality TV performer Donald Trump in dominating the news cycle through his controversial posts on Twitter and statements and campaign rallies has demonstrated.

The social conditions of post-truth, digital disinformation and partisan publics have changed both the context in which PR work gets done and also the practice of PR itself. Instead of operating as a centrist function that brings balance to public debate and dampens down instability, using the orthodox approaches of media relations and persuasion, some aspects of post-classical PR are increasing the volatility of facts, knowledge and opinion in society through divisive public communication and carelessness with matters of truth. The changes are profound and the field could benefit from a new grammar to support discussion of the wake that these early examples of post-classical PR have already left behind and are still generating in the form of waves of harmful and divisive discourse in society. PR is a trade that has made money from the epistemological fragility of post-truth and it continues to contribute to and participate in the political economy of fake news by delivering content that audiences want to see and that meets their confirmation biases. Digital confections, such as the promotional presence of Kylie Jenner, Beppe Grillo in Italy and the Brexit Party in the United Kingdom, look viable and are engaging to audiences, but are essentially inauthentic. The scale and speed of their success at the time of writing (September 2019) suggests that the spinners and modern-day digital Sophists of post-classical PR are offering clients a winning formula that will continue to prevail in post-truth society.

Index

Printed in the United States
by Baker & Taylor Publisher Services